Good
Writing!

Good Writing!

MARY MEISER

University of Wisconsin—Eau Claire

Allyn and Bacon

Boston   London   Toronto   Sydney   Tokyo   Singapore

Editor: Eben Ludlow
Production Coordinator: Aliza Greenblatt
Cover Designer: Hothouse Designs
Editorial/Production Service: P. M. Gordon Associates

Library of Congress Cataloging-in-Publication Data

Meiser, Mary Jordan.
    Good writing! / Mary Meiser.
      p. cm.
    Includes index.
    ISBN 0–02–380155–7
      1. English language—Rhetoric.   2. English language—Grammar.
    3. College readers.   I. Title.
    PE1408.M454   1995
    808'.042—dc20   94–12808
                                                             CIP

Printed in the United States of America

10 9 8 7 6 5 4 3 2   99 98 97 96 95

For Susan
my best pen pal,
who learned the value of writing,
across two oceans, a year, and a day

Contents

CHAPTER 2   *Reading and Writing Connections* 41

CHAPTER 3   *Writing from Personal Experience* 59

CHAPTER 4   *Working Through the Processes of Writing*

CHAPTER 5   *Generating and Exploring Topics* 121

CHAPTER 6   *Writing to Inform, Writing to Analyze* 158

CHAPTER 7   *Reading and Responding to Arguments* 189

PART TWO   A Writer's Handbook   243

CHAPTER 9   *Working with Sentences* 245

PART THREE Evaluating Writing 341

PART FOUR Student Essays for Revision and Editing Practice

Preface

From nearly 30 years of working with students, I know well the disparity that arises in composition courses: students with academic potential but undeveloped writing skills. Thus, in this text I wish to acknowledge and celebrate students' intelligence and creativity, as well as to assure them that all they lack is experience with academic writing. From that basic assumption, I want to talk them through the processes of reading and writing in a systematic way, building skills in ways congruent with current research on language and writing. This text, then, is based on what we know about the processes of acquiring written language. Consequently, it is process-oriented and interactive.

Students work through the processes of generating, drafting, revising, and editing. Multiple drafts are assumed and essential for building skills and confidence. Revising is viewed from the perspective of content first: what to include, what to delete, what to change or move. Revising is then viewed from the perspective of sentences: completeness and clarity. Editing remains the final process of readying text for another's eyes: adherence to standards and conventions of written American English. This text is interactive in that students are asked to respond thoughtfully and analytically, first to themselves, then to peers and instructor. Students are also asked to work together. Not only does such collaboration and discussion assist learning, but also it makes learning more fun.

Similarly, students learn from reading and discussing other writers' work. This text thus uses many writing samples, mainly from other students, both in the rhetoric and the handbook. The writing tasks most often ask students to respond in full discourse. Most teachers know the discouragement associated with sentence-level work that fails to transfer to paragraphs or short essays. Composing is a messy business, and single sentences don't help students prepare for the many choices they must make in full discourse writing. Consequently, this text seeks to prepare them for the "messy business" of composing. Only the handbook section features sentence-level work, acknowledging that some students will need to focus on a specific skill for a short time. But for the most part, skills work is assumed to be a part of revising and editing within student drafts.

PART ONE   A RHETORIC AND READER

After an introduction to the importance and role of writing, students are asked to explore the concepts of purpose, audience, and context in Chapter 1. They next work through the writing processes in a collaborative project. In this way, they verbalize every aspect of developing a text, and their instructor can clarify, elaborate, or guide them as needed or desired. Chapter 2 shows students the relationship between reading and writing processes and introduces them to writing as an academic tool. Readings from Sandra Cisneros and Kate Chopin form a thematic base for activities. In Chapter 3, with a focus on narrative and descriptive writing, students explore writing from personal experience. Richard Wright, Maxine Hong Kingston, Sandra Cisneros, and Thomas Whitecloud provide views of life from the perspective of various cultures and, at the same time, show the universality of human experience. Seven student writers, ranging in age from 19 to 40-something, provide another poignant and thoughtful view of experience. Chapter 4 takes student writers through the process of writing, from generating to revising and editing. As they develop their own personal-experience essays, students examine two student drafts and learn to ask the questions that prepare an essay for other readers' eyes.

In Chapter 5, students move into strategies for academic writing. Systematically, students are asked to try out various strategies for generating and exploring academic topics. Activities are grouped around thematic readings, and in some cases the readings themselves become the focus of student response. Chapter 6 focuses student attention on exposition and analysis. Six student essays provide experience in applying criteria for expository writing. A group analysis project on the topic "If Women Ran America" takes students through processes needed for academic reading and writing. In Chapter 7, students explore argumentative writing. Again student essays are the basis of reading and writing activities. Chapter 8 continues student experience with argumentative writing. Here students are introduced to common problems in reasoning. After analysis of a student position paper, students are asked to develop their own position paper.

PART TWO   A WRITER'S HANDBOOK

In the handbook, students will find variety. Some tasks are traditional, whereas others are contemporary. Similarly, some tasks use a provided text, and others require students to create their own text. Again, students are expected to interact with what they read, thoughtfully and analytically. The goal is understanding and application, ultimately the internalization of the rules and conventions of standard written American English.

The handbook first addresses problems with sentence boundaries (fragments, run-ons, comma splices), as well as other sentence problems such as misplaced modifiers and parallelism. It then moves systematically through coordination and subordination, including embedding. Students should view the revision of sentences as separate and preparatory to the editing of sentences. Editing sentences addresses problems of usage. Punctuation (everything outside of that used in syntax) and other mechanics rules are discussed in the final section: apostrophes, colons, commas, quotation marks, capitalization, and spelling.

The handbook has a variety of exercise formats: sentence, paragraph, and short essay. Students are asked to observe and then formulate the rules as often as possible. Many of the exercises are drawn from student work or from interesting real-life news topics.

PART THREE   EVALUATING WRITING

This section of the text is generally not found in composition texts, despite its importance to novice writers. Inexperienced writers in particular seldom understand just how teachers and others judge whether or not a piece of writing is acceptable. In Evaluating Writing, they learn about criteria that can both guide the development of a text and serve as the measure of its success. Students are taken through the process of evaluating student responses to a specific writing task. Students first read excerpts from "To Kill a King," on which the writing task was based. They next examine the writing task and criteria for evaluation. Finally, they apply these criteria to student responses to "To Kill a King." After students have achieved some understanding of and comfort with the evaluation process, they are asked to apply evaluation criteria to other student pieces. This section should assist instructors as well. Through it, they can demonstrate that evaluation is neither as subjective or mystifying as it may appear. Instructors can then ask students to assist in developing criteria for evaluating their own drafts in narrative, expository, and argumentative writing.

PART FOUR   STUDENT ESSAYS FOR REVISION AND EDITING PRACTICE

Students need sustained experience in revising and editing texts if they are to achieve writing competency. Although these processes must be applied to their own texts, students nonetheless benefit from experience with texts other than their own. Such practice is non-threatening and, as such, offers an opportunity for rigorous discussion and decision-making. The essays also provide instructors with models for group or whole class work.

Six paragraph-length and six full-length student essays provide full discourse practice in revision and editing. The full-length essays can be used in conjunction with personal experience, expository, and argumentative writing tasks or separately.

PART FIVE   KEEPING TRACK OF WRITING SKILLS AND PROBLEMS

Students are introduced to the concept of logs in the handbook section. The logs provide a systematic way to analyze error patterns in everything from punctuation to spelling, from failure to develop essays to problems with controlling ideas. Separate logs for revision, editing, and spelling reinforce the idea that revision and editing are separate processes, that content should be revised before attention is placed on correction. The logs also provide an easily accessed record of progress or persistent problem areas. With this information, instructors can easily form groups needing additional instruction on specific skills, as well as groups ready for more advanced instruction. Once students understand the importance and "mechanics" of the process, the logs should become their responsibility.

ACKNOWLEDGMENTS

I wish to thank not only the students whose writing appears in this text but also those who unwittingly contributed to my learning as a teacher and, ultimately, as a writer.

I also wish to thank my reviewers. Their insightful comments informed every chapter and guided my judgments of what might best serve both students and teachers as a practical resource in composition:

Barbara Beauchamp, County College of Morris

Thomas D. Cameron, Austin Community College, Rio Grande Campus

Toni Empringham, El Camino Community College

Stella Kaplan, Pace University

Diane Martin, Eastfield College

Mary Sue Ply, Southern Louisiana University

Larry Silverman, Seattle Community College

Carol Wershoven, Palm Beach Community College

Linda F. White, Stephen F. Austin State University

M. M.

Good
Writing!

PART ONE

A Rhetoric and Reader

CHAPTER 1

Becoming a Writer

WHY WE WRITE

Is Writing Old-fashioned?

With the wondrous telecommunications of the 1990s, it's not surprising that many people tend to think of voice rather than print when they want to communicate. In the time it takes to punch in 10 to 15 numbers, America and the world are accessible; families, friends, and businesses are linked—mere seconds away, 24 hours a day. For example, my son thinks nothing of calling home from such diverse places as the coastal highway between Los Angeles and San Diego or 31,000 feet over the Rocky Mountains. Being confined to a car or plane offers no barrier to communication these days; we can be wherever we want to be by punching in a series of numbers. Even when no one is physically present, we have easy access through answering machines and electronic mail. What's more, as we become part of a call-waiting triangle, even busy signals are no barrier to instant communication. Today, audio- and videotape, microchip, and satellite are a way of life. Consequently, print communication may appear to be as old-fashioned as a quill pen and inkwell.

But it isn't. The status and availability of the fax machine, for example, indicate that writing is still a major means of communication. And cards and letters retain their importance in both the world of personal relationships and the world of business. Further, our world revolves around written documents—everything from a job contract to a product guarantee, from marriage licenses to wills, from rules of conduct to laws governing our cities, states, and nations. Our most important documents, from the very beginning of settlement in

America, have always been written. And even informally today, it's common to hear someone respond, "Put that in writing." We still expect important agreements to be written rather than oral. Analysis and evaluation nearly always require a written form, from the simple report cards of primary school to complex reports of the chief executive officer in a *Fortune* 500 company. Print communication is, and will continue to be, an important medium of communication.

Nonetheless, given the ease, efficiency, and sophistication of voice communications today, students understandably wonder just why they are required to take at least one composition course. Are colleges simply maintaining an old-fashioned course? Are teachers making too much of writing skills? Just why are students required to expend considerable time and effort in a composition course? Is it merely to satisfy a traditional college requirement? The response to these questions lies in the nature of writing itself. Writing is not just communication in the traditional school sense; it is, rather, an integral part of the thinking and learning process.

✦ Writing is a way of discovering what we mean, as well as what others are trying to tell us.

✦ Writing is a way of remembering and manipulating information, of preserving it for later reflection and better understanding.

✦ Writing is a way of thinking, of taking apart ideas and concepts, of examining relationships and meaning.

In brief, writing helps us make sense of ourselves, others, and our world. It is, simply put, a powerful tool, not just for college but for the world at large—a world that grows increasingly more complex, a world that depends on our ability to communicate well in both oral and written language.

How Does Writing Help Us?

Writing Helps Us Learn.   At times, you will write as a process of inquiry and discovery, not just from books but also from your own experiences and observations. We can run ideas and memories through our heads, but without writing them down, they quickly slip away. Further, without writing, we would have far less success in reflecting on their significance. Our memories are limited and subject to a very natural distortion. Writing, then, provides us with the means to capture experience and, ultimately, to learn from it. At other times, you will write to remember or to sort out class-related information.

Writing notes, for example, is a common activity both in and out of college. Through notes, we sort out various kinds of information, provide timely information for others, and generally preserve information for later use. When we read, we use writing to outline, summarize, or annotate important areas. Most students learn quickly that writing while reading saves them from rereading, especially in preparing for exams. Although there are many reliable studies illustrating the power of writing in college, students seem to know almost instinctively that writing is a valuable tool.

Through writing, we are able to bring together ideas from many different sources—our reading, our discussions, and our personal experiences and observations. We can connect these ideas, clarify our understanding of them, and finally, relate them to new information or new ideas. Writing makes this process concrete—something we can see and manipulate—and therefore makes it easier. Writing also makes us active learners, virtually forcing us to interact with what we are reading or hearing, to interact with our brains and not just eyes or ears. Writing, then, is not just something to be used during times of examinations. It is, rather, a lifelong skill we can draw upon whenever we need or wish to learn.

Writing Helps Us Know Ourselves and Others Better. Experienced writers often remark that through writing, they have come to know themselves, others, and the world around them in important ways. It might be that in the process of working out our ideas in print, we become more deliberate and thoughtful. Writing slows us down somewhat; in many cases, slowing down benefits our thinking processes. And quite often, we may not even know exactly what we feel or mean until we have written it out. The process of writing can help us in many ways: to understand our ideas and to explore them more systematically and thoroughly; to help us deal with conflicting ideas and emotions; and to help us solve both personal and professional problems. If we choose to save our writing, we have a wonderful record of how we felt about something or someone, and quite possibly, why we felt that way. Or we have a record of how we solved a problem or which alternatives we might yet pursue. Writing can be discovery, a special way of coming to know; through it, we have a powerful means of connecting self, others, and a world of ideas.

Writing Helps Us in the World of Work. You might associate writing only with school tasks, and therefore you may think of it as something you'll leave behind when you complete your studies. However, we live in an information society, where the processes of gathering, analyzing, and dispersing information are essential. Much of what you learn in college relative to content knowledge will eventually become obsolete. Research has yielded new information in nearly every field of study and has forced us to discard both what we know and how we deal with that knowledge. A new and better mousetrap has evolved everywhere. But process skills such as oral and written language will become more and more valuable. The ability to sift through information, analyze it, and communicate your findings clearly and accurately will be invaluable to you and any employer.

BECOMING A WRITER

Learning to Talk, Learning to Write

When you learned to talk, you were in an ideal environment for gaining language skills quickly and effortlessly. You were immersed in oral language and encouraged to use it every waking hour. You had a genuine purpose for using it: to communicate with others, to be part of a family and community. Making errors was a normal and expected part of the learning process; everyone knew that with more exposure to language and more experience in using it, you'd be fine. And you were. The process of learning to talk was, in many ways, joyful and effortless. It was natural, unschooled, and continual between birth and starting school. When you entered school, you were already quite a sophisticated talker. Learning to write, however, is seldom as easy.

Although there are some parallels between learning to talk and learning to write, there are significant differences. Learning to write is not a natural, unschooled process. We are not surrounded by print every waking hour, nor are we continually urged to communicate through it. And our purposes for writing are less obvious and less clear than for talking. Our audience is remote, and thus we have to work harder at making ourselves understood, as well as in anticipating what our audience knows and needs to know. Further, writing appears to carry a certain vulnerability with it; our mistakes with spelling or grammar, for example, are visible, permanent in a way speech is not. Moreover, a tolerance for errors in writing, even from beginners, is far lower. People seem to forget that learning to write takes time, a great deal of time, and sustained experience—just as learning to talk did. Only recently have educators realized that providing beginning writers with an environment similar to that of beginning speakers would really make a difference for those writers. Consequently, teachers are working hard to ensure the writing classroom is a safe environment—one where mistakes are viewed as part of the learning process, where processes and strategies for writing are modeled, and where working with others is expected and valued.

Amazingly, most young children believe they can write. What's more, they like to. Free from restrictions of topics, rules, and time, children leave their mark everywhere. Those scribbles on walls, appliances, and every available surface represent authentic writing. Children believe adults can read their scribbles, and sometimes they are offended when adults ask for a translation. You may have been one of those children, writing before you started school, writing before it became complex and demanding in a school setting. Michael Rafferty, coming to college as a nontraditional student after military service, discovered that he was. The result was this essay for his composition course:

The Boxes

A question was posed to me recently, "when did you first start writing?" This question would have been hard for me to answer, if it had not been for a rather alarming discovery I made last week. I suppose the traditional response would have been, in kindergarten like everyone else. But thanks to my mother's pack rat tendencies, an archive of my early childhood grammatical expressions were unleashed to the world.

My mother and I were sitting around the old dining room table viewing some archaic family photo albums. There were two common phrases being aired that night, "oooh look at this," and "that's so cute." Of course each of these phrases were emanating from my mother. I suppose I could have enjoyed the session more if it was not for the minuscule dust particles irritating my eyes to the point of watering. Funny thing is, Mom thought the tears soaking my face were tears of joy or something.

After about an hour, I finally thought the session was coming to an end. That's when it happened. Out of the last photo album fell a pile of old Mother's Day cards drawn in crayon. Instantly I knew that this was truly my first viable link to the literary world. The earliest known date on the cards was Mother's Day 1970. At the

conception of this card I would have been just about
fours years of youth. Most people would think that a four
year old human would not exactly be a trademark writer,
but let me tell you I was. For each card I created ended
in one specific way. "Write your name in the boxes" was
printing at the tail of every card. This was followed by
a sequence of misshaped box-like formations.

I was so overcome by this trademark technique, I
called my grampa and gramma to verify my findings on the
cards I had given to them. The grandparents did not hesitate to inform me that they also knew of this practice.

Since my early childhood, my writing has been infre-
quent at best. To this day I can say I have written fewer
than five letters to friends or family. It has been much
easier to just pick up the phone, and much quicker.
Primarly, over the last six years my writing has been
restricted to filling out forms and paperwork.

Although writing is becoming an added pleasure to my
life, I doubt it will ever be as original as "The Boxes."

Michael Rafferty

Writing Activity

Like Michael, you might have a writing memory tucked away.
Wander around in your memory a bit. Many students find they have
images of writing on a wall or sidewalk, of creating fantastic stories, or
of making up a secret written code. Others find they suddenly see their
drawings and stories displayed on the refrigerator. If wandering
around in your memory doesn't produce an image of you as a child
writer, check with family or friends. I recently found some notes from
my son and daughter, for example, and I doubt they recall writing
them. My son told me to stop covering him with a blanket, that he
didn't want to end up a "pes of bernt bakon" (piece of burned bacon).
My daughter told me that I "hert her fealings" after disciplining her;
she also drew a picture of herself in tears, complete with sound effects
written in invented spelling. Many caretakers have both a box of saved
child writings and good memories of those early efforts.

As you think about yourself as a child writer, let your pen, pencil,
or computer wander freely. The very act of "thinking on paper" may
produce the memories. Write down words or phrases as they pop up.

These may trigger more memories. Don't feel pressured to write in sentences. Exploring ideas, making lists or notes, and keeping things simple are essential first steps in the writing process. Also feel free to talk with classmates. One person's experiences may be the key to your own or may unlock more detailed recollections. Talking, by the way, is an excellent way to begin any writing task.

Do this writing task in your journal. You may use these notes for a later assignment.

WRITING IN SCHOOL

If most young children consider themselves writers, why do so many adolescents and adults believe themselves to be "nonwriters"? The answer may lie somewhere in their experiences with writing in school. School writing is often linked to reporting what we know rather than to discovering new knowledge; school writing may also translate into criticism and grades. Therefore, writing was no longer the self-initiated, free, and flexible activity it had once been. And along with concerns about the limits of the assignment and the correctness of the product, came false notions of what writing is all about. These false notions are so common that both within and out of school they have held many potential writers hostage. A few of the most widely heard are these:

✦ **Good writers are born, not made.** Although some people may appear to be naturally gifted, they most likely have worked hard and long at their writing. It's true, of course, that some people are better writers than others, just as some people are better musicians or athletes. Along with sustained interest and motivation, there may be some natural talent. But without working to develop it, no writer, musician, or athlete would become "good." The naturalness arises from years of experience, from turning complex actions into routine actions.

✦ **Good writers get everything right the first time.** No one, no matter how skilled or talented, gets everything right the first time. That just isn't the way writing works. Good writers expect to write several drafts. They know that revising and editing are essential parts of the writing process, allowing them the freedom to get down what they want to say before being concerned with the best way, or the correct way, to say it.

✦ **There's only one right way to go about writing.** Writing is a complex activity, and each of us brings different skills and experiences to the process. Consequently, each of us has to find the best way to go about writing. Although there are many strategies to help us, there is no single correct way to go about the process. If we take the time to try various strategies, we find that some work well. Similarly, if we pay attention to how, when, and where we work most efficiently, we develop habits that help us take on a writing task. The more we understand about ourselves as writers, the better. But there will never be a single, right way to go about the process. There are no formulas, no magic.

◆ **The written product is more important than the process.** Because students are used to being graded on the final product, they quite rightly consider that product important. And it is important: it is the cumulation of a great deal of thought and effort. However, the process of developing that product is just as important. Without a good writing process (prewriting, drafting, revising, and editing), a good product is very unlikely, if not impossible. The process is also critical to learning to write more effectively and easily. And sometimes, very good things happen in process, regardless of the quality of the final product. We might learn to handle some part of writing better, or to become more comfortable with it, even if the final product isn't as good as we would like it to be.

Writing Activity

Again, in your journal, walk around in your memory. This time try to recall some of your experiences with writing in school. Most students have rather sharp memories of a specific writing task that challenged, frustrated, or satisfied them. A specific teacher who encouraged their writing is also a common memory. Sometimes the memories are linked to the tools of writing: big, fat yellow pencils, rough gray paper with lines to guide the formation of letters, bright crayons or chalk, the magic of a computer. You might even recall some writing "rules" that baffled you. Don't be surprised if you have stored both good and not-so-good memories of writing in school. We all have them.

You might capture your memories in list or note form. You don't have to write in sentences unless you want to. Save these writings. You may use them later.

STANDARD WRITTEN ENGLISH: THE LANGUAGE OF SCHOOL

The Dialect Nobody Speaks

Because their English differs from that of books, some students believe they can't write well. However, none of us speaks the English of books, magazines, and newspapers. We have to learn that variety of English, called Standard Written English, because it is a dialect with its own rules and conventions. Writing, in other words, is not just speech written down. What is both expected and acceptable in our speech may be quite different from what is expected and acceptable in our writing. When we talk, for example, we can and do use incomplete and ungrammatical sentences:

A. "Looking good!"

B. "What next?"

C. "He don't know that." (he doesn't)

D. "I'm taller than him." (than he is)

E. "Me and Jonah are friends." (Jonah and I)

These utterances are understandable. They work fine as communication. And for most people, they are acceptable. The exceptions would be "He don't" and "Me and Jonah," especially in school and business. "I'm taller than him" would probably be noticed only by English teachers. This nongrammatical form has become common and quite acceptable in most informal language settings. The key is knowing which language settings require Standard (school) English and having the versatility to use it when needed. It is not a matter of being understood, but rather, of fitting in. If you plan to work within a language community that uses Standard English, you need to know that dialect. It is, in brief, a matter of being practical. And being practical does not mean that you have abandoned or devalued your home dialect in any way. You have simply added to your versatility with English.

Each of us speaks a dialect that marks us as belonging to a certain ethnic group, gender, social class, and geographic region. No American dialect is superior to any other. Each is logical, grammatical, and systematic; each provides its speakers with a rich and effective means of communication. With the exception of speech related to age or profession, we retain our original dialect throughout our lives. Only when we change our role or status do we find it necessary to acquire another dialect. Thus people who enter academic, professional, or business situations may find they need to acquire the dialect labeled as standard. In fact, knowing and using the correct forms might be considered a survival skill.

Some students use two dialects daily, that of home and that of school, thus demonstrating an enviable versatility with English. In learning Standard Written English, these students gained another dialect and expanded their versatility further. Just as we use our spoken dialect to fit in with family, friends, and immediate community, we use Standard Written English to fit into academic, professional, and certain work environments. For this reason, time and effort invested in learning Standard Written English are worthwhile. Career goals are being well served.

UNDERSTANDING WRITING

The Processes of Writing

Although it might appear to be a single process, writing is actually a series of processes: generating and exploring ideas (prewriting), drafting, revising, and editing. Each of these processes contributes to our ability to write a competent paragraph or essay. If we skip generating and exploring ideas, we run the risk of producing a very limited, and perhaps pretty dull, piece. If we fail to revise, we may end up with a disorganized or incoherent piece. We might also end up with too much material, thus boring our reader, or too little, thus confusing the reader. If we ignore the editing process, we may end up with errors in spelling, grammar, and punctuation. In brief, each process provides us with a focus and allows us to think about different aspects of developing our piece.

It would be a mistake, however, to think that these processes are linear and orderly; that is, that we proceed as though they were locked steps, start to finish. We can and do use any of the processes throughout our writing time. For example, while revising, a writer might discover the need for more material. At that point, he or she would go back to generating and exploring ideas. Or while generating and exploring ideas, a writer might turn to drafting, writing in paragraph form as a means of exploring an idea. Understanding the focus of and strategies for each of the writing processes is important. This knowledge helps us utilize each process fully, and at the same time, moves us through the entire process of developing a paragraph or essay.

Generating and Exploring Ideas

The process of generating and exploring ideas is also referred to as prewriting. During this process, writers use many strategies to discover and explore ideas for writing, including reading, writing, and talking. You might be familiar with some specific strategies such as making lists, brainstorming, responding to specific questions, or mapping. You'll learn and practice these, and many other strategies, as you work through this textbook. What's important is that you find out which strategies work well for you.

Drafting

Drafting is the process of putting ideas on paper or computer screen. When writers draft, they move beyond words and phrases to sentences and paragraphs. Drafting is what most people refer to as writing, but drafting is more specific. It refers to developing and refining a written text; it also implies multiple drafts rather than one draft. Most people find a discovery draft, a really messy head-to-paper draft (or head-to-computer-chip draft), a necessity. A discovery draft frees writers from being orderly or neat; its very purpose is freedom to think, getting ideas out of the head in whatever form and order they come. In another draft, those ideas will be worked with; they will be put into some logical order, developed fully, and polished. And in yet another draft, sentences will be clarified and corrected. For some writing assignments, you will write only a first draft, a discovery piece. But for most, you'll work through several drafts. Think of multiple drafts as an opportunity to concentrate on different aspects of writing at different times.

Revising

Revising occurs when writers are satisfied with the content of the paragraph or essay, when they have a good sense that "this is what I want to say." Writers have to be quite certain that what they want to say and what they actually say match. Revision is the process that helps them achieve that certainty. During revision, writers reread the paragraph or essay, slowly and thoughtfully. They may decide to add material, delete material, or change the order of material. They then check on how ideas flow and how readers would get from one idea to the next without getting lost. Revision also occurs on the sentence level. Writers decide if sentences are clear and effective, and make changes in those that aren't. Finally, writers check on individual words, deciding if another would be more precise or effective. Revising is the writer's preparation for the reader, and it is a demanding task. Shifting the point of view from "I wrote this" to "How will someone read this?" requires considerable time and, often, a bit of help from peers or teacher. You'll learn revising strategies—specific ways of looking at your written text and making changes as needed—as you work through writing assignments. Work with peers will also provide you with experience in revising.

Editing

Editing is the one writing process that should stay in its place—last. When writers edit (editing is also known as proofreading), they are concerned with correctness. If writers worry about being correct too early in the writing process, they can literally stop themselves from writing. Or they can spend a great deal of time making a sentence correct, only to throw it out during revision. Many students, having been penalized heavily for incorrect spelling, grammar, or punctuation, are understandably concerned about being correct. They also know the final draft will be judged against the standards of written American English. As a result, they find it difficult to leave editing until the very end. Putting editing last, however, is important. Otherwise, writers may actually block the other writing processes and fail to gain the fluency they need. Editing is an important process, and learning to do it well is a critical writing skill. Because it is so critical, you may be asked to keep a personal editing log. In it, you will list the errors you typically make, as well as their corrections. A pattern will show up, and with that knowledge, along with explanations as needed, you'll be able to find and correct errors during editing.

A good way to think about the processes we use in developing a piece of writing is to work collaboratively. With a small group of classmates, you will explore a topic, then draft, and finally revise and edit a brief essay. In doing so, you will both experience and discuss each of the writing processes. You'll make each process a focus, visible and concrete, as you develop and refine your ideas. Each of you will be responsible for writing a single paragraph for this essay. But before you see how this collaborative project works and learn more about your topic, you need to review a few basics about the paragraph.

A BASIC STRUCTURE: THE PARAGRAPH

A Single Idea

A paragraph may be loosely defined as a group of sentences about a single topic. The average paragraph has 100 to 150 words. However, it may be slightly longer in formal writing and considerably shorter in other places, such as newspapers and magazines. Generally, we adjust paragraph length to help our readers. If we have a great deal to say about a single topic, we will do it in several short paragraphs rather than one lengthy one. Doing so will keep readers more alert and ease eyestrain. Sometimes a single paragraph is in itself a short essay, requiring no further development of the topic. At other times, a single paragraph is one of several in an essay, each paragraph contributing to the development of the essay's topic.

Every paragraph you write will be about "something": It may describe something or somebody, question something, explain something, analyze something, define something, argue something. "Something" is usually identified in the topic sentence of the paragraph. Here are some examples:

> John Lennon was one of the most influential musicians of modern times.
>
> Natural disasters bring out the best in Americans.
>
> Television violence has negative effects on young viewers.

Each of these sentences has a key word or phrase that tells the reader what to expect in the paragraph. For example, what is meant by "influential"? The reader would expect details and examples to "prove" that Lennon was indeed influential. A paragraph about natural disasters bringing out the best of Americans could describe the acts of care and kindness, of bravery even, found during hurricanes and floods. A paragraph supporting the idea that television violence has negative effects would first of all have to provide examples of television violence and then illustrate the negative effects.

The topic sentence serves as a reminder: this paragraph is about something. Every sentence in that paragraph then serves to develop the idea, the something. Not every paragraph will have an explicit topic sentence, but every paragraph nonetheless is organized around a single something. Very experienced writers sometimes omit the topic sentence, but they never violate the idea of developing a paragraph around a single something. However, student writers usually state their topic sentence. Because it helps unify the ideas within the paragraph, a stated topic sentence helps them stay on track.

For example, if you decide to write about natural disasters bringing out the best in Americans, you would be choosing specific acts of kindness or bravery related to natural disasters, such as hurricanes or floods. If you then thought about some acts of kindness or bravery related to an apartment fire, you would have to set them aside. Your topic sentence specifically noted natural disasters, not acts of human destruction. You could, of course, come up with a new topic sentence that included man-made destruction. More likely, however, you would stick with a more focused, limited topic sentence, and then eliminate any idea that doesn't directly relate to it.

Remember: The topic sentence states the main idea of the paragraph. All sentences within the paragraph relate to and develop that main idea.

Developing the Idea

One strategy for developing a paragraph evolves from the idea that each sentence derives directly from the sentence before it; it responds to that sentence in some way. Considered this way, the paragraph is a series of sentences that carry both the reader's expectation and the writer's response. For example:

Bart Simpson is every teacher's worst nightmare.

The reader expects to learn why Bart is a "worst nightmare." The next sentence thus might define "worst nightmare." It could be something to the effect that Bart is mouthy, unproductive, and defiant. From there the reader would expect several examples of Bart in action. The writer could describe Bart's language in the classroom, his efforts to avoid homework or class activities, and finally the language and acts of defiance against authority. Anyone who was a regular watcher of *The Simpsons* could easily supply details and examples for a paragraph on this single topic.

Ways Topic Sentences Evolve

Topic sentences can evolve in two ways: (1) We might think of a general idea—like Bart Simpson being a teacher's nightmare—and then fill in all the details and examples that fill out that general idea.

(2) We might have the details and examples first and work toward the general idea that becomes our topic sentence. We might have been making notes about *The Simpsons,* listing all the things Bart does to drive teachers crazy, and then come up with a sentence that acts as the main idea: "Bart is a teacher's worst nightmare." Any method that you use or that just occurs is fine, as long as you check that the topic sentence really matches the details or examples.

Placing the Topic Sentence

Although typically placed as the first sentence of a paragraph, topic sentences may come as the last sentence or somewhere in the middle. In this way, writers vary their writing style.

At the Beginning.   If you put the topic sentence first, you provide readers with a clear statement of intent for your paragraph. Whenever you write to inform or to explain something, the topic sentence as the first sentence is best. You want your reader to grasp your main idea quickly. School essays and exams, business reports, and on-the-job writing often require a clearly stated topic sentence as the first sentence.

At the End.   If you develop a paragraph using inductive reasoning (where you have gathered specific examples or evidence from which you draw a conclusion—the Sherlock Holmes approach), the topic sentence will quite naturally be at the end of the paragraph. For example:

> Grease and dirt covered the kitchen counters. A stack of dirty dishes filled the small sink, traces of ketchup, wilted lettuce, and hamburger juice providing a slash of color. A trash can was overflowing with paper plates and beer cans, some half filled with stale liquid. The floor was covered with yellow footprints formed from beer and dirt. *It was clear that no one had cleaned up after the party.*

Collaborative Writing Activity: A Place in the Family _____

Although psychologists study the effects of birth order on our personalities and intelligence, many people simply draw conclusions from their own experience and observations. Only children, for example, suffer from descriptions marking them as self-centered, but they also are considered very bright and articulate. Firstborns are viewed as natural leaders, whereas later-born children are seen as more flexible, better able to deal with whatever turns up. Popular belief says that middle children are lost in the family shuffle, or they may be the family mediators. And the last born, everyone's baby, may be considered completely loveable or totally manipulative. There may be a bit of truth in all of the descriptions, if we can manage to be objective about the topic.

Since you and your classmates have had extensive experience with "A Place in the Family," you will use this topic for your collaborative writing project.

Some Ground Rules

1. For this writing task, you will have to agree on a position and support it—even if that position doesn't represent your personal experience. For example, your experience as a firstborn may be very positive. In group discussion, however, you discover that most of the examples and details show that being a firstborn is a somewhat negative experience. Because your group's best and most abundant material supports "negative," your group will probably choose to write it up that way. You will have to agree to go along with it.

2. You will write as "I," as though the group were a single person developing this piece of writing. For this writing task, it doesn't matter that each paragraph shows a different writing style.

3. Your group has to make a decision on whether "I" is male or female. Many times, the examples are genderless, but now and then an example is clearly male or female. If you intend to use that example, you have to make all the paragraphs correspond to that gender.

4. Sharing writing with others is a bit scary at first. It's natural to feel that yours isn't good enough or to fear that someone might criticize it. But sharing writing is very important, and everyone has exactly the same doubts and fears. Your job is to help make that piece of writing better, and you can do that through gentle but honest questions and comments:

   Tell me more about _____.

   What do you mean by _____?

   Could you give me another example of _____?

Would this work as well without _____?

That is a really good idea. How about adding to it?

I had a bit of trouble here _____.

Each of you knows a good bit about telling stories clearly and effectively—going straight to the heart of the matter—so apply that knowledge as you work with one another. Each paragraph should go to the "heart of the matter," demonstrating that this place in the family is either positive or negative.

5. Build trust in your group. You bring different experiences and abilities to your group, and everyone has something good to contribute to this project. Honor each person's contribution.

6. Remember the purpose of this writing task: to discuss and work through each of the writing processes. The end product may not be very good, but the process will be very good. Keep that perspective. As you work through this textbook, you will gain knowledge and experience that will eventually pay off in a better product. But right now, concentrate on the process.

The following paragraphs illustrate how some students responded to the writing task. Notice how a topic sentence reflects the main idea of the paragraph. What information do you expect based on the topic sentence? Also notice the placement of the topic sentence. Why are some topic sentences at the end of the paragraph? What other clues does the writer give to indicate where he or she is heading with the paragraph, or in some cases, where the group is headed with the essay?

Firstborn

At first, I felt being the oldest child in my family was going to be great. Each time my mother and father produced another offspring I knew I would have one more soldier under my command. Another slave to satisfy all my eldest sibling needs. But then reality set in and I knew it would not be quite so easy.

In the Middle

Occasionally I feel neglected because I'm the middle child. When I look in family albums, I see tons of pic-

tures of my older sister as the baby. She has a whole
album of pictures devoted to her. There are not half as
many pictures of me as a baby. Pictures of my younger
brother as a baby fill another album. My parents knew my
younger brother was their last child so they took roll
after roll of film of him.

The Baby

   I can still remember my two older sisters glaring
icily through the window at me as I pulled into our driveway with my new car. At the time, I couldn't understand
why my sisters were so upset with me. It only seemed fair
that a freshly licensed 16-year-old should be rewarded
with a new car. Now I realize how many advantages I had
being the youngest in my family.

Your instructor will group you according to your place in the family: firstborn or only child, middle child, youngest child. In preparation
for group work, spend some time thinking about your place in your
family. What were the advantages? The disadvantages? What specific
examples can you bring in support of advantages or disadvantages?
Make a list and bring it to your group for discussion. You will find others have remarkably similar experiences, although some may be more
dramatic than others. Your group will want to choose the very best
support to defend your place in the family as a great or not-so-great
place to be, or to build a description, a role. For example, some groups
choose a label, such as "leader" or "mediator," and then use details and
examples to show how being a firstborn makes one a leader or being
a middle child leads to being the mediator. Similarly, some groups use
a word like "spoiled" as the controlling idea for their essay. "Spoiled
rotten," incidentally, has been used to describe both the firstborn and
the baby.
   Remember you will be going public with your ideas. You are not
required to reveal anything you don't feel comfortable with.

Exploring the Topic.   With your group, tell the stories of your
place in the family. Your individual lists will merge into a single list.
Perhaps the easiest way to start is with two lists: positive and negative
experiences. Then, evaluate the experiences: which are the most vivid,
most telling, most interesting? Where do you have the most material?
The best material? Choose a focus for your essay:

Being _____ is positive.

Being _____ is negative.

As a _____ I feel _____.

_____ are _____.

The controlling idea for the essay will come from the material and the focus it suggests to you. If you decide being a firstborn means being set up as *the* example, you have a focus:

Firstborn = *The* example

Your next task is to choose the material to support that focus, the controlling idea for the essay:

The example for siblings = get punished as warning to sibling
                            meeting high expectations:
                              student, athlete, musician
                            criticized more often
                            friends scrutinized

You then need to take some of these points and be more specific by way of examples and details that show the reader what you mean:

get punished as warning to sibling = minor stuff made into big deal

Example: was 15 minutes beyond curfew and was grounded for two weeks.

Meet high expectations = Grades

Example: "C" in math resulted in conference with teacher, inquisition, and monitoring of homework for a month. Idea of "C" as competent—not for firstborn—supposed to get "A".

Drafting.   When the group has decided on its focus and supporting material, divide up the work. Each person should write a single paragraph. For example, one person would develop the paragraph on being grounded for a 15-minute infraction, another would develop the paragraph on high parental expectations relative to grades, and so forth.

Remember, your topic sentence expresses the main idea of the paragraph. Every sentence in the paragraph develops that idea and that idea only.

Talk with group members about your paragraph, especially if you feel you need more ideas or help with getting things down on paper. Drafting does not mean writing in isolation. Some people like to draft in a quiet place, alone, but others need and enjoy the company of peers.

Revising.   When you believe the content of your paragraph is complete, you are ready for revision. Return to the ground rules on pages 18–19, and review the kinds of questions needed for revision. Your instructor will let you know whether or not to make copies of your paragraph. Sometimes groups work orally, the writer reading his or her piece to the group. At other times, the writer furnishes each group member with a photocopy.

As you work with the paragraphs, you have some major decisions:

A. Is the topic sentence clearly stated?

B. Do the details and examples fit the topic sentence?

C. Does the writer need more or different examples?

D. Do the sentences follow one another naturally and logically?

E. Are the sentences complete?

F. Are the words active and interesting?

G. Where does this paragraph fit in the larger essay? Does it make a difference whether it is first, in the middle, last?

Because we are so close to what we write, understanding in our heads what we intend to say, other readers are an important part of revision. They bring "fresh eyes." They don't know what we intended, only what we have on paper. For this reason, revising as a peer activity is important.

When you are satisfied with the content of your paragraph, you are ready for the final process, editing.

Editing.   As you work through this text, you will learn more about both revising and editing. For now, do the best that you can in your group. Usually, some group members are able to help others. Part Two of this text contains a reference for editing; check it for examples and explanations. Your instructor may provide some whole-class or small-group instruction. Editing skills take a long time to develop, so don't be frustrated or embarrassed if yours are in an early stage. Ask for help.

Remember what editing is for: to make our writing conform to standards of American written English. At this point, you are asking questions about correctness.

Ask questions about every sentence:

✦ Is the sentence complete? (Who or what is doing something? What about it?)

✦ Are subject and verb both singular or both plural?

✦ Is tense (time) either all present or all past?

✦ Does each sentence have an end mark (period, question mark)?

✦ Does each sentence start with a capital letter?

✦ Is every word spelled correctly?

Summing Up. Your instructor will provide you with information about putting your place-in-the-family essay together. But even if you don't turn your individual paragraphs into a single essay, you have worked and talked through all of the processes needed to develop a paragraph or a multiple-paragraph essay. You know from experience that there are no formulas, rules, or recipes that ensure an acceptable piece of writing. However, you also know that writing is not an act of magic—hard work, to be sure, but not magic. Learning to write well takes considerable time and effort, as well as motivation. And for most students, especially those with jobs and family responsibilities, learning to write well is a major commitment. However, the outcome is also a major accomplishment, a lifelong skill.

UNDERSTANDING PURPOSE, AUDIENCE, AND CONTEXT

If someone asked why you are writing, your first response might be something to this effect: "Because I have to." With school tasks, we often feel that way! However, a second response to that question would probably indicate a specific need to communicate something to someone. In brief, you'd have a purpose, an audience, and a context for writing. These would help you decide what to include, as well as what your tone and language would be like. For example, a note telling a friend to meet you or one telling a roommate to clean up the kitchen would probably illustrate different tones and language choices. Similarly, a note telling your boss why you were late for work would illustrate yet another tone. In the workplace, a report on the effectiveness of a certain machine has different requirements than a report outlining customer dissatisfaction with a product. When we write, then, we consider purpose, audience, and context:

Purpose   Why we write; what we want to accomplish in this piece of writing.

Audience   To or for whom we write; our readers.

Context   The situation or place in which our writing will be understood; academic, work, cultural, political, social, etc.

But regardless of why and for whom we write, we have to ask and answer a basic set of questions:

✦ What do I want to accomplish in this piece?

✦ What will readers expect from me?

✦ What will readers already know? Need to know?

✦ How will I develop my ideas?

✦ How will I organize my ideas?

✦ How much information is enough?

✦ How much information is excessive?

✦ What information is my best information?

✦ Do I need outside resources?

✦ What language is most appropriate?

✦ What tone is most appropriate?

✦ How will readers get a sense of me, the writer?

These are practical questions. The answers to them reflect some of the choices we make as we work through the writing process. Our purpose may make some choices for us. For example, if a job application requires a cover letter, I would know that I must explain clearly and briefly both why I want this job and why I should be considered for it. I would also know I have to use formal language and a standard business letter format, as well as Standard Written English spelling, usage, and mechanics. However, I would still have other questions to answer: How much information about me is enough, and how should I organize it? Every time we write, we make decisions that guide the development of that piece of writing. And every piece of writing shares questions of purpose, audience, and context—even within a common form such as newswriting.

ANALYZING THE NEWS

As you examine the news pieces that follow, determine the purpose of each. Also consider the audience: (1) What assumptions can you make about the audience? (2) Does it make any difference if the reader's social or cultural background differs from the writer's? (3) What do readers expect and why? Finally, consider the questions that each writer had to ask and answer; how successful was each news writer?

Two Mexican Adventures

CONGRATULATIONS!!!
You have been selected to receive one of the following exciting holidays of your choice:

**A Mexican Vacation that includes 2 round trip
Airfare and Hotel accommodations for 2**
(Not Including Meals)

Your Choice of Mazalan, Puerto Vuarta, Cancun
(Suggested Retail Value $1,100.00)

YOU MUST CALL WITHIN 72 HOURS to claim your holiday.
Call toll free
1-800-232-0000
Monday-Friday 9:00 A.M.-9:00 P.M. Eastern Standard Time

Rules: No Purchase Necessary. Must be at least 18 years old. Some restrictions apply.

A. What is the stated purpose of this "good luck" piece of writing? Are there other purposes involved? How do you know? What is the writer counting on from the reader?

_____

_____

_____

B. As a reader, how do you feel about a company that is offering you a trip to a place whose name it cannot spell correctly (Mazalan =

Mazatlán? Puerto Vuarta = Puerto Vallarta? Is this a case where Standard Written English (or Spanish) makes a significant difference in effect and confidence?

_____

_____

_____

C. What information is given? Lacking?

_____

_____

_____

D. Does this piece of writing accomplish its purpose?

_____

_____

_____

Mexico also figures in the next example. However, the context changes radically, and our view of "Mexico" shifts to a critical descriptive word. How many of us would recognize a Mexican redhead parrot? Or would it be enough to simply know "parrot"?

A. What is the writer's purpose?

_____

_____

_____

B. Did the writer provide enough information in this piece? What questions do you as a reader have? Do you really need them answered or are you just curious?

_____

_____

_____

The British Act and Speak Out

Next determine how these two pieces of British "news" provide insights into purpose, audience, and context.

SARAH GIVES HUSBAND ROYAL ROASTING

London—A paint bucket, a pair of shears, and a grudge against her prospective ex-husband have made a celebrity of Lady Sarah Graham-Moon.

Lady Sarah, who is divorcing Sir Peter Graham-Moon after 25 years of marriage, says she has dumped paint over her husband's BMW and trimmed four inches off the left sleeves of 32 of his suits in the past few weeks.

She also confessed to anyone who inquired that she had distributed 70 prime bottles from his wine cellar around the village of East Garston, about 60 miles west of London.

Sir Peter has said nothing, and the police said no complaints had been lodged.

A. Although the general purpose of newswriting is to inform, what do you think the writer of this piece intended?

_____

_____

_____

B. Did you enjoy this piece? Why? Did the specific pieces of information the writer chose to include provide a certain effect? What if the writer had included only the incident about dumping paint? Would the effect be the same?

_____

_____

_____

Now consider this excerpt from a letter from the vice chairman of the Cambridge Women's Luncheon Club:

Our first lunch will be on Wednesday 10th October, at the University Arms, when Dr. Colin Lattimore, a very eminent and knowledgeable Speaker will tell us about the History of the Longcase Clock.

After much heartsearching we have decided to revert to a three course sit-down lunch with a more varied menu of higher quality. The buffet did not prove to be popular with everyone, and in the interests of peace and harmony, the Hotel has agreed that the entire lunch will be silver served.

Do please make sure that one of the officers is informed of absence at least 48 hours before the lunch, otherwise a place will be laid for you and a meal provided. Empty seats are so daunting to a speaker.

I hope you will enjoy our new programme and that the luncheons will provide you with the opportunity to make some new friends and maybe startle your family with your newfound knowledge.

A. How do you envision the audience for this letter? When you write a letter, do you have a mental picture of your audience? How does knowing your audience help the writing process?

_____

_____

_____

B. What is the letter's obvious purpose? Could there be a more hidden purpose or agenda? What makes you think so? Have you ever received a letter in which you did as much reading between the lines as reading of actual lines?

_____

_____

_____

C. How does the language match the audience and purpose? In letters you may have written or received, has the language been appropriate to the purpose and audience, namely you? How does the tone of this letter strike you? What does tone have to do with purpose and audience?

_____

_____

_____

D. Although they are generally understood by speakers of both languages, American and British English are not identical. What differences do you notice in the letter? What do they suggest to you as a speaker of American English? Can writing represent or suggest our cultural upbringing? Does tone sometimes relate to the culture of the writer?

_____

_____

_____

Dear Ann Landers

Now examine the following letter written to advice columnist Ann Landers. Before you read it, quickly run through what you already know about purpose: Why do people write to a distant advice columnist? What kind of response might they expect? What do you know about Ann Landers? Can you anticipate the type of response she might give? Does she have any advantages when she writes a response? For example, can she draw on experts or research to help her?

Dear Ann Landers:

Are people becoming more insensitive, more vicious, crueler and maybe crazier as time goes by? I wonder where mankind is heading when I read about the hideous things that are happening all around us. For example:

A lawyer in Maryland pleaded guilty to breaking into the home of a friend's estranged wife to look for documents that had to do with the couple's divorce. He encountered the family kitten running loose in the kitchen, became annoyed by the "nuisance underfoot," picked up the kitten and tossed it into the microwave. He then "accidentally" turned the oven on. Of course the poor little thing died instantly.

When the woman discovered the kitten she was horrified. The man was prosecuted for this heinous act and pleaded guilty. His defense was that he had been drinking and "wasn't thinking straight." The penalty—are you ready for this?—probation!

What is this world coming to when a person can break into a home, nuke the family pet and not be punished? Again I ask, are people becoming crueler, more vicious and crazier?

—Richmond, VA

• • •

Before you read Ann Landers' response, think about how you would respond. Do you have all the information you need in order to make an appropriate response? What would you want to learn before responding? How would you get the information you need? What would be your purpose in responding to Richmond? What do you know about her/him from the letter?

_____

_____

_____

_____

Dear Rich:

Check the Bible and you will find that the cruel, vicious and crazy have been among us for a long time. Because of the advances in communication, however, we not only hear about atrocities the moment they happen but get instant replay in our living rooms on TV. Now back to that poor cat. My friends at the *Baltimore Sun* informed me that the lawyer was sentenced to one year in prison, which was then suspended, given 18 months probation, required to receive alcohol counseling and do 40 hours of community service and fined $1000 plus court costs. He also faces disbarment proceedings.

• • •

Meet the Bride and Groom

We've been looking at these diverse pieces of writing with an eye and ear for their purpose, audience, and context. In other words, we want to know why a piece was written, for whom it was written, and the situation that helps us make sense of this type of writing. We have also looked at specific language and tone in some of the pieces. How is language the product of both purpose and audience? What do writers reveal about themselves in their choice of language? Examine the two wedding announcement pieces with that question in mind. Do we learn as much about the writer as about the bride and groom?

WEDDING 1

"VALLEY" SPEAK BRINGS THEM TOGETHER

Eeeww, like, totally awesome. Faye Cregger met Victor Velasquez by accepting a double dare to walk up to him and talk to him in "valley" speak, which spoofs the way some California teen-age girls speak.

Like, ya'know. Faye wasn't expecting too much of a response. "To my surprise, he spoke back in valley talk," she said. "Weeks after meeting him, I found out that he had just learned to valley talk two days before we met."

In addition to their shared linguistic skills, the couple said they make a good pair because they're both short, "which makes us very compatible. At least it helps when kissing."

Victor proposed in 1990 on his birthday, Nov. 28, while they were out for dinner.

They were married Feb. 15 in St. Patrick's Catholic Church, Doylestown. They had a Mexican/American wedding with a few Mexican traditions.

WEDDING 2

Laura Bartell and Stanley Harr were married on Feb. 29 in the First Unitarian Society Meeting House, Madison. The Rev. Max Gaebler and Judge Angela Bartell, the bride's sister-in-law, officiated.

The bride is a partner in the international law firm of Shearman & Sterling, working in its Manhattan office. The daughter of Joyce Bartell and the late Gerald Bartell, she is an honors graduate of Stanford University and of Harvard University Law School, where she was on the 'Law Review.'

The bridegroom taught music in the Madison Public Schools for 25 years, principally at West High School. He graduated from North Central College in Naperville, Ill., where his late father was dean of the theological seminary. He also has a master's degree in music education from UW-Madison.

A. Although the purpose, audience, and context are determined by the fact that both these pieces are public wedding announcements, how has each writer provided a thoroughly individual announcement? What is the effect of each on you as a reader?

_____

_____

_____

B. Does your personal preference of writing style affect how you responded to each piece? Does your background influence how you respond?

_____

_____

_____

Making a Match

Again, note how purpose and audience influence choice of language in these pieces of writing. Does gender or age appear to make any difference in the type of information provided? Do you think geography has any influence on the information?

FROM A SOUTHERN CALIFORNIA NEWSPAPER

Able bodied 33, tall and good looking and fit physically and mentally. Seeks in shape lady for exercising, bicycling, the beach, summer fun and romance.

Attractive, intelligent, philosopher college student, mystic, misfit, intro-vert, 25 in North County. Seeking similar/interested lady, 18-25, to spend time with.

East County urban cowboy looking for urban cowgirl 40-48, country western dancing. Live East County. Fishing, camping, like classic vehi-cles. Blue eyes, 5'10", 175 lbs. white (shy).

Here's the good stuff. I'm handsome, tall (6'1"), fit (180 lbs), strawberry blond (and not losing it), green eyes (two), self-employed and secure (no debt). Christian, can cook. Interests include art, antiques, football and lots of golf. Now for the other stuff: I smoke and drink and use pro-fanity on occasion. I'm a perfectionist but not perfect. I work too much, and care too much. I'm notorious for running away to Mexico on short notice. If you are a very attractive, intelligent woman (28-33) that is happy with yourself, share similar interests and realities and have no children, you probably don't exist! But if you do, I would enjoy meeting you!

Vegetarian goddess, seeking confident 6'+ Pices-Cancer-Capricorn (higher consciousness). I'm vivacious, sensual, shapely, holistic, metaspiritual, intense, deep, playful, young, happy, intelligent, multifac-eted. Let's fly!

FROM A COLLEGE ALUMNI MAGAZINE

NYC lady, 60-ish, youthful, vibrant. Enjoys adventures, travels, city/country pleasures. Searching for harmony with healthy, intelligent, witty man with zest.

LA arts professional, attractive 50s. Serene, loving. Seeks single male, integrity, achievement.

Widower. Early 60s. Interests include Boston Symphony, Harvard foot-ball, tennis, theatre, travel. Democratic politics. Seeking nonsmoking woman with similar interests.

Journalist/artist, 60s, male, NYC. Children grown, politics left, music classical. 5'8", high energy, successful, happy. Seeks lovable, intellectual, active woman to share the rest of our lives.

FROM A MIDWEST METROPOLITAN NEWSPAPER

Intelligent, young, handsome, successful European 6'2", 190, seeks commitment-oriented woman, to 28, prefer blonde, red, light brown hair, blue eyes, sturdy full build, household-oriented with strong desire for having children. Exceptional opportunity for sincere, serious woman. No cigarette smokers.

I am a single white professional female, age 28. Do you enjoy long walks through the suburbs, shopping at Target [a discount store] on Sunday afternoons, fine dining at the Embers [low-cost restaurant not known for its decor or chef], and discussing cars? Do you find the music of Barry Manilow inspiring? If so, please do not reply.

A. How does the language of these ads convey a sense of personality?

    _____

    _____

    _____

B. Would you be tempted to respond to any of them? Why or why not?

    _____

    _____

    _____

People often make fun of matchmaking ads. But as a piece of writing, they are as legitimate and important to their writers as any other piece of writing. What's more, the ads demand careful attention to language. Every word counts heavily in the message and impression it creates. Other considerations such as the effect of humor or satire also enter into this type of writing. Similarly, the degree of formality or informality says something about the writer.

As you look back on these news articles,

✦ Which would you give high marks for engaging you as a reader?

_____

_____

✦ Which depended heavily upon a cultural context for reader acceptance and understanding?

_____

_____

✦ Which had definite "rules and regulations" (spoken or unspoken) for including specific information?

_____

_____

Be sure to have specific reasons and examples to support and illustrate your response.

ANALYZING THE NEWS: HOW OUR PURPOSE FOR WRITING EMERGES

When we write, we have a specific purpose for doing so. We may not always think of it consciously, especially in everyday writing, but it is there nonetheless. These purposes vary, everything from describing a cell under a microscope to narrating the week's events in a letter to a friend, from defining a principle of psychology to arguing for better day care or a smoke-free environment. Understanding the purpose of our writing helps us make other decisions. For example, if our purpose is to describe a cell, we would organize information differently than if we wished to argue for better day care. Sometimes your purpose for writing will be clear immediately; at other times, you have to explore topics. The following activity will show you how exploring topics can lead to purpose.

TRYING OUT THE PROCESS

Group Activity

Follow along as one member of the group reads the article aloud. Think about the different writing topics the article suggests. When you have a list of topics, discuss them.

A. Why would you be writing this particular essay? Would your primary purpose be to inform or explain? To argue for or against a point of view or an action? To describe something or someone? To narrate an incident? Although you might include description, for example, in a piece that is argumentative, your primary purpose would be argument. Consider, then, your true purpose for writing the piece.

_____

_____

_____

B. When you have determined purpose, consider the audience. To whom would you direct this writing? What do you know about this audience? Are they likely to agree or disagree with you? What kind of language and tone would be most appropriate for this audience?

_____

_____

_____

As you consider topics suggested by the following article about Bulgarian diplomats visiting the United States, think about purpose. Keep a record of the topics, no matter how far out or unlikely they may appear at first. Some of our best writing topics surface when we allow our minds to travel freely. Then follow the general directions already provided.

ARTICLE 1

DIPLOMATS MISTAKEN FOR GYPSIES

St. Anthony, Minn. (AP)—A delegation of Bulgarian diplomats who were ordered out of a grocery store after the manager mistook them for Gypsies plans to file a human-rights complaint over the incident.

Dana Penoff, a U.S. State Department interpreter escorting the group, said Sunday that she would talk to state government officials Monday about filing the complaint.

The diplomats and journalists visiting the Twin Cities as part of a U.S. Information Agency tour were forced to leave the Apache New Market Friday, she said.

"They just wanted to see what a neighborhood shopping center was like," Penoff said Saturday. "Almost immediately after we walked in, we heard this announcement that there was a suspicious group, that every shopper should be alert. It turned out that every one of us was being followed and watched," she said. Penoff said she tried to tell store owner-manager Vern Berggren that the Bulgarians were guests of the United States. He said, "Put everything down and leave. We don't want your kind of people in this store," she said.

Berggren said he was concerned after hearing reports that bands of roving thieves struck stores in Minnesota and Wisconsin on March 24. Law enforcement officials used the term *Gypsies* when comparing notes about the shoplifting incidents last weekend.

When you read this article, stereotyping and discrimination may have been high on your list of possible writing topics. Or you might have discussed shoplifting, real or imagined. Americans' response to foreigners, guests, or immigrants may have generated some topics as well. In any event, you should have a list of topics, along with the specific purpose that would guide your development of an essay on each topic.

If the general topic were stereotyping, for example, you might have come up with more refined topics such as these:

✦ Why people stereotype others

✦ How stereotypes harm various racial or ethnic groups

✦   School programs addressing stereotyping

✦   Athletic logos that stereotype

Each of these topics has writing to explain or inform as its purpose. The emphasis would be on the subject matter, stereotyping. By restating the topic, however, we could shift our purpose to one of argument, where the emphasis would be on convincing our readers that we have a valid and logical point. For example:

✦   Schools should stop using stereotypic logos, such as those depicting Native Americans.

✦   Professional sports team should stop using Native American logos (e.g., Washington Redskins, Cleveland Indians).

✦   Schools have to do a better job with multicultural education.

You have many options when you explore topics and determine your purpose for writing. Although some academic assignments are given to you, many others allow you to choose. Trying out topics and thinking about purpose, especially with classmates or friends, is a good start to the writing process.

Now continue your work with topics and purpose with articles on a stressed-out Florida student and tuna for cats—or humans?

ARTICLE 2

STUDENT BARRICADES HIMSELF IN OFFICE

Tallahassee, Fla. (AP)—A Florida State University student who barricaded himself in a state Capitol office early today demanded marijuana, liquor and doughnuts, authorities said.

The man, who had a two-way radio, told police he was armed, but authorities do not believe he took any hostages, said Leon County Undersheriff Larry Campbell.

No one was injured, and no shots had been fired. As a precaution, police diverted traffic around the building and kept out state workers.

The Legislature is not in session, but several hundred full-time staff members were scheduled for work. David Coburn, chief of staff for House Speaker T. K. Wetherell, said they were sent home with instructions to call in later.

`"There are some jumpy people out there. These kind of incidents make you wonder about your security," he said.

A dozen members of a police SWAT team and six hostage negotiators entered the building at 9:30 A.M. to try to get the man to surrender, said sheriff's spokesman Dick Simpson.

Simpson identified the man as a student at the state university in Tallahassee but did not release his name.

ARTICLE 3

TUNA TURNS OUT TO BE CAT FOOD

Newark, N.J. (AP)—Federal agents have seized 38,640 cans of cat food that had been labeled tuna for human consumption.

The $6\frac{1}{2}$ ounce cans, confiscated Monday from a Teterboro warehouse, were labeled Ocean King Chunk Light Tuna in Water but instead contained decomposed tuna fit only for sale as pet food, the Food and Drug Administration said.

Some of the cans were sold, the FDA said. The agency said all canned foods are sterilized during processing, so it isn't dangerous. "But who wants to eat decomposed cat food?" asked Lillian Aveta, an FDA compliance monitor.

M. Chu, president of Ocean King in New York City, did not immediately return calls Monday. The cans belonged originally to a lot of 25 million to 50 millions cans produced in 1985 at a cannery in St. Andrews, Canada, the FDA said. The Canadian government closed the cannery because of unsanitary conditions.

The tuna was supposed to be labeled 7th Heaven cat food in the United States. "But at some point, some cans were relabeled as tuna," Aveta said. "We don't know yet how many, or when or by whom."

The investigation was prompted in July by complaints in Minnesota, including one from Darlene La Musga of St. Paul, who opened the can and took a bite.

"I went to pull off the label, and I saw there was another label underneath," she said. "It said . . . 7th Heaven cat food. It gagged me, and I threw up in the waste basket."

ARTICLE 4

SUPPLIER: CHUNK MEAT REALLY WAS TUNA

La Crosse—The supplier of IGA brand tuna that was recalled after some consumers found a cat food label under the outer label says the cans contained tuna meant for humans, not cats. . . .

Some customers called it a shock to find the pet food label under the outer wrapper. Vicki Rundquist of Deer Park said she was recycling cans earlier this week when she discovered the double labels and suddenly felt ill to her stomach.

Darlene La Musga said she opened a can of tuna Wednesday in her mother's kitchen in St. Paul, took a bite and prepared to make tuna salad. "I went to pull off the label, and I saw there was another label underneath," she said. "It said Tuna Treat and it also said 7th Heaven cat food. It gagged me, and I threw up in the waste basket."

CHAPTER 2

Reading and Writing Connections

When we write, we also draw upon our reading skills, especially when we're revising or editing. Revising and editing depend upon our ability to read carefully—to step out of the role of writer and become a reader. Thus, although this is a text about writing, it is also a text about reading. You will be asked to read carefully and thoughtfully, to observe, to analyze, and, finally, to evaluate written texts.

RESPONDING TO WHAT WE READ

As individual readers, we approach a written text with a personal frame of reference. All of us are influenced by our past experiences, as well as by our present situations. Each person's age, gender, and ethnicity affect how that person responds to a piece of writing. Even if several people share similar backgrounds, each will nonetheless bring an individual response to what is read. We weave our own images, sensations, and emotions into what we read; we blend emotional and logical responses. We bring ourselves to those marks on a page, interact with them, and take something away. Someone in an unhappy relationship, for example, will bring sad experiences and emotions to a reading that explores relationships. Someone who has experienced or observed racial discrimination will bring those images and feelings to a reading dealing with race relationships. This response is what makes reading so powerful, and good writing so important.

RESPONDING THROUGH WRITING

A Reading Journal

To learn more about responding to writing, you will keep a reading journal. You will be asked to write various types of entries in your reading journal. At times, you will explore your knowledge or beliefs about a topic before and after you read. At other times, you may find yourself summarizing the main ideas, arguing with them, asking questions, or connecting with your own experiences in some way. In your journal, you will be writing to explore ideas—another writer's, your own, a classmate's, a friend's—and to make connections. Later you may be asked to communicate those ideas and your responses to them more formally. The journal, however, is simply a place to explore—freely and honestly. Don't worry about complete sentences, grammar, spelling, or punctuation. What's important here are your ideas, understandable only to you.

Responding as You Read. As you read, respond to words, phrases, passages—anything that interests you, confuses you, intrigues you, angers you. One way to make this process more orderly is to divide your journal page into two halves. On the left-hand side, write down words or sentences that evoked a response as you read. When you've completed the reading, respond more fully on the right-hand side of the journal.

Responding After You Read. Sometimes you'll be asked to share your ideas with classmates, focusing on questions raised by that piece of reading, or perhaps to develop your own questions about what you read.

A HOUSE OF MY OWN

Sandra Cisneros

Sandra Cisneros, a noted Hispanic writer, is best known for The House on Mango Street.

Not a flat. Not an apartment in back. Not a man's house. Not a daddy's. A house all my own. With my porch and my pillow, my pretty purple petunias. My books and my stories. My two shoes waiting beside the bed. Nobody to shake a stick at. Nobody's garbage to pick up after.

Only a house quiet as snow, a space for myself to go, clean as paper before the poem.

In your journal:

What questions does Sandra Cisneros raise for you?

Do you think males and females might have different responses?

What two things would you have in a house of your own?

BEAUTIFUL AND CRUEL

Sandra Cisneros

I am an ugly daughter. I am the one nobody comes for. Nenny says she won't wait her whole life for a husband to come and get her, that Minerva's sister left her mother's house by having a baby, but she doesn't want to go that way either. She wants things all her own, to pick and choose. Nenny has pretty eyes and it's easy to talk that way if you are pretty.

My mother says when I get older my dusty hair will settle and my blouse will learn to stay clean, but I have decided not to grow up tame like the others who lay their necks on the threshold waiting for the ball and chain.

In the movies there is always one with red lips who is beautiful and cruel. She is the one who drives the men crazy and laughs them all away. Her power is her own. She will not give it away.

I have begun my own quiet war. Simple. Sure. I am one who leaves the table like a man, without putting back the chair or picking up the plate.

In your journal:

What are your most immediate responses to Cisneros's ideas? Why?

Before you read "The Story of an Hour" by Kate Chopin (1851–1904), examine for a moment, in your journal, your own knowledge and feelings about marriage. Do you, for example, believe that a marriage vow is sacred, that marriage is for life, regardless of individual happiness or fulfillment? Do you consider love to be complex? Or is it fairly straightforward—you either love or do not love someone? Do you believe the death of a spouse or partner is always a tragedy?

In order to form some point of identification with Chopin's story, respond to the following:

My definition of marriage is _____

I got this definition through _____

As you read Chopin's story, keep your reading journal beside you. Jot down words, phrases, and passages that evoke strong images or responses in you; write questions you might have concerning things you wonder about or don't understand.

THE STORY OF AN HOUR

Kate Chopin

Knowing that Mrs. Mallard was afflicted with heart trouble, great care was taken to break to her as gently as possible the news of her husband's death.

It was her sister Josephine who told her, in broken sentences; veiled hints that revealed in half concealing. Her husband's friend Richards was there, too, near her. It was he who had been in the newspaper office when intelligence of the railroad disaster was received, with Brently Mallard's name leading the list of "killed." He had only taken the time to assure himself of its truth by a second telegram, and had hastened to forestall any less careful, less tender friend in bearing the sad message.

She did not hear the story as many women have read the same, with a paralyzed inability to accept its significance. She wept at once, with sudden, wild abandonment, in her sister's arms. When the storm of grief had spent itself she went away to her room alone. She would have no one follow her.

There stood, facing the open window, a comfortable, roomy armchair. Into this she sank, pressed down by a physical exhaustion that haunted her body and seemed to reach into her soul.

She could see in the open square before her house the tops of trees that were all aquiver with new spring life. The delicious breath of rain was in the air. In the street below a peddler was crying his wares. The notes of a distant song which some one was singing reached her faintly, and countless sparrows were twittering in the eves.

There were patches of blue sky showing here and there through the clouds that had met and piled one above the other in the west facing her window.

She sat with her head thrown back upon the cushion of the chair, quite motionless, except when a sob came up into her throat and shook her, as a child who has cried itself to sleep continues to sob in its dreams.

She was young, with a fair, calm face, whose lines bespoke repression and even a certain strength. But now there was a dull stare in her eyes, whose gaze was fixed away off yonder on one of those patches of blue sky. It was not a glance of reflection, but rather indicated a suspension of intelligent thought.

There was something coming to her and she was waiting for it, fearfully. What was it? She did not know; it was too subtle and elusive to name. But she felt it, creeping out of the sky, reaching toward her through the sounds, the scents, the color that filled the air.

Now her bosom rose and fell tumultuously. She was beginning to recognize this thing that was approaching to possess her, and she was striving to beat it back with her will—as powerless as her two white slender hands would have been.

When she abandoned herself a little whispered word escaped her slightly parted lips. she said it over and over under her breath: "free, free, free!" The vacant stare and look of terror that had followed it went from her eyes. They stayed keen and bright. Her pulse beat fast, and the coursing blood warmed and relaxed every inch of her body.

She did not stop to ask if it were or were not a monstrous joy that held her. A clear and exalted perception enabled her to dismiss the suggestion as trivial.

She knew that she would weep again when she saw the kind, tender hands folded in death; the face that had never looked save with love upon her, fixed and gray and dead. But she saw beyond that bitter moment a long procession of years to come that would belong to her absolutely. And she opened and spread her arms out to them in welcome.

There would be no one to live for her during those coming years; she would live for herself. There would be no powerful will bending hers in that blind persistence with which men and women believe they have a right to impose a private will upon a fellow-creature. A kind intention or a cruel intention made the act no less a crime as she looked upon it in that brief moment of illumination.

And yet she had loved him—sometimes. Often she had not. What did it matter? What could love, the unsolved mystery, count for in face of this possession of self-assertion, which she suddenly recognized as the strongest impulse of her being!

"Free! Body and soul free!" she kept whispering.

Josephine was kneeling before the closed door with her lips to the keyhole, imploring for admission. "Louise, open this door! I beg; open the door—will you make yourself ill. What are you doing, Louise? For heaven's sake open the door."

"Go away. I am not making myself ill." No; she was drinking a very elixir of life through that open window.

Her fancy was running riot along those days ahead of her. Spring days, and summer days, and all sorts of days that would be her own. She breathed a quick prayer that life might be long. It was only yesterday that she had thought with a shudder that life might be long.

She arose at length and opened the door to her sister's importunities. There was a feverish triumph in her eyes, and she carried herself unwittingly like a goddess of Victory. She clasped her sister's waist, and together they descended the stairs. Richards stood waiting for them at the bottom.

Someone was opening the front door with a latchkey. It was Brently Mallard who entered, a little travel-stained, composedly carrying his gripsack and umbrella. He had been far from the scene of the accident, and did not even know there had been one. He stood amazed at Josephine's piercing cry; at Richards' quick motion to screen him from the view of his wife.

But Richards was too late.

When the doctors came they said she had died of heart disease—of the joy that kills.

In your reading journal, respond to the following questions:

Thinking About Content

1. Early in the story, Mrs. Mallard is described as weeping with wild abandonment, a "storm of grief." This is a strong, very poetic image. Do you change your image or notion of Mrs. Mallard's "storm of grief" as the story progresses? Explain.

2. The final line of the story: "When the doctors came they said she had died of heart disease—of the joy that kills." What is meant by "the joy that kills"? Do you believe the doctors were correct? How do you know?

3. In your own words, characterize Mrs. Mallard's marriage and life. What in the story leads you to these conclusions?

Thinking About Writing

1. Reread paragraphs 5 and 6. Chopin is creating a mood which is somewhat unusual for a story about death and loss. What details make us think more about life than about death?

2. Who tells this story? Would the story be different if it had been written in the first person (I)? Rewrite the opening paragraphs, about the first 25 lines, in the first person. Then, consider the difference between first and third person "telling." Which version do you like better? Why?

3. List some of the images which provide us with the sense of life and freedom that Mrs. Mallard was experiencing. How does Chopin connect with our senses?

Personal Connections

1. Reread Mrs. Mallard's first response to news of her husband's death, paragraphs 3 and 7. Have you ever responded this way to some personal tragedy or bad news? Do you think males and females respond differently? Explain.

   _____

   _____

   _____

2. Do you think personal freedom is stressed too much in American culture? Not enough?

   _____

   _____

   _____

3. Imagine Kate Chopin sitting across from you, having a cup of coffee in the student center. What would you say to her? What would you want to know from her?

   _____

   _____

   _____

Making Connections

Writing a hundred years ago, Kate Chopin offered us a view of women in her society. Sandra Cisneros, a contemporary writer, offers us another. Despite a century between them, are there similarities?

Group Activity

Discuss the following questions thoroughly. If you disagree, ask questions to learn more about this person's viewpoint. If people disagree with you, try to clarify your views through more specific details, examples, and reasons. You may want to keep some notes from this discussion: What surprised you? Amused you? Puzzled you? Disturbed you? Did you think about some very different points of view because of your classmates?

1. Do males and females respond differently to important events, show joy and sadness in significantly different ways? Does culture play a role in such response? Provide examples.

2. Do males and females have significantly different ideas about marriage? About degrees of freedom within marriage? Do different cultures have different ideas about marriage? Why would it be important for a culture to develop its own notion of courtship and marriage? Are cross-cultural relationships doomed from the start? Are attitudes about cross-cultural relationships changing in the 1990s?

3. How do young people build ideas about love and marriage? Are these ideas always valid?

4. Do humans need relationships? Does living alone result in an unfulfilled life? Is being alone the same as being lonely?

5. Are relationships complicated in the 1990s?

As a literary piece, "The Story of an Hour" represents one type of reading task common to school settings. The following excerpt, taken from a college sociology textbook, represents another. Although its authors also discuss love and marriage, their purpose is very different from Chopin's. In your reading journal, respond to the following questions before you read:

1. Do you know anyone who married solely for economic reasons? For reasons of gaining social status? Given the "hype" of love in modern America, do you think anyone would admit to marrying for any reason but love?

2. What are your views on marrying for reasons other than love? How has your culture influenced your thinking? Your family?

Keeping a journal for textbook reading is a good study habit. On the left-hand side, jot down words, phrases—anything from the text that strikes you. Note any ideas that are confusing, difficult, and so on. When you complete your reading, review what you've just recorded. Then, on the right-hand side, respond more fully to those notes.

THE LOVE REVOLUTION AND THE RISE OF FEMINISM

THE LOVE REVOLUTION

The basic principle of the modern love revolution was to connect love with marriage. Love existed in previous societies, to be sure. But it simply was not expected to be the reason for marrying someone. In tribal societies, kinship rules that specified, for instance, that one should marry one's cousin on the father's side but not on the mother's side obviously excluded love as a motive for marriage. Similarly, where marriage was a matter of family politics or economics, the sentiments of the individual counted for very little. By the mid-twentieth century, though, marrying for love became *the* dominant ideal, so much so that one is embarrassed to admit marrying for any other reason. This change, which came about gradually in the 1700s and 1800s, may be referred to as the *love revolution.* [p. 126]

ECONOMIC AND POLITICAL RESTRICTIONS ON LOVE

. . . Marriages were just too imporant economically for other considerations to enter in very much. The man who wanted to be a property owner running his own farm or small business had to be married and he chose a wife who could help him with the work, oversee the servants and apprentices, and, if possible, bring in some money or property to get started. The woman had even less choice in the matter. She needed a husband in order to have an economic establishment in which she could share; if she wanted any kind of career or social status, she would have to do it by helping her husband's trade. . . .

The fact that people did not live long contributed to a somewhat mercenary attitude toward marriage. Since men were generally older than their wives (though not necessarily by much), many women were left widowed. If a widow inherited a substantial business or farm and her children were still too young to run it, she would very likely remarry in order to have a man to help work the enterprise. On the other hand, the life expectancy of women was shorter than that of men, mainly because many women died in childbirth. When this happened, a widower married again as fast as he could, since a wife was needed, not for sentimental reasons, but in order to have someone help run the household business. [pp. 129–130]

. . . [In the 1700s] Marriages became more a private affair between the couples themselves, less of a political or business arrangement. . . . As business moved out of the home, the work of wives (at least in the middle class) became less crucial economically. As the private domestic sphere emerged, women found themselves confined within it [the house and family]. . . .

> For although men now needed little from marriage besides sex and
> domestic help, women still found themselves economically dependent
> upon a husband. To ensure their own economic well-being it was
> important to attach men to themselves personally, and with a strong
> and lifetime tie if possible. This is what the new love ideal did. . . . [It]
> made [love] the emotional insurance that kept a woman and her loyal
> breadwinner tied together "until death do us part." [pp. 136–137]

In your journal, respond to the following questions:

Thinking About Content

1. How does this factual look at love and marriage as it emerged in the nineteenth century compare with Kate Chopin's fictional look at marriage during the same time period?

2. What is meant by political or economic marriages? Does either or both of them exist today? How do you know?

3. If society has changed its views on sex, love, and marriage throughout the course of world history, what are the implications for the future generations? What do you think sociologists will be writing fifty years from now? A hundred years from now? What in this reading led you to these conclusions?

Thinking About Writing

1. This type of writing, very common in academic settings, is expository writing. How would you characterize it?

2. Kate Chopin's story is an example of fictional narration. How is it different from exposition? What differences did you notice in your reading of each type of writing?

Personal Connections

1. Do you think "until death do us part" is considered important in a modern love relationship? Is this phrase still part of marriage vows?

2. Based on the information in the above reading, do you believe that marriage was more or less complex before the twentieth century? Do you think marriage in the twenty-first century will be complex?

Writing Activity 1 _____

Turn back to your reading journal responses. Review your notes, paying attention to questions where you had quite a bit to say or strong personal ideas. Mark these areas with an asterisk (*). Your ideas on one of these questions will form the basis of your writing task. Choose one question; write it on a clean sheet of paper; then list the various ideas you have already explored in response to it. What do these ideas suggest? Do you have a main idea, a single point of view, in these notes? If yes, write it down. Does it answer the question? Can it serve as the main idea? If so, it may be your topic sentence for a brief piece of writing.

A REMINDER: USING TOPIC SENTENCES

In academic writing, the topic sentence expresses the main idea of the entire paragraph; it makes a point. The topic sentence is helpful in that it prepares us for what the paragraph is all about. As readers, we gear up for a specific discussion on a single point; we look for details, examples, or reasons to support that single point. Stating a topic sentence can also help us when we write. It boldly reminds us that we have promised to discuss a single point and, thus, that we have to stick to it. Not all paragraphs, however, have an explicit, stated topic sentence.

We develop paragraphs around the main idea through various means of supporting detail. Sometimes we use examples, sometimes we use reasons, and sometimes we use both. We use examples and reasons every day in conversations. When someone asks, "What do you mean?" the response is likely to be an example. When someone asks, "Why?" the response is likely to be a reason. We use examples when we describe our world and the people and things in it; we use examples when we want to illustrate a point; and we use examples when we analyze an idea, event, or problem. We use reasons most often when we argue or evaluate.

Although we don't even have to think very hard to come up with supporting details in conversations, while writing we usually spend more time and thought on choosing just the right ones, mainly because we won't get a second chance. When we talk, we can continually add, change, and modify according to the needs of our listener. In writing, we have to anticipate the needs of a distant reader. It's one of the reasons why writing is demanding and time-consuming.

Writing Activity 2

Write a brief piece based on one of the questions following "A House of My Own," "Beautiful and Cruel," "The Story of an Hour," or "The Love Revolution and the Rise of Feminism." Use the question as a base for your response, forming a topic sentence that will guide you in developing your answer. Here are some student examples:

"Until death do us part" has not anywhere the meaning it had, because our society generally doesn't care about ethics, morals, the long term, or religious practices like it once did.

Matt

Culture plays a role in the ways that males and females respond to significant events.

Mark

Sexual freedom has definitely weakened the marriages of the 1990s.

Laura

As you consider your topic sentence, review your notes again. Then ask why as a means of addressing the topic and thinking about the ideas you need to support your topic sentence. Have you already answered "Why?" in your notes? Continue to jot down ideas as they occur to you, in any order. Then review the list and decide if you want to include all the ideas. In a single paragraph, you need to be very focused, developing your topic sentence clearly and economically. Perhaps one reason or example is all you need. This student focused on one television show to make his point:

The Image of Relationships

In the age of soap operas, Al Bundy, and frequent divorces, young people are building ideas about love and marriage that can scar a child's image of it forever. The daytime soaps romanticize affairs, sex outside of wedlock and glamorous people whose love for someone changes every time there's an advertisement. This is not a good impression on a young person trying to start a relationship they can enjoy. For a couple trying to take the final step of marriage, <u>Married with Children</u> shows life after marriage doesn't exist. It's plagued with constant quarreling between spouses and their children. It portrays marriage as torture or punishment for making a relationship permanent. People may laugh at the couple's arguments, but soon the image is subconsciously with them. Today's skyrocketing divorce rate only enforces the sitcoms' message. Society must do something to offset these negative and unrealistic images of relationships.

Joe Cronick

Supporting Your Ideas

When you think about "why," reasons may come readily to mind. But you need to support those reasons. Otherwise, you're asking someone to just accept your word for it, "Because I say so." In academic writing, you need to present your reader with facts or experiences that provide a basis for your reasons. Facts are statements that can be verified, that can be proven to be accurate and true. For example, if you were to say something to the effect that more marriages end in divorce today than ten years ago, you should be able to present government figures, statistics, to prove it. Someone else could look up these statistics and verify that your statement is accurate. Experiences provide details of some event that either you experienced yourself or saw. In using experience to support your topic sentence, you let the reader see and hear what you saw and heard. Or you may use someone else's experience, something you heard directly from that person or even through television, radio, or film. It is even possible to present an imaginary experience, something you only thought about.

What's important is recreating the experience in a way that a reader can visualize it, hear it, imagine it. You want to show, not tell. Through vivid words, tapping into a reader's senses (sight, sound, touch, hearing, taste), you can bring the reader into the experience. There is considerable difference between a sentence that tells:

The boy seemed nervous.

and one that shows:

The boy shifted from foot to foot, sneaking looks at the police officer; when he opened his mouth to respond, the words came tumbling out in nonsense syllables.

Providing readers with specific detail, then, is essential in supporting your ideas.

Thinking About Order

When you have decided on content—what you want to include—think about the order in which you want to present it. If you are using several reasons, you need to decide whether to use the strongest or weakest first. If you are using more than one example, you need to decide whether it would be better to start or end with the best one.

Putting It All Together

Write a rough draft. Don't worry about grammar, punctuation, and spelling at this point. They're important, but not at the point where you are still thinking about getting the ideas down on paper.

REVISING

When you are satisfied that you've made your point—said what you want to say—you're ready to start revising. Use the following questions as a guide:

1. Is my topic sentence clearly stated? Will my readers understand immediately what this paragraph is all about?

2. Have I supported my topic sentence with specific details, reasons, or examples? If not, add material.

3. Have I strayed from my topic, added in some idea which really isn't related to my main idea? If so, delete this material.

4. Have I repeated myself? If so, delete material.

5. Will the organization of my ideas make sense to my readers? Will they be able to follow my ideas easily? If not, rearrange the ideas to reflect a logical flow: least to most important, most to least important, chronological.

6. Have I connected my ideas so my readers can move easily from one sentence to the next? If not, consider the relationship between the ideas:

    A. An addition to what you just said:

    furthermore   equally important
    additionally   also

Married with Children shows life after marriage doesn't exist. Furthermore, it portrays marriage as torture or punishment for making a relationship permanent.

B. **An example of what you just said:**

for example
for instance

Culture plays a role in the ways that males and females respond to significant events. For example, most American males wouldn't cry at a wedding, even their own.

C. **An explanation of what you just said:**

for example   in other words
for instance   namely

Sexual freedom has weakened the marriages of the 1990s. In other words, premarital sex has had an effect.

D. **A comparison with what you just said:**

also   similarly
in the same way

The daytime soaps romanticize affairs. Similarly they promote sex out of wedlock.

E. **A contrast with what you just said:**

however   nevertheless

Society must do something to offset these negative images of relationships. However, it appears unlikely to do so given the current popularity of the daytime soaps.

F. A result of what you just said:

because therefore

consequently as a result

but

Sexual freedom weakened many marriages in the past
decade. Consequently, couples of the 1990s are rejecting
it.

Be careful not to overuse these connectors. Using too many of
them is just as distracting as using too few.

Writing Partner Activity

Exchange your draft with a writing partner. Don't say something
like "This isn't very good." No one, no matter how experienced or
skilled, writes a good early draft. It's just that, a draft, something to
work with and shape into a better draft. At the same time, don't say
something like "It's okay" either. You can't help one another if you
don't respond honestly—and no early draft, as just noted, is "very
good."

Use the questions in the preceding list as a guide to evaluating the
paragraph. Additionally, use these questions as a general guide:

1. What do you mean when you say _____?

2. Give me an example of _____.

3. Explain the part (or sentence) about _____.

4. Prove what you say about _____.

5. Be more specific about _____.

In addition to pointing out areas for improvement, be sure to comment on what the writer has done well. No matter how rough the
draft may appear at this point, it no doubt contains some real potential for development. Let the writer know that you are interested in an
idea or that you noticed an especially vivid word. Help your partner by
being specific and honest about areas that need work. Discuss all comments and suggestions with your partner.

After you have thought about your writing partner's suggestions
for your draft, decide which of them you will use. The draft is yours,
no one else's, and you must be the one to decide what stays and what
goes. However, if your partner had trouble following your ideas or felt

that you had too much or too little information, chances are other readers will have similar problems. Revise your draft for content and organization.

Editing Activity

When you are satisfied that your draft says what you want it to say, and in the order you wish to say it, you're ready to check individual sentences for completeness.

Read each sentence slowly, placing a piece of paper over the rest of the writing. This technique will force you to read only one line at a time, to concentrate on it alone. Ask yourself two questions: Is the sentence complete? Is it separated by end punctuation?

Is the sentence complete? Can it stand alone and make complete sense to a reader? Remember the difference between speaking and writing: When we speak, we often use incomplete sentences. Because our listener is right there, it doesn't matter. He or she can follow us quite easily, or ask questions or request repetition if needed. But when we write, we have no immediate feedback, no face-to-face context to help us. Therefore, we have to follow a different set of rules to ensure that our readers really can follow our ideas easily. Making certain our sentences express a grammatically complete idea is one of those rules.

Incomplete sentences are often referred to as *fragments*, the word itself indicating a "piece of something." Sometimes our brain is racing ahead of our hand, and we end up making connections in our head that aren't there on the paper. Because we may be thinking in complete sentences, we punctuate the fragment as though it were a complete, independent word group. Check that the word group starting with a capital letter and ending with a period, question mark, exclamation point, or semicolon is actually an independent sentence, relying on nothing else for its meaning. If you discover that the word group can't stand alone, read the sentence just before and just after it. Can you attach the fragment? Do you want to? You may decide to make a new sentence out of the fragment.

Is each sentence separated by end punctuation (period, question mark, exclamation point, semicolon)? If not, you may have a *run-on*, two independent sentences side by side, no punctuation or connectors between them. If you find that you have independent sentences separated only by a comma, you have a *comma splice* or *comma fault*. Correcting a run-on or comma splice requires you to think through the relationship between the two sentences: Do you want to emphasize the relationship through use of a connector word? Is the relationship so close that you could use a semicolon, with no connector needed at all? Do you want to separate the sentences completely by adding end punctuation?

If you think you may have seen fragments and comma splices in professional writing, you're right. Professional writers use them occasionally to achieve a particular effect. But they do so deliberately, with confidence that no reader will be derailed or annoyed by the very occasional fragment or comma splice. As readers, we expect writers to help us follow their ideas efficiently and accurately. Without definite sentence boundaries, we simply can't do that. We are forced to reread every word group, trying to figure out where each begins and ends. And we would no doubt be very irritated, perhaps stop reading altogether. For this reason, as writers we need to check sentence boundaries carefully.

Writing Partner Activity

Check each other's drafts for fragments, run-ons, and comma splices. Although there may be other types of errors, concentrate only on sentence completeness. Put an asterisk (*) next to any sentence that you believe is faulty. Discuss the paragraphs when you have both completed your sentence check. Consider various options for making needed corrections.

Refer to Part Two, "A Writer's Handbook," for assistance.

CHAPTER 3

Writing from Personal Experience

Most often, we begin writing as a way of sharing our experience. From the first crayon mark on the wall to a school essay, we draw upon our personal world—events, people, thoughts and dreams, hopes and dashed hopes. Personal-experience writing is powerful because it arises from our very core. Writing about personal experience can also be very satisfying, providing an exploration that might be left unsaid or quite limited in the give and take of conversation. Through writing, then, we can explore ourselves and our world in important ways. Narration is one of the most basic and most important of these.

NARRATION

When you read Sandra Cisneros's and Kate Chopin's pieces, you were reading narratives. Although narratives don't usually state their main idea explicitly, we nonetheless could form a very good idea of Cisneros's or Chopin's main idea. We also grasped its significance; what Cisneros and Chopin told us mattered. Telling a story that matters is at the heart of narration. We want to care about the people and events, and we want what happens to reflect our human experience, such as growing up or dealing with relationships. Narratives are a powerful means of connecting us not only with others, but also with ourselves.

Characteristics of Narration

Narration is one of the most common forms of writing we encounter, often starting as early as age one or two through picture books. Oral narratives, in many cultures, take the place of written forms; they contain the same elements as the written form, and capture listeners through the same techniques. Narratives tell a story, most often presenting a series of incidents, recording a slice of life through time. That time may be five minutes or five years. Generally, narratives are linear; that is, they take us from point A to point B; first this happened, then this happened. Within this structure, the writer can emphasize an incident, paint a verbal picture, and highlight feelings. However, some narratives start at the end and then return to the real beginning through flashbacks. We often see this technique in movies or television programs, where we know the outcome and then follow the story line to learn how people and events reached that outcome. It can be a very effective strategy for keeping the reader's attention.

Although it seems easy enough to get from point A to point B to point C, there are potential problems. If the writer jumps ahead too quickly, not preparing us for the outcome, we'll probably become confused. Or if the writer leaves out important details, we will become equally confused and, most likely, irritated. If the writer gets sidetracked, wandering off the story line, we will get bored and put aside the narrative. We may also get bored if the writer doesn't use enough specific detail, enough examples, to draw us into the story. Good narratives depend upon selecting words that provide the reader with a concrete sense of person, place, events. The connection between writer and reader lies in our senses—touch, taste, hearing, sight, and smell—and the ability to evoke both physical and emotional images and associations.

Effective narratives, those that leave us with a sense of "I'm really glad I read this," have captured us through the writer's attention to specific detail, as well as through the careful ordering of that detail. Spatial description may play a large role in narratives. The writer has to consider the ways in which our eyes move over an object, person, or scene. We usually start at a set point and return to that point, taking in everything en route. Sometimes, we focus on a single detail first, a dominating detail that draws us to it before we shift our gaze to other things. Descriptions may be realistic, such as those in dictionaries and encyclopedias—or police reports, for that matter, but they may also be nonrealistic, painting a picture not as it would appear with a camera but with an artist's brush. This type of description, not intended as scientific accuracy, provides us with a picture nonetheless, often a mood or atmosphere essential to the narrative. In Richard Wright's narrative, we see both.

Before you read this excerpt explore your ideas on discipline in your reading journal.

✦ Do you believe parents have an obligation to discipline their children? In what ways?

✦ Do disciplinary practices get passed from generation to generation, a child repeating the same type of discipline as was practiced with him or her?

✦ Do children have rights? Have you had any experience with an adult as lawgiver? If yes, can you recall your feelings, responses, and so on?

As you read, keep your double-entry journal open. On the left-hand side, write down words, phrases, or sentences that evoke strong responses in you; ask questions or argue.

THE KITTEN

Richard Wright

Richard Wright was among the most gifted writers of the 1940s and 1950s, one of the voices exploring themes of racial inequality and injustice. Born in Mississippi, he moved from one urban center to another, and finally, to Paris, where he died in 1960. "The Kitten" is taken from Black Boy, *his autobiography.*

In Memphis we lived in a one-story brick tenement. The stone buildings and the concrete pavements looked bleak and hostile to me. The absence of green, growing things made the city seem dead. Living space for the four of us—my mother, my brother, my father, and me—was a kitchen and a bedroom. In the front and rear were paved areas in which my brother and I could play, but for days I was afraid to go into the strange city streets alone.

It was in this tenement that the personality of my father first came fully into the orbit of my concern. He worked as a night porter in a Beale Street drugstore and he became important and forbidding to me only when I learned that I could not make noise when he was asleep in the daytime. He was the lawgiver in our family and I never laughed in his presence. I used to lurch timidly in the kitchen doorway and watch his huge body sitting slumped at the table. I stared at him with awe as he gulped his beer from a tin bucket, as he ate long and heavily, sighed, belched, closed his eyes to nod on a stuffed belly. He was quite fat and his bloated stomach always lapped over his belt. He was always a stranger to me, always somehow alien and remote.

One morning my brother and I, while playing in the rear of our flat, found a stray kitten that set up a loud, persistent meowing. We fed it some scraps of food and gave it water, but it still meowed. My father, clad in his underwear, stumbled sleepily to the back door and demanded that we keep quiet. We told him that it was the kitten that was making the noise and he ordered us to drive it away. We tried to make the kitten leave, but it would not budge. My father took a hand.

"Scat!" he shouted.

The scrawny kitten lingered, brushing itself against our legs, and meowing plaintively.

"Kill that damn thing!" my father exploded. "Do anything, but get it away from here!"

He went inside, grumbling. I resented his shouting and it irked me that I could never make him feel my resentment. How could I hit back at him? Oh, yes. . . . He had said to kill the kitten and I would kill it! I knew that he had really not meant for me to kill the kitten, but my deep hate of him urged me toward a literal acceptance of his word.

"He said for us to kill the kitten," I told my brother.

"He didn't mean it," my brother said.

"He did, and I'm going to kill 'im."

"Then he will howl," my brother said.

"He can't howl if he's dead," I said.

"He didn't really say kill 'im," my brother protested.

"He did!" I said. "And you heard him!"

My brother ran away in fright. I found a piece of rope, made a noose, slipped it about the kitten's neck, pulled it over a nail, then jerked the animal clear of the ground. It gasped, slobbered, spun, doubled, clawed the air frantically; finally its mouth gaped and its pink-white tongue shot out stiffly. I tied the rope to a nail and went to find my brother. He was crouching behind a corner of the building.

"I killed 'im," I whispered.

"You did bad," my brother said.

"Now Papa can sleep," I said, deeply satisfied.

"He didn't mean for you to kill 'im," my brother said.

"Then why did he *tell* me to do it?" I demanded.

My brother could not answer; he stared fearfully at the dangling kitten.

"That kitten's going to get you," he warned me.

"That kitten can't even breathe now," I said.

"I'm going to tell," my brother said, running into the house.

I waited, resolving to defend myself with my father's rash words, anticipating my enjoyment in repeating them to him even though I knew that he had spoken them in anger. My mother hurried toward me, drying her hands upon her apron. She stopped and paled when she saw the kitten suspended from the rope.

"What in God's name have you done?" she asked.

"The kitten was making noise and Papa said to kill it," I explained.

"You little fool!" she said. "Your father's going to beat you for this!"

"But he told me to kill it," I said.

"You shut your mouth!"

She grabbed my hand and dragged me to my father's bedside and told him what I had done.

"You know better than that!" my father stormed.

"You told me to kill 'im," I said.

"I told you to drive him away," he said.

"You told me to kill 'im," I countered positively.

"You get out of my eyes before I smack you down!" my father bellowed in disgust, then turned over in bed.

I had had my first triumph over my father. I had made him believe that I had taken his words literally. He could not punish me now without risking his authority. I was happy because I had at last found a way to throw my criticism of him into his face. I had made him feel that, if he whipped me for killing the kitten, I would never give serious weight to his words again. I had made him know that. I felt he was cruel and I had done it without his punishing me.

But my mother, being more imaginative, retaliated with an assault upon my sensibilities that crushed me with the moral horror involved in taking a life. All that afternoon she directed toward me calculated words that spawned in my mind a horde of invisible demons bent upon exacting vengeance for what I had done. As evening drew near, anxiety filled me and I was afraid to go into an empty room alone.

"You owe a debt you can never pay," my mother said.

"I'm sorry," I mumbled.

"Being sorry can't make that kitten live again," she said.

Then, just before I was to go to bed, she uttered a paralyzing injunction: she ordered me to go out into the dark, dig a grave, and bury the kitten.

"No!" I screamed, feeling that if I went out of doors some evil spirit would whisk me away.

"Get out there and bury that poor kitten," she ordered.

"I'm scared!"

"And wasn't that kitten scared when you put that rope around its neck?" she asked.

"But it was only a kitten," I explained.

"But it was alive," she said. "Can you make it live again?"

"But Papa said to kill it," I said, trying to shift the moral blame upon my father.

My mother whacked me across my mouth with the flat palm of her hand.

"You stop that lying! You knew what he meant!"

"I didn't!" I bawled.

She shoved a tiny spade into my hands.

"Go out there and dig a hole and bury that kitten!"

I stumbled out into the black night, sobbing, my legs wobbly from fear. Though I knew that I had killed the kitten, my mother's words had made it live again in my mind. What would that kitten do to me when I touched it? Would it claw at my eyes? As I groped toward the dead kitten, my mother lingered behind me, unseen in the dark, her disembodied voice egging me on.

"Mama, come and stand by me," I begged.

"You didn't stand by that kitten, so why should I stand by you?" she asked tauntingly from the menacing darkness.

"I can't touch it," I whimpered, feeling that the kitten was staring at me with reproachful eyes.

"Untie it!" she ordered.

Shuddering, I fumbled at the rope and the kitten dropped to the pavement with a thud that echoed in my mind for many days and nights. Then, obeying my mother's floating voice, I hunted for a spot of earth, dug a shallow hole, and buried the stiff kitten; as I handled its cold body my skin prickled. When I had completed the burial, I signed and started back to the flat, but my mother caught hold of my hand and led me again to the kitten's grave.

"Shut your eyes and repeat after me," she said.

I closed my eyes tightly, my hand clinging to hers.

"Dear God, our Father, forgive me, for I knew not what I was doing. . . "

"Dear God, our Father, forgive me, for I knew not what I was doing," I repeated.

"And spare my poor life, even though I did not spare the life of the kitten. . ."

"And while I sleep tonight, do not snatch the breath of life from me. . ."

I opened my mouth but no words came. My mind was frozen with horror. I pictured myself gasping for breath and dying in my sleep. I broke away from my mother and ran into the night, crying, shaking with dread.

"No," I sobbed.

My mother called to me many times, but I would not go to her.

"Well, I suppose you've learned your lesson," she said at last.

Contrite, I went to bed, hoping that I would never see another kitten.

In your journal, respond to the following questions:

Thinking About Content

1. In your own words, characterize the main characters: child, father, mother. What specific details in the story led you to these characterizations? What is the nature of the family relationships? How did you form these ideas?

2. Do you believe the boy is portrayed as a victim? Is Wright looking for sympathy from his readers?

Thinking About Writing

1. Wright provides both a physical and psychological description for his readers. List words, phrases, and so on that provide us with these descriptions.

2. How is the use of dialogue essential to this story? Would you have the same reactions if there were no dialogue?

3. From whose point of view is the story presented? How might the story change if another person related the incident?

Personal Connections

1. Children and adolescents often feel victimized by adults, people in authority (e.g., parent or caretaker, teacher). Have you ever been in a situation where you believed you were treated unfairly, picked on, victimized? What, if anything, did you do?

2. Do you believe Wright's action was justified? Do you know of situations where children had to take desperate measures to preserve themselves? Do you know of situations where children manipulated adults for the sheer pleasure of it?

3. As a child or young adolescent, were you ever in a situation where you could push an adult into a corner? What did you do?

4. What are your beliefs on disciplining children and adolescents? Is parent as lawgiver an appropriate and necessary role?

WRITING ACTIVITY

In your journal, explore any of the questions you were asked in "Personal Connections." This writing is strictly for yourself, so concentrate on remembering, thinking—don't worry about grammar and spelling for this type of exploratory writing. You may use this writing for a formal writing assignment later.

WHITE TIGERS

Maxine Hong Kingston

Maxine Hong Kingston has focused her writing on growing up female as a first-generation Chinese-American. "White Tigers" is taken from her award-winning autobiography, The Woman Warrior.

My American life has been such a disappointment.

"I got straight A's, Mama."

"Let me tell you a true story about a girl who saved a village."

I could not figure out what was my village. And it was important that I do something big and fine, or else my parents would sell me when we made our way back to China. In China there were solutions for what to do with little girls who ate up food and threw tantrums. You can't eat straight A's.

When one of my parents or the emigrant villagers said, "Feeding girls is feeding cowbirds," I would thrash on the floor and scream so hard I couldn't talk. I couldn't stop.

"What's the matter with her?"

"I don't know. Bad, I guess. You know how girls are. 'There's no profit in raising girls. Better to raise geese than girls.'"

"I would hit her if she were mine. But then there's no use wasting all that discipline on a girl. 'When you raise girls, you're raising children for strangers.'"

"Stop that crying!" my mother would yell. "I'm going to hit you if you don't stop. Bad girl! Stop!" I'm going to remember never to hit or to scold my children for crying, I thought, because then they will only cry more.

"I'm not a bad girl," I would scream. "I'm not a bad girl. I'm not a bad girl." I might as well have said, "I'm not a girl."

"When you were little, all you had to say was 'I'm not a bad girl,' and you could make yourself cry," my mother says, talking-story about my childhood.

I minded that the emigrant villagers shook their heads at my sister and me. "One girl—and another girl," they said, and made our parents ashamed to take us out together. The good part about my brothers being born was that people stopped saying. "All girls," but I learned new grievances. "Did you roll an egg on *my* face like that when *I* was born?" "Did you have a full-month party for *me?*" "Did you turn on all the lights?" "Did you send *my* picture to Grandmother? "Why not? Because I'm a girl? Is that why not?" "Why didn't you teach me English?" "You like having me beaten up at school, don't you?"

"She is very mean, isn't she?" the emigrant villagers would say.

"Come, children. Hurry. Hurry. Who wants to go out with Great-Uncle?" On Saturday mornings, my great-uncle, the ex–river pirate, did the shopping. "Get your coats, whoever's coming."

"I'm coming. I'm coming. Wait for me."

When he heard girls' voices, he turned on us and roared, "No girls!" and left my sisters and me hanging our coats back up, not looking at one another. The boys came back with candy and new toys. When they walked through Chinatown, the people must have said, "A boy—and another boy—and another boy!" At my great-uncle's funeral I secretly tested out feeling glad that he was dead—the six-foot bearish masculinity of him.

I went away to college—Berkeley in the sixties—and I studied, and I marched to change the world, but I did not turn into a boy. I would have liked to bring myself back as a boy for my parents to welcome with chickens and pigs. That was for my brother, who returned alive from Vietnam.

If I went to Vietnam, I would not come back; females desert families. It was said, "There is an outward tendency in females," which meant that I was getting straight A's for the good of my future husband's family, not my own. I did not plan ever to have a husband. I would show my mother and father and nosey emigrant villagers that girls have no outward tendency. I stopped getting straight A's.

And all the time I was having to turn myself American-feminine, or no dates.

There is a Chinese word for female *I*—which is "slave." Break the women with their own tongues!

I refused to cook. When I had to wash dishes, I would crack one or two. "Bad girl," my mother yelled, and sometimes that made me gloat rather than cry. Isn't a bad girl almost a boy?

Thinking About Content

1. What does Hong Kingston reveal about traditional Chinese views and values with regard to gender?

2. How does she respond to these traditional values? Does growing up Chinese-American in California make her life more or less "troublesome"?

Thinking About Writing

1. Hong Kingston uses dialogue very effectively. Choose an example of dialogue where you can hear and see the scene. Why would the effect be different if she just told you what others had said, without the dialogue?

2. Hong Kingston writes: "And all the time I has having to turn myself American-feminine, or no dates." Why doesn't she give us more detail here? Why does she go on to a different aspect of being female?

Personal Connections

1. How does your culture view and value females? Males? How do you know? How do you feel about it?

2. Do families, regardless of the culture, sometimes value one sex more than the other? If so, what may be the consequences of such a practice?

Before you read the following excerpt by Sandra Cisneros, reflect in your journal on your early childhood for a moment. Are there memories of what it felt like to be safe? Are there "sense" memories—smells, sounds, sights that even today bring back feelings of safety, of home (and *home* may be someone or somewhere other than your street address)?

HAIRS

Sandra Cisneros

"Hairs" is from Sandra Cisneros's best known book, The House on Mango Street.

Everybody in our family has different hair. My Papa's hair is like a broom, all up in the air. And me, my hair is lazy. It never obeys barrettes or bands. Carlos' hair is thick and straight. He doesn't need to comb it. Nenny's hair is slippery—slides out of your hand. And Kiki, who is the youngest, has hair like fur.

But my mother's hair, my mother's hair, like little rosettes, like little candy circles all curly and pretty because she pinned it in little pincurls all day, sweet to put your nose into when she is holding you, holding you and you feel safe, is the warm smell of bread before you bake it, is the smell when she makes a little room for you on her side of the bed still warm with her skin, and you sleep near her, the rain outside falling and Papa snoring. The snoring, the rain, and Mama's hair that smells like bread.

Thinking About Content _____

1. Why do you think Cisneros has written about the different types of hair in her family?

2. What, for you, is the center of Cisneros's narrative? What captures your attention? Why?

Thinking About Writing _____

1. Reread Cisneros's description of hair. What senses are touched with her words?

2. What other sense images does she bring to us?

Personal Connections _____

1. Did Cisneros's narrative bring back any childhood memories you hadn't thought of before you read it?

2. As adults, do we need positive childhood memories?

The following draft was written by Jennifer Rogalsky, an 18-year-old freshman. In it she offers a view of memories and family.

A FEAR OF FORGETTING

Jennifer Rogalsky

When growing up, those most important to children are their parents. Every child needs warmth, security, and the presence of parents. The greatest loss a child could bear is the loss of a parent, yet the greatest fear is for the child to forget that parent.

At the age of 12, I suffered the loss of my mother to cancer. Every 12-year-old thinks she knows everything, which, of course, I thought I did. Looking back, I realize there was much I had to learn, to help me deal with the loss as I got older. I naturally remember the most important things about my mother. She was bright, stubborn, and beautiful, and loved me very much. It is the little things I've forgotten, and fear very much that I won't remember them.

Without a doubt, my mother's family would be more than willing to remind me of her small, yet significant actions, but it seems perhaps everyone has forgotten my mother, as she is rarely spoken about. I'm sure this is not true, for those I have spoken to seem overjoyed that I want to hear stories and such, as they are also happy to speak of and remember her. Yet there is one relative, whom I greatly fear speaking to--my father.

At times, not only do I feel the loss of my mother, but also my father. I see him differently, as he is no longer together with my mother. Realizing he is the one I should, and need to talk to to remember our beloved, I feel an even greater fear--his reaction. After seven years of silence, there is no telling what kind of feelings he has been keeping inside.

It is so frightening to think I may not remember my mother--I see her memory fade each day. Some have told me, "You were so young," or, "It has been seven years," or that it may even be my way of dealing with her death or my grieving. Everyday it becomes more frustrating as I wish there were more pictures, videotapes, letters, or personal items. I have to realize all I have left are other people resources.

The feeling I get when others talk of my mother is almost indescribable. When I hear of her habits, her appearance, or talents, I feel like someone is describing me. Apparently, to many, our appearances and personalities are like one; therefore, I often think people don't need to remind me of what my mother was like, for they see her in me.

Events such as family reunions or even personal conversations are integral in restoring my memory of my mother, yet these events only last so long. I can relate the memories that friends and relatives have of her to my own experiences, yet in the back of my mind is the reoccuring thought--I have nearly forgotten her once before, how can I be sure I won't forget her again.

This fear of losing my mother's memory has just occurred recently after seven years of slow memory loss. I can only hope that now that I have realized this problem, I can continue to make progress. The loss of a parent is a tragic enough experience. I am just lucky to have real-

ized my need for rememberance now and am glad I still have
the resources--friends and relatives--to remind me and
help rid me of the fear of forgetting.

Thinking About Content

1. Why does Rogalsky refer to her father in an essay essentially about her mother?
2. Why is she afraid to even talk to her father about her mother?
3. Why is Rogalsky so frustrated as a young adult?

Thinking About Writing

1. Rogalsky tells us, "It is the little things I've forgotten." Should she have told us what those "little things" are?
2. Could Rogalsky have added dialogue to her essay? What difference might it make?

Personal Connections

1. What did you find most touching or surprising about Rogalsky's draft?
2. Can you visualize your parent, hear your parent, and so on? What stands out as the most vivid impression?

Before you read the following piece, write in your reading journal whatever words come to mind when you think of *mirrors*. What associations does this word bring to mind?

MIRRORS

Susan Kenney

Susan Kenney is a contemporary professional writer. This excerpt is taken from her book In Another Country.

My father died suddenly when he was forty and I was twelve. For years after his death I was bitterly resentful of his abrupt departure: I tried to keep the memory of him, his voice, his face, the color of his hair, the way he moved, the clothes he wore, and noted the anniversary of his death each year as it came around. Five years, ten years, twelve, and he had been dead as long as I knew him; fifteen, twenty-five, the years passing so quickly that soon he would be dead as long as he had been alive. I regarded that anniversary with an almost physical dread; we are alive so little and dead so long, and even in the memories of those who want to keep us we fade away.

Thinking About Content

1. We have a tendency to distort our memories, making them better or worse than the actual event or person. Do you think Kenney's memory has distorted her father's image? Explain.

2. "Mirrors" is a very suggestive title. Why might Kenney have used it for this section of her childhood memories?

Thinking About Writing

1. Notice how Kenney uses lists after "I tried to keep the memory of him" and for counting time. Why is this an effective method for her purpose?

2. The sentence "we are alive so little and dead so long" is a very effective one. What did Kenney do to achieve such a nice balance between the ideas?

Personal Connections

1. Anger directed at a person who has died is not an uncommon response among children, adolescents, and adults alike. Have you ever experienced this type of anger or known someone who has? Analyze why it occurs and why it can be considered a natural response.

2. Reflect on times when, as a child or young adolescent, you have been most angry with an adult. Is there a pattern?

3. Kenney notes "even in the memories of those who want to keep us we fade away." Do you believe such fading away is natural and good? Have you ever experienced a fading away? How did you finally deal with it?

4. If you were reflected in mirrors by someone who knows and cares for you deeply, what might the reflections be?

5. Sometimes, people view us as the "very image" of a parent or grandparent. Has this ever happened to you, and if it has, how did you feel about it? How would you feel if someone said this to you? In what ways could you be "the very image"?

Jennifer Urman wrote the following personal-experience essay in freshman composition when she was 19 years old. In it, she reflects on another kind of anger and resentment at losing a father.

Before you read the following essay by Jennifer Urman, respond to the following in your journal:

Divorce is _____.

Second families are _____.

PASSAGE

Jennifer Urman

I distinctly remember my father stopping by the roadside to teach me about cotton fields. "This is how thread is made," he would explain, and "How do you think these plants get water way out here in the desert?" He loved to play Master Educator; I was his doting pupil. He took me to Encanto Park on Sundays, where we sailed my plastic sailboat and raced rocket ships and chased geese that pestered us for bread crumbs and popcorn. I ran to my father when the geese bit my fingers because he was all that was strong and good and great in my life. My father was my teacher, my playmate, and my refuge.

My fourteenth summer shattered my world. I was an hysterical adolescent, melodramatic and demanding. Because of my parents' divorce, I was caught between two families, belonging to neither. I was probably looking for some reason to choose between the two. I am not quite sure. In any case, my father became my scapegoat. His hurt looks when I pulled away from his embraces, his fury when I lashed out at my half-sister in a jealous rage, and his uncomprehending anger when I matched my stubborn will with his own; all of these are imprinted on my mind as pre-emptory to our eventual parting of the ways. We topple our childhood gods from their lofty pedestals farther than they ever deserve to fall. That summer I was stony-faced and unforgiving, not realizing, too young to understand the failings of human nature. Youth is willing to sacrifice so much for its impatient ideals. . . .

Five summers have passed. But I am there again and again, reliving the final moments of my fourteenth summer.

The airplane cabin is a little world all itself, a pressurized corridor muffling voices and stifling engines at take-off. It is a good place to think. Leaving the heat of Arizona for my family in cool, green Wisconsin seems momentous to me. My father stands outside the fence, one hand in his pocket, the other dangling a cigarette. He wears sunglasses against the scorching Arizona sun. They hide his eyes and all expression. Seeing him standing there, all alone, I feel regret, sorrow, pity, anything but the tension and frustration of the wasted summer. These are useless tears. It is suddenly clear he is lonely and lost. There are so many hard lessons to learn, all of this growing up to do.

Thinking About Content

1. Is this essay about the father or the daughter? Why?
2. Compare Jennifer's anger and resentment with that of Susan Kenney. Are they similar or different? Explain your response.
3. Is this essay just about anger or about something more universal to our experience, to growing up? Refer back to sentences or passages that support your view.

Thinking About Writing

1. Quickly review the content of each of the three paragraphs. What has the author done in each and why? How does each serve her purpose in writing this essay? Note the time frame in each paragraph. Why does Urman write the third paragraph as though she were still fourteen years old?
2. What is the tone of this essay? Do you think Urman was trying to evoke sympathy? Do you think she was merely recording?
3. List some words, phrases, or sentences that you found to be especially effective.

Personal Connections

1. Do you believe young adolescents often become, as Urman describes herself, "melodramatic" or "demanding" when faced with some crisis? Can you recall a time when you could have been described in this way?

2. Have you ever been in a situation where, like Urman, you realize as an adult that your response was "youth sacrificing so much for its impatient ideals"?

3. With an American divorce rate at 52 percent early in the 1990s, the chances of children experiencing a sense of abandonment by one parent or facing remarriage and subsequent half-siblings are greatly increased. What are your thoughts on these critical family situations?

4. Urman believes, "We topple our childhood gods from their lofty pedestals farther than they ever deserve to fall." Do you agree with her? Explain your response.

Writing Activity

In your journal, explore further one of the ideas in "Personal Connections": adolescent demands, unrealistic expectations, sibling rivalry, melodrama, impatience, anger.

Like Jennifer Urman, Marjorie Harnden wrote the following essay, "Christmas Time," as her personal-experience essay in a college composition class. When she wrote this essay, Harden was in her early twenties, looking back to a family incident that happened when she was still in high school.

Before you read this essay write in your journal the name of some holiday or ritual that has special meaning for you. Quickly list all the things associated with this holiday or ritual, including family members and any specific roles they play—or you expect them to play.

CHRISTMAS TIME

Marjorie Harnden

The Christmas of my junior year in high school is one I will never forget, not because I got a lot of presents or all the relatives came down, but because of what happened. My father went to jail on Christmas Eve. He was not a bad man, just sometimes a careless one. He was on probation for writing bad checks, and he must've done it again on Christmas Eve. He was apprehended at Shopko just before supper time, and his car was left in the parking lot, full of Santa's surprises for the wonderful morning.

When we found out what happened, we four kids were furious. How dare he ruin Christmas for everyone? What kind of father goes to jail on Christmas Eve? Nobody would get any presents. I looked to my mother just in time to see her wipe away a painful tear, and then it occurred to me. I faced my siblings and said, "I know we all feel bad, but how do you think Dad feels? I bet he feels like a real failure right now. How would you like to spend Christmas in jail? He's probably worrying about what we're going to think of him. And we all know he wouldn't do something like this on purpose. Accidents happen."

I paused for their reaction. Mom held her breath, looking first from one thoughtful face to another. My sister Mary spoke first. "She's right. He probably feels terrible." Amy began to cry. Mary continued, suddenly inspired. "Let's wait for Christmas! We can have it when Dad gets home. It's only a couple of days, and we can have it like he never was gone!" She was overwhelmingly supported.

When Dad got home two nights later, walking in the door with a tired and apprehensive look on his face, Christmas Eve dinner was steaming on the table. His four daughters came roaring downstairs to greet him, a massive flurry of hugs and kisses. Tears of joy and relief brimmed in his eyes, and he exclaimed, "I'm the luckiest father in the world!"

For the first time I had realized that my parents aren't just my father and mother; they are real people with dreams of their own. Parents also make mistakes, and they can feel just as bad as any kid. The lesson I learned became a valuable one as I grew up understanding why they did things the way they did. That gave me respect for their decisions, a respect I might not have had otherwise.

Thinking About Content

1. Do you think the four daughters are typical? Why or why not?
2. In your experience, are teenagers generally so forgiving?

3. Are parents under pressure to "do the right thing"? In this case, has the father done "the right thing"? How many different ways can you view his action?

4. How would you characterize Harnden's relationship with her father? What leads you to this characterization?

Thinking About Writing

1. In the final paragraph, Harnden makes a number of assertions about parents: "they are real people with dreams of their own"; "parents also make mistakes"; "they can feel just as bad as any kid." Do you have enough information to accept these statements? Are there too many of them?

2. In that same paragraph, Harnden says of herself: "I grew up understanding why they [parents] did things the way they did." Does this conclusion match the story she related? Where might she have concluded her essay?

3. If Mrs. Harnden, Marjorie's mother, had written this essay, how would it change?

Personal Connections

1. Harnden says, "Accidents happen," with reference to her father's lapse of judgment in writing more bad checks. Do you think his deliberate violation of the law and probation was justified? Have you ever faced a situation where you "did wrong" in order to "do right"?

2. Many people believe that Christmas has lost its original significance, has become little more than a commercial event, and has increasingly brought stress to people, especially those struggling financially. Do you agree with this judgment? Why?

3. Think of a holiday or ritual most celebrated or held in high regard by your family or culture. What would ruin it for you?

4. How do children learn to be as forgiving and generous as Harnden and her sisters? Do you think it is difficult to respond as they did?

5. Holidays, whether religious or cultural, carry expectations for those who have grown up with them. What expectations do you have for a particular holiday or ritual? Have you ever been angry or frustrated when those expectations weren't met?

BLUE WINDS DANCING

Thomas Whitecloud

Whitecloud, a Chippewa Indian, wrote this essay while a student at the University of the Redlands (California) in 1938. He later earned a medical degree, served as a military surgeon in Europe during World War II, and practiced medicine in the West.

There is a moon out tonight. Moon and stars and clouds tipped with moonlight. And there is a fall wind blowing in my heart. Ever since this evening, when against a fading sky I saw geese wedge southward. They were going home. . . . Now I try to study, but against the pages see them again, driving southward. Going home.

Across the valley there are heavy mountains holding up the night sky, and beyond the mountains there is home. Home, and peace, and the beat of drums, and blue winds dancing over snow fields. The Indian lodge will fill with my people, and our gods will come and sit among them. I should be there then. I should be at home.

In my Wisconsin, the leaves change before the snows come. In the air there is the smell of wild rice and venison cooking; and when the winds come whispering through the forests, they carry the smell of rotting leaves. In the evenings, the loon calls, lonely; the birds sing their last songs before leaving. Bears dig roots and eat late fall berries, fattening for their long winter sleep. Later, when the first snows fall, one awakens in the morning to find the world white and beautiful and clean. Then one can look back over his trail and see the tracks following. In the woods there are tracks of deer and snowshoe rabbits, and long streaks where partridges slide to alight. Chipmunks make tiny footprints on the limbs; and one can hear squirrels busy in hollow trees, sorting acorns. Soft lake waves wash the shores, and sunsets burst each evening over the lakes, and make them look as if they were afire.

That land which is my home! Beautiful, calm—where there is no hurry to get anywhere, no driving to keep up in a race that knows no ending and no goal. No classes where men talk and talk, and then stop now and then to hear their own words come back to them from the students. No constant peering into the maelstrom of one's mind; no worries about grades and honors; no hysterical preparing for life until that life is half over; no anxiety about one's place in the thing they call Society.

I hear again the ring of axes in deep woods, the crunch of snow beneath my feet. I feel again the smooth velvet of ghost-birch bark. I hear the rhythm of the drums. . . . I am tired. I am weary of trying to keep up this bluff of being civilized. Being civilized means trying to do everything you don't want to, never doing anything you want to. It means dancing to the strings of custom and tradition; it means living in houses and never knowing or caring who is next door. These civilized white men want us to be like them—always dissatisfied, getting a hill and wanting a mountain.

Then again, maybe I am not tired. Maybe I'm licked. Maybe I am just not smart enough to grasp these things that go to make up civilization. Maybe I am just too lazy to think hard enough to keep up.

Still, I know my people have many things that civilization has taken from the whites. They know how to give; how to tear one's piece of meat in two and share it with one's brother. They know how to sing—how to make each man his own songs and sing them; for their music they do not have to listen to other men singing over a radio. They know how to make things with their hands, how to shape beads into design and make a thing of beauty from a piece of birch bark.

But we are inferior. It is terrible to have to feel inferior; to have to read reports of intelligence tests, and learn that one's race is behind. It is terrible to sit in classes and hear men tell you that your people worship sticks of wood—that your gods are all false, that the Manitou forgot your people and did not write them a book.

I am tired. I want to walk again among the ghost-birches. I want to see the leaves turn in autumn, the smoke rise from the lodgehouses, and to feel the blue winds. I want to hear the drums; I want to hear the drums and feel the blue whispering winds.

There is a train wailing into the night. The trains go across the mountains. It would be easy to catch a freight. They will say he has gone back to the blanket; I don't care. The dance at Christmas. . . .

Northward again. Minnesota, and great white fields of snow; frozen lakes, and dawn running in dusk without noon. Long forests wearing white. Bitter cold, and one night the northern lights. I am nearing home.

I reach Woodruff at midnight. Suddenly I am afraid, now that I am but twenty miles from home. Afraid of what my father will say, afraid of being looked on as a stranger by my own people. I sit by a fire and think about myself and all the other young Indians. We just don't seem to fit in anywhere—certainly not among the whites, and not among the older people. I think again about the learned sociology professor and his professing. So many things seem to be clear now that I am away from school and do not have to worry about some man's opinion of my ideas. It is easy to think while looking at dancing flames.

Morning. I spend the day cleaning up, and buying some presents for my family with what is left of my money. Nothing much, but a gift is a gift, if a man buys it with his last quarter. I wait until evening, then start up the track toward home.

Christmas Eve comes in on a north wind. Snow clouds hang over the pines, and the night comes early. Walking along the railroad bed, I feel the calm peace of snowbound forests on either side of me. I take my time; I am back in a world where time does not mean so much now. I am alone; alone but not nearly so lonely as I was back on the campus at school. Those are never lonely who love the snow and the pines; never lonely when the pines are wearing white shawls and snow crunches coldly underfoot. In the woods I know there are the tracks of deer and rabbit; I know that if I leave the rails and go into the woods I shall find them. I walk along feeling glad because my legs are light and my feet seem to know that they are home. A deer comes out of the woods just ahead of me, and stands silhouetted on the rails. The North, I feel, has welcomed me home. I watch him and am glad that I do not wish for a gun. He goes into the woods quietly, leaving only the design of his tracks in the snow. I walk on. Now and then I pass a field, white under the night sky, with houses at the far end. Smoke comes from the chimneys of the houses, and I try to tell what sort of wood each is burning by the smoke; some burn pine; others aspen, others tamarack. There is one from which comes black coal smoke that rises lazily and drifts out over the tops of the trees. I like to watch houses and try to imagine what might be happening in them.

Just as a light snow begins to fall, I cross the reservation boundary; somehow it seems as though I have stepped into another world. Deep woods in a white-and-black winter night. A faint trail leading to the village.

The railroad on which I stand comes from a city sprawled by a lake—a city with a million people who walk around without seeing one another; a city sucking the life from all the country around; a city with stores and police and intellectuals and criminals and movies and apartment houses; a city with its politics and libraries and zoos.

Laughing, I go into the woods. As I cross a frozen lake I begin to hear the drums. Soft in the night the drums beat. It is like the pulse beat of the world. The white line of the lake ends at a black forest, and above the trees the blue winds are dancing.

I come to the outlying houses of the village. Simple box houses, etched black in the night. From one or two windows soft lamp light falls on the snow. Christmas here, too, but it does not mean much; not much in the way of parties and presents. Joe Sky will get drunk. Alex Bodidash will buy his children red mittens and a new sled. Alex is a Carlisle man, and tries to keep his home up to white standards. White standards. Funny that people should be ever falling farther behind. The more they try to imitate whites the more tragic the result. Yet they want us to be imitation white men. About all we imitate well are their vices.

The village is not a sight to instill pride, yet I am not ashamed; one can never be ashamed of his own people when he knows they have dreams as beautiful as white snow on a tall pine.

Father and my brother and sister are seated around the table as I walk in. Father stares at me for a moment, then I am in his arms, crying on his shoulder. I give them the presents I have brought, and my throat tightens as I watch my sister save carefully bits of red string from the packages. I hide my feelings by wrestling with my brother when he strikes my shoulder in token of affection. Father looks at me, and I know he has many questions, but he seems to know why I have come. He tells me to go on alone to the lodge, and he will follow.

I walk along the trail to the lodge, watching the northern lights forming in the heavens. White waving ribbons that seem to pulsate with the rhythm of the drums. Clean snow creaks beneath my feet, and a soft wind sighs through the trees, singing to me. Everything seems to say "Be happy! You are home now—you are free. You are among friends—we are your friends; we, the trees, and the snow, and the lights." I followed the trail to the lodge. My feet are light, my heart seems to sing to the music, and I hold my head high. Across white snow fields blue winds are dancing.

Before the lodge door I stop, afraid. I wonder if my people will remember me. I wonder—"Am I Indian, or am I white?" I stand before the door a long time. I hear the ice groan on the lake, and remember the story of the old woman who is under the ice, trying to get out, so she can punish some runaway lovers. I think to myself, "If I am white I will not believe that story; if I am Indian, I will know that there is an old woman under the ice." I listen for a while, and I know that there is an old woman under the ice. I look again at the lights, and go in.

Inside the lodge there are many Indians. Some sit on benches around the walls, others dance in the center of the floor around a drum. Nobody seems to notice me. It seems as though I were among a people I have never seen before. Heavy women with long black hair. Women with children on their knees—small children that watch with intent black eyes the movements of the dancers, whose small faces are solemn and serene. The faces of the old people are serene, too, and their eyes are merry and bright. I look at the old men. Straight, dressed in dark trousers and beaded velvet vests, wearing soft moccasins. Dark, lined faces intent on the music. I wonder if I am at all like them. They dance on, lifting their feet to the rhythm of the drums, swaying lightly, looking upward. I look at their eyes, and am startled at the rapt attention to the rhythm of the music.

The dance stops. The men walk back to the walls, and talk in low tones or with their hands. There is little conversation, yet everyone seems to be sharing some secret. A woman looks at a small boy wandering away, and he comes back to her.

Strange, I think, and then remember. These people are not sharing words—they are sharing a mood. Everyone is happy. I am so used to white people that it seems strange so many people could be together without someone talking. These Indians are happy because they are together, and because the night is beautiful outside, and the music is beautiful. I try hard to forget school and white people, and be one of these—my people. I try to forget everything but the night, and it is a part of me; that I am one with my people and we are all a part of something universal. I watch eyes, and see now that the old people are speaking to me. They nod slightly, imperceptibly, and their eyes laugh into mine. I look around the room. All the eyes are friendly; they all laugh. No one questions my being here. The drums begin to beat again, and I catch the invitation in the eyes of the old men. My feet begin to lift to the rhythm, and I look out beyond the walls into the night and see the lights. I am happy. It is beautiful. I am home.

Thinking About Content

1. Whitecloud, a Chippewa Indian, lived in both the white and Native American cultures. How does he give his readers a sense of being between two cultures? How do we learn what each culture is like, at least according to Whitecloud?

2. Why does Whitecloud both long for and fear going home to northern Wisconsin, ancestral home of the Chippewa?

Thinking About Writing

1. Like Richard Wright, Whitecloud provides both a physical and psychological description of this environment. Choose one example of each and explain how Whitehead brought you into the description, allowing you to share his environment and himself.

2. Whitecloud writes in the first person, *I.* What is the advantage of using *I?* The disadvantage?

Personal Connections

1. Whitecloud describes his Wisconsin home in vivid detail, letting us see and hear it. We can then better understand his emotions upon returning home. Do you have a place that is special, where you feel in touch with yourself?

2. Have you ever felt caught between two worlds—not necessarily of race or ethnicity, but also the worlds of child/adult, home/school, country/city? Explain.

As a student from a war-torn Central American country, Ruth Aida Cañas had family memories unlike most of her classmates. For her personal-experience essay she chose a positive one, but one born of tragedy.

Before you read this piece, reflect in your reading journal on a family member or friend who is especially dear to you. Have you ever told this person how deeply you care, how important he or she is to you?

"I LOVE YOU, CHAVA"

Ruth Aida Cañas

"Your brother is going to the mountain," my mom said on an unforgettable 30th of December, 1980. I was just a little, shy, ten year-old girl who did not know anything about the war in El Salvador, my country. How could I have understood the peril of my brother's leaving?

My brother could not avoid being active: he thought that the war in El Salvador, his country, needed to stop immediately. He could not stand looking at the starvation, exploitation, and poverty that most Salvadorans suffered. An enthusiastic, straight-A student, Chava left his studies, family, comfort, friends--everything--to fight and stop the hated war.

We did not hear from him after he left. My mom missed her only son. She was proud of him because Chava was not just a great student, but also an excellent son and a fantastic brother; he used to help my mom clean the house, wash the clothes, and take care of us, his sisters. He even took a job on a farm to earn a little extra money; one Christmas with that money he bought presents for each member in our family instead of buying things for himself. I learned from him to be courageous because he chose to fight with the Salvadoran's guerrillas, even though he knew that going to the mountain was dangerous.

However, his dreams of an El Salvador without strife never came true; he was killed in 1981. No one knows where his body rests, or how he was killed. His precious life was taken; all his ideals were stolen with his death. I did not understand that he was not going to come again because I was not old enough to realize all the consequences that his death had.

My mom and sisters cried when they found out about the murder of my brother, but I could not cry. I reproached myself for not reacting as a sister who loved her brother. Yet, there is something for which I reproach myself even much more: I never told him how much I admired him and what I felt for him.

Now, I have lost him, and there is nothing I can do. Nevertheless, I have understood what his departure meant: I know how generous he was by giving his life to building an El Salvador where everyone would have a dignified life. Sometimes I have wanted to be sure he can hear me from the divine place where he is, and tell him: "I love you Chava; I have missed you all my life."

Thinking About Content

1. What portrait of Chava emerges from Cañas's essay? Can we trust her memory? Why?

2. How do you picture Ruth Cañas? Why? Is the significance of this essay found in Chava or in Ruth?

3. Cañas never mentions her father. What will the reader assume? Is that assumption justified?

Thinking About Writing

1. Is Cañas looking for sympathy in this essay? How does she control the tone?

2. Could Cañas have provided the reader with more detail about the state of El Salvador when Chava left for the mountain?

Personal Connections

1. Did Ruth Cañas's narrative nudge your thinking about what's important in life, in families?

2. Even if you have never had to face war in America or in your country, through television war has been brought into every home. In America, we have also witnessed "civil war" born of urban poverty and hopelessness. Reflect on those images.

As a young girl, Catalina Ruge, the author of the following essay, experienced her first sense of betrayal. Looking back as a college freshman, she shares that moment.

DIARY

Catalina Ruge

When I was 13 years old, I kept a diary. All of my personal thoughts, feelings, and experiences were secure in between the hardcover of my Hello Kitty Personal Diary, or so I thought. I came home one afternoon after ballet lessons, my knees weak and my heart racing, I had just seen Felipe, my future husband. No one was aware of my wedding plans yet, not even Felipe. "I have to make a note in my diary to change the best man; Camilo is Felipe's best friend now," I said to myself.

I walked into my room and headed straight for my desk. The light shining off the brass handle of the third drawer always made me think of the invaluable treasure that lay in there, my wedding plans. But today there was something in between me and that gleaming handle. Laughter made me look up only to find my Hello Kitty Private Diary in the hands of my cousin. He had read it all. The only gleaming I could see now were the tears in my eyes.

I felt betrayed that day, as if someone had trespassed the boundaries of my privacy. My cousin's hurtful words made it all the more painful. The life spelled out in the pages of the diary was no longer mine. It became the object of a big joke. Although the whole incident is now a joke; thinking back, I realize how much of who I am today is a result of that occurrence.

Since then, I have been afraid to tell people what I'm feeling. Afraid that they will take my feelings and turn them into a big joke. I haven't kept a diary since.

Thinking About Content _____

1. Was Ruge's daydream unusual? Her need for privacy?
2. Is there a gender difference here? Do both male and female adolescents have private hopes and dreams? The same type of hopes and dreams?

Thinking About Writing _____

1. How has Ruge organized her essay? Why?

2. Ruge tells us that her "cousin's hurtful words made it all the more painful." What might be the effect on the reader if those "hurtful words" had been revealed?

Personal Connections _____

1. Have you ever felt betrayed by a family member or close friend? Has anyone ever revealed your secret thoughts, things said in confidence? How did you feel? Are there lasting effects, like those Catalina Ruge relates?

2. Ruge tells us "the life spelled out in the pages of the diary was no longer mine." Have you ever felt as though your life was no longer yours?

Writing from Personal Experience _____

In your journal, you have already explored many ideas growing out of your experience as a member of a family, a community, a culture, including some of the following:

✦ Relationships between child and parent or caretaker

✦ Adult as lawgiver

✦ Child as victim

✦ Anger at abandonment through death or divorce

✦ Fading memories

✦ Growing up

✦ Adolescent self-righteousness

✦ Adolescent demands

✦ Expectations and regrets

Review your journal and put an asterisk (*) next to those which offer the most potential for your personal-experience paper. Then go back to the starred entries and choose one. You will use this entry to develop a discovery draft. But first, you need to think about the significance of that choice.

THINGS TO CONSIDER: THE "SO WHAT?" FACTOR

When readers finish our narrative, we want them to understand why we have written it. We don't want them to finish reading and think, "So what?" We want them to know the significance of our narrative. Keeping these questions in front of you is important as you consider your subject from a reader's viewpoint:

✦ Why is this event or person significant to me?

✦ Will my reader understand this significance?

✦ Will I be able to convey my thoughts and feelings on this topic?

As you read the next two student narratives, think about their significance. Why did David Schwartz and Tom McDonald focus their narratives on these people?

David Schwartz was "forty-something" when he wrote this piece in freshman composition. Out of all his life experience, he chose to write about a special "father." Why?

UNFORGETTABLE FATHER ROSSITER

David Schwartz

My first encounter with the man was early in my freshman year at Regis High School. As usual, I was late for homeroom and was trying to retrieve books from the chaotic mess of my locker. With my familiar breakfast carrot hanging from my mouth, I really was trying to hurry when out of nowhere came this booming voice proclaiming "YOU BOOB!" Only one voice existed that could strike terror amongst the masses like that--our principal, Father John Rossiter, affectionately known as "Rock." There he was, an imposing figure with fire in his eyes, lumbering toward me with a half limp, a constant reminder of the Korean War. Ranting and raving, he let me know that being late wasn't tolerated. As terror stricken as I was, I continued to chomp on my carrot and tried not to convey fear. Seeming somewhat amused at my half-hearted attempt at calling his bluff, he shooed me off to class. Psychology books tells us how impressionable we are in youth, but I had no idea just how big an impact this chance encounter would have on the rest of my life.

Our relationship began to develop from that moment on, spanning over twenty years. I soon learned that beneath his tough rocklike exterior beat the unselfish heart of a man with immense compassion. Behind the scenes at Regis, he never denied a Catholic education to a student unable to pay for it. Something could always be worked out, from part-time work at the school or in the private sector, to a ten-year payment plan. If all else failed, he anonymously made tuition payments himself.

Tuition wasn't the only reason for reaching deep into his own pockets. Like today, the sixties were troubled times. For the less fortunate, that meant struggling to make ends meet. In his Buick we had dubbed the "Green Hornet," he made the rounds more than once to Regis families in need, delivering bags of groceries—anonymously, of course.

Haircuts were a similar matter. Part of a Catholic education was discipline, and one of the rules was that students' hair had to be cropped so close that bristles, as he called them, had to be visible on the back of the neck. Long hair, sported by that new singing group the Beatles, didn't fit with the program. Here again, if an occasional haircut was out of our price realm, he would foot the bill. I wore a regular path driving the Green Hornet between Regis and Tony's Barber Shop, shuttling classmates back and forth to get their locks shorn--on his tab.

Looking back, it comes apparent his niche was being there when you needed him. He readily identified with students like myself, who always seemed to have an uncanny knack for sniffing out trouble. In later years, he told me what a hellion he had been in his youth and how a teacher he had never forgotten had reached out to him. Likewise, he inspired us with nurturing, understanding, and support. Rock strongly encouraged us to always do our best as we traveled through life. In that respect, he was more like a father figure.

As with my own father, I sometimes wondered what life would be like when he no longer walked this earth. I found out all too soon. Six years ago, on a cold, snowy January day, a deranged individual entered his church and ended his life. I wasn't prepared. He had always been there; I couldn't imagine him not being there.

Reflecting after the funeral, I reassessed my own life and realized it was time to follow a path I had planned long ago but never finished--the pursuit of a teaching degree. It was as if his death held his final inspiration for me--to pass the torch.

Tom McDonald, writing as an 18-year-old freshman, also reflects on a person who made a difference in his life.

SHAKING HANDS WITH GOD

Tom McDonald

Isn't it funny how life, when we're least expecting it, throws people or events our way that teach us that it is not all about us? Or that we don't have it so bad? The 1988 ELCA San Antonio youth gathering did that for me. Ron did that for me.

In the summer of 1988, my church shared buses with other area churches to go to the great Lutheran youth gathering held in San Antonio, Texas. My true reasons for going weren't religious, and when you get right down to it, weren't very respectable. Simply put, I went for the girls. Upon boarding the bus, I was more than pleasantly surprised to see that there was a great selection of available females to choose from. In fact, I was so busy scoping, I didn't even notice <u>him</u>.

In about the fifth hour of the first day of our ten-day trip, our pastors, always looking to "broaden our horizons," paired us with a complete stranger from a different church. Their task for us was to introduce ourselves and essentially make friends with our fellow Lutherans. "No problem," I thought, "Maybe I'll end up with one of the girls I've been watching."

To my dismay, I was not only paired with a male but he was a somewhat disfigured, unhealthy vision of a male. Smiling with a hairelip as he approached me, he winked at me with constantly watery eyes through Coke-bottle glasses. Then the scrawny figure that made me so uncomfortable to look at held out one of his three-fingered hands in greeting.

"Hi. I'm Ron," he said with a smirk, "but you can call me Ron." He followed this tension breaker with a boyish smile that drew me in.

"Hi Ron," I said, trying to ignore his deformities at all costs. "I'm Tom."

Putting one of his odd-looking hands on my knee he again offered his free hand for me to shake. Uncomfortably, my hand met his, and I was forced to look at him. Despite my typical teenage male attitudes, I began to see in front of me a very able, accepting person.

As we moved on, from day to day, Ron and I became very close, playing dumb bus games together and comparing notes on the girls on the bus, some from my town and some from his. Despite myself and my poor intentions, I was beginning to change my focus from strictly girl-watching to learning how to have and be a friend. This change was all Ron's fault, but he wasn't done yet.

On about the third day of the gathering, Ron and I attended a youth dance held at the local college, where we would be spending the night. I have never danced before, and assumed the same of Ron. I thought that we could hang out around the sides and watch the more confident people dance. To my surprise, Ron left me at the side and wove his way through the crowded dance floor, cracking jokes about his six fingers and making friends as he went. I couldn't make myself go out onto that dance floor, no matter how much I really wanted to, bringing to mind a stirring question. Who was the handicapped one now?

Yes, life taught me a huge lesson over those ten days. Through Ron, who excelled at things that at first appearance seemed impossible for such a seemingly defective body, I learned that the only handicaps are those of the mind. Now, when I see Ron at a ball game or showing off his skills on the latest video game or piano keyboard (which I recently found was another of his innumerable talents) I realize how lucky I was to meet him and learn the lesson he had to teach. Now, I realize what an honor it is to know him and to shake his hand.

Group Activity

In a personal narrative, the point may or may not be explicitly stated, but it should be very clear to the reader. This is your experience: how it touched you; why it touched you; why you have chosen to relate it in this essay. The point and significance usually link us as fellow travelers on this earth—feelings, thoughts, and emotions that we may share to a certain degree. Effective narratives help us reflect on ourselves and our world, sometimes with joy and laughter, at other times with pain or anger, and now and then, with the simple wonder of being alive. With your group, review and comment on the significance of the personal narratives you have read thus far. Give specific reasons why you believe some are more memorable than others. Then, share your idea for your own personal narrative. Good discussion is a valuable way of exploring the signficance of the topic. You want your readers to feel as you do, that what you have chosen to narrate was well worth the effort.

CHAPTER 4

Working Through the Processes of Writing

When you worked on the "Place in the Family" writing task, you and your classmates not only worked through the writing process; you talked about it as well. Now we'll talk about writing once more, paying close attention not only to the various processes we all use when we write, but also to strategies that help us through them.

GENERATING

Every time you explored ideas, either alone or with your classmates, you were readying yourself for potential writing tasks. Reading and responding, talking to others, and making notes for yourself are all good strategies for generating ideas for writing. There are many other strategies, which we'll explore in Chapter 5, but for now we'll stick with some general ideas about getting started and staying with the process.

You probably associate generating or discovering ideas with the start of a writing task. However, we also find ourselves generating ideas while we draft. Sometimes, it's only in the act of writing that we discover that we need more or different material. At that point, we have to return to strategies that help us generate ideas. One of those strategies, strange as it may seem, is getting away from writing.

All through the writing process, we face times when we need to get away from the writing task. It's very normal to feel worn down and out of ideas, and to wish for the entire draft to go up in flames. Writing, even when it's going well, is hard work. Inexperienced writers sometimes feel guilty for doing just what they need to do—take a break. We can never really shut down the brain, so even if you think you're not working on your writing assignment, you probably are. It's somewhere in your brain, even if you are not consciously aware of it. Professional writers refer to this process as incubation. The ideas are there, growing and changing until the moment when they are born consciously.

You will try out many generating strategies in the weeks ahead. Once you discover which of them work best for you, you can apply them both when you start an assignment and when you get stuck. Seeing words appear on the paper is tangible evidence that you're working on the assignment. Some people do the strategies in their heads; it's the way they always work. Others can't function that way at all. Some writers need more "people" assistance than others, finding that talking through the writing task or certain segments of a draft is a tremendous help. What's important about generating is knowing what helps you.

DRAFTING

Discovery Drafts

Drafting is the process of developing the written text. Most people think of drafting as the writing itself—not revising or editing but developing the content that will later be revised and edited. When we start to write in paragraph form, we usually think of it as drafting. Once we have a workable draft, we go on to the process of revising it. A special form of drafting is the discovery draft, which is a generating strategy for many writers. It's a good way to get many ideas down quickly, simply letting ideas evolve without concern for how they match or whether they are even usable. Discovery drafts often appear messy and are generally unintelligible to everyone but the writer. However, because some writers do a form of drafting in their heads, they turn up with a fairly organized discovery draft. This student's discovery draft turned out to be rich resource for a personal-experience essay:

What a jerk! I just came from the blue-gold room [student union] for a coffee and a smoke where I heard this guy ranting to a friend. The subject was Native American

rights and I couldn't believe my ears. Apparently this
man is some big activist, probably employed to look out
for native americans rights. His endless condemnation of
the "white, upper-middle-class drug culture" and its
responsibility for drug and alcohol abuse among Native
Am.s was typical of the fanatic without a cause. That
isn't what bothered me. It was the way he talked about a
list of indian leaders that didn't approve of his philosophy in every aspect. This firey, radical, irrational,
condemnation of his ENEMIES belied his true pathetic
nature. I tried first to listen objectively to what he
was saying, then I tried assuming that all the things he
said are true. Anyway you slice it, this guy was power
hungry, afraid of other leaders, a back-stabber, interested only in his own views, not interested in general
debate ...

When you examine this discovery draft, you find that Roy was
really letting off steam on paper. It's not focused. There are many
ideas in it, and Roy would have to pick one to center his essay on.
He's written a narrative account of an incident that had just happened to him, just as though he were talking to us about it. But if
we were talking, we'd be asking Roy questions about this incident
and pushing him to describe the scene and the object of his anger
more clearly and fully.

Group Activity

Write down statements or ideas from Roy's discovery draft that
you believe would be good ones as the focus of an essay. Then discuss
each idea in terms of the type of essay it might lead to. For it to be a
personal-experience essay, a narrative, it would have to focus on Roy.
How could Roy use what he has described to say something significant
about himself, about his own experience, his view of self and world?
What could lead to an expository essay, one that informs or explains,
where the emphasis is on the subject being discussed, not the writer?
What could lead to an argumentative essay, where the emphasis is on
the reader, on efforts to bring the reader around to acknowledging or
accepting the writer's point of view? List each potential topic and the
possible purpose of the essay, and then discuss what would be needed
to support the idea. Refer back to the draft for ideas. Prepare your
group's work for full class discussion.

First Drafts

The first draft of an essay is usually the most difficult. However, sometimes people make it more difficult by worrying about grammar, sentences, punctuation, and spelling—in other words, worrying about Standard Written English. Writing Standard American English is important, if only because it is the written dialect of school and business. But we attend to it in a final draft and not before. When we are in the process of getting things down on paper, we don't need to be concerned about getting things down correctly. Although worrying about correctness is understandable and normal, especially among inexperienced writers, it can get in the way. If we're thinking, "Is this correct?" we're not thinking, "What else can I say?"

In our first drafts, we need to attend to the content, to what we want to say. When we are satisfied with the content, we can turn to revising and editing. Multiple drafts are the way in which we work our essay into an understandable, correct, and interesting paper. Sometimes, you will write only a first draft. But most of the time, academic writing requires several drafts.

Writing Activity

A. You have been considering a personal experience topic—something that has real significance for you and will be worth the effort of writing. Now it's time to write a discovery draft. Keep in mind that this draft may be a real mess, understandable to you only. Save every scrap of writing from this project. You may want to return to the generating papers.

B. When you have completed the discovery draft, review it. If you have handwritten your discovery draft, use ink of a different color for the next step. Circle with the different color anything you wish to save in the discovery draft. Then, review what you have circled, and place numbers on each circle to indicate a potential order for using this material. You may change your mind later, drop some material, add some material, or rearrange, but for now, the numbers will serve as a general indicator of order.

C. Evaluate your audience and purpose:

Who is your audience for this essay? What would you expect your audience to know? Have you assumed too much background knowledge? Are you using any special terms, vocabulary associated with a specific place, group of people, workplace, hobby, activity, and so on?

What is the purpose of your essay? What are you trying to do?

D. List what you believe you need to do to shape the discovery draft into a good draft, concentrating on what you want to say and the order in which you want to say it. At this point, ignore problems with sentences, grammar, punctuation, and spelling. All you need to do here is make a list, like the kind you make when you have ten things to do on a very busy school day.

Allowing Time

One of the more difficult factors in writing is time—allowing enough time for the entire process. All of us procrastinate when it comes to a tough task, and writing is a tough task. However, with the strategies for generating ideas and the freedom of a discovery draft, you should be able to get going. The next problem with time lies between drafts and the due date. You will need a pretty good draft for peer response, so your first deadline comes on the date for small-group activity. The draft for peers will probably be a second one (not counting the discovery draft), and then you will have yet another for additional revising and editing.

An advantage of writing with a word processor or computer is the physical ease with which we can work on a draft. The mental work is just as hard, but deleting, changing, and rearranging material are far easier with the machine. If you are unable to work with word processing, you can take a scissors to the draft, cutting up parts, moving them, or omitting them. It is a perfectly good way to work, the way most people worked before the advent of the computer.

Set this draft aside for at least a day, preferably longer. The more distance you can get, the better. The shift from writer to reader is a significant one, one that improves with distance from what we have written.

Writing Partner Activity

If you would like additional help with your discovery draft, get together with your writing partner.

When you read, read your draft aloud, in its entirety and with no additional comments on it. When you discuss the draft with your partner, take notes on what he or she says.

When you listen to your partner read, concentrate on what you are hearing, without making any comments at this time. At the completion of the reading, write down your understanding of the main point (or points) and most important details or examples. Also note things that you would like to learn more about or that were particularly interesting. Spend only three or four minutes writing these notes. Then read and discuss your notes with your partner.

Writing Activity: From Discovery Draft to Draft 1

Review your comments (and any from a classmate) on the discovery draft. Then take the plunge into the next draft. This draft will be your first solid draft. Don't worry about sentence structure, grammar, punctuation, and spelling at this point. Concentrate only on developing what you want to say. If you get stuck during this drafting process, try one or more of the following strategies:

WIRMI: What I Really Mean Is . . .   When you are bogged down trying to get an idea out of your head and onto paper, or when you are struggling with getting the sentence to say what you want it to, switch from writing to talking to yourself. Say to yourself, "What I really mean is _____." You should then have something tangible to work with.

Notes Only.   Another strategy is to stop writing in sentence form and write only in phrases—short notes for yourself. Your brain can handle only so many tasks at once. Cutting back to phrases will lighten the load.

Visual Notes.   Working with an idea visually, not just in the head, is another useful strategy. Notation techniques are usually very helpful: write alternative phrasing, words, and the like one under another so you can emphasize or see the various options more clearly; put boxes around words or ideas so as to focus your concentration on them; draw lines or arrows from one idea or word to another. You will consider relationships more carefully if you see your thinking "in the lines."

Make Do.   Try "making do." Even though you know that what you put down is not the full idea or the right word or the way you want the sentence to read—put it down. Tell yourself that it's okay for now. You may not be satisfied, but you have let yourself move on. When you come back to the unfinished part, you will be able to see it with fresh eyes.

Take a Break.   When you're stuck, spinning wheels for an hour and getting more and more frustrated, take a break. If you have been sitting at a desk for an extended period of time, with nothing going right or nothing going at all, it's time to do something else. The ideas will run around in your head, regardless, and when you return to write, chances are you will return refreshed and ready with some ideas of what to do next. Letting ideas incubate is a good practice in any case. After you generate ideas, allowing some time for them to sit in the head is not wasting time. Similarly, while drafting, thinking about the next unsolved problem in your draft is often more productive when you are not sitting at a desk or computer. Some of your best thinking may occur when you are walking to class, driving to work, relaxing in the student union, or making a sandwich.

REVISING

Revising an essay requires a new set of eyes. When we draft, we try to get our ideas down on paper, concentrating on what we want to say, the content. When we revise, we take another look at that content, this time concentrating on how we might improve it. Sometimes, we add material; other times, we delete it. Or we might change the organization of our material. In revising, we also take another look at our sentences, hoping to make them clearer or more "alive," more interesting. And finally, we examine individual words and phrases, usually asking ourselves if we can make them more precise or vivid.

Revisions in Student Drafts

Before you begin revising your draft, read the following drafts and take notice of the changes made by two students in their revision process.

AY'S DRAFTS

Ay's native language is Hmong, an Asian language derived from Chinese. A refugee from Laos, Ay wrote this personal-experience essay about her job in a refugee camp in Thailand.

Compare Ay's drafts:

1. What changes did Ay make in content, in keeping or deleting information?

2. What changes, if any, did Ay make in how she organized information?

3. What changes did Ay make in sentences, in revising for clarity and editing for correctness?

4. What word changes did Ay make, both for effectiveness (e.g., vividness, precision) and for correcting to Standard Written English?

DRAFT 1

The worst job I have ever had took place in Ban

Vinai Camp. I was employed by a short Hmong woman who *whose*

garden ~~for a~~ *was her* living. My job was to get a bag full of

pigs fices for her garden. For my job, I had to travel

a long distance in order for me to get to my

destination. Everyday, I walked passed a high bamboo

fence built along narrow dirt road.∧ ~~before I passed or~~

To get to the other side of

camp I had to walk across a huge log

~~crossed a big log to the other side of the camp~~. After

that, I passed fruits stands, Thai Restaurants, and

food stands. I turn right as soon as the open market

dissappeared from view. I walked toward a smaller part

of the camp reserved only for Thai to raised their

livestocks. I looked for pigs houses that have ~~fices~~ *dung*

underneath the wood. When I found it, I crawled

underneath. I felt the pigs above me moved on the

wooden floor as I gathered crumbled dry green ~~fisces~~

with my hand into my rice bag. When the bag was full,

I crawled on my knee and hand out of the suffocoting cage. I was glad that my task was completed as I walked toward home. I thought of nothing except of how my wages for the day was going to be spend.

DRAFT 2

Ten years ago, I was employed by a short Hmong woman whose garden was her living. My job was to get a bag full of pig manure for her garden. ~~For my job,~~ I had to travel a long distance ~~in order for me to get~~ to my destination. Every day, I walked passed a high bamboo fence that was built along-side a narrow dirt road. To get to the other side of the camp, I had to walk across a huge log. Once I got to the other side, an open market was set along the road: Thai restaurant, food stands, fruits stands, clothes stands, and aroma merchandise stands. The ~~smells~~ of the fresh fried noodles with garlics, fruit drinks, noodles soup, cold coffee, filled my nostrils. My stomach cried for food, but I was unable to do anything for I was out of money. I let the thought of food drift out of my mind and continued on with my plan. As soon as the open market dissapeared from my view, I knew that my destination to where Thai raised their livestock was not far away.

Once I arrived to it, my eyes scanned pig houses that contained manure. When I found them, I crawled underneath. The pigs above moved, causing manure to dropped onto my hairs and clothes. I felt sick to my stomach∧but I gathered enough couraged to gather crumbled dry green dung, with my hand, into my rice bag. When my bag was full, I was glad to get out of the suffocating cage. I was glad that my tasked was completed because that was the worst job I have ever had.

DRAFT 3

Ten years ago, I was employed by a short Hmong Woman whose garden was her living. My job was to get a bag full of pig manure for her garden. I had to travel a long distance for my job. Every day, I walked passed a high bamboo fence that was built along-side a narrow dirt road. To get to the other side of the camp, I had to walk across a huge log. When I got to the other side, an open market was set along the road: Thai restaurants, food stands, fruits stands, clothes stands, and merchandise stands. The aroma of the fresh fried noodles with garlics, fruit drinks, noodles soup, cold coffee, filled my nostrils. My stomach cried for food, but I was unable to satisfy it for I was out of money. I let the thought of food drift out of my mind and continued on with my work. As soon as the open market dissappeared from my view, I knew that my destination to where Thai farmer raised their livestock was not far away. Once I arrived, my eyes scanned pig houses that contained manure. When I found them, I crawled underneath. The pigs above moved, causing manure to dropped onto my hair and clothes. I felt sick to my stomach, but I gathered enough courage to gather crumbled dry green dung with my hand into my rice bag. As soon as my bag was full, I crawled out of the suffocating cage. I was glad that my tasked was completed because that was the worst job I have ever had.

Ay Moua

TODD'S DRAFTS

Todd's essay relates one of the most profound experiences of his life, the death of his mother.

Compare Todd's two drafts:

1. How did Todd strengthen his essay through more specific description and detail?
2. List some of the sentence changes Todd made to cut down on wordiness.

DRAFT 1

Sudden Change

I was on my way home from a weekend spent with my friends. Approaching my house, neighbors were surprisingly gathered in my driveway. With the car still running, I was instructed to hurry to the hospital. [~~The reason being that~~ my mom had~ˆa~ suffered heart attack.][Trying to stay as optimistic as possible, by telling myself that everything was going to be fine.] One short block away from the hospital, I was unexpectedly stopped by my sister's boyfriend, Adam. ~~To my surprise~~, the news he brought drastically change the rest of my life.

With tears in his eyes, Adam hesitantly approached my car. In a compassionate voice and a startling look, he muttered, "I'm really sorry." Those three breathtaking words∧along with his expression∧were all I needed to realize that my mom was dead! The ~~remaining~~ drive to the hospital was one of pure hell. I kept hoping this was just a horrible nightmare and that I would soon wake up. Hysterically rushing into the hospital, I was directed toward my father. "We lost her∧~~B~~ud" was all he said as we grasped one another in tears. The remaining time spent there was a complete blurr, as I repeatedly broke down in disbelief and despair, realizing I was not dreaming.

The next two days were filled with funeral arrangements and the facing of close friends and relatives. ~~Being a person~~ who ~~usually hides his feelings,~~ this part was really important and necessary to me. Talking about all the good memories and hearing how my mom positively affected everyone was really helpful in my coping with the tragic situation.

~~Having a great deal of dependence on my mom,~~ ~~this inevitable situation~~ forced me to grow up a great deal and take on bigger responsibilities. Things that seemed so simple before became more difficult without her around. ~~Simple things, such as attending school~~, now became more difficult. I was in my first year at college and now was experiencing another change to go along with the ones college brings upon you. This change being a challenge to me; the challenge of dealing with an adverse situation, one of many life throws at you.

People handle tough situations in many different ways. I feel character is developed by how a person deals with tough situations, life being full of them. Seeing this loss as a test of my character, I tried to think positive about the future and what it held. Spending a lot of time remembering many great experiences with my mom, I felt fortunate to have had nineteen years of them. ~~She was a very caring woman who concerned herself with other people's wants and needs before her own.~~

This entire experience has made me develop as a person and notice a variety of things about life and myself. I realize how precious life is and how quickly it can be taken away. ~~In regards to that idea~~, I find myself living for the day and not letting many opportunities pass by me. Also, I find myself expressing

my feelings to others more frequently than in the past

~~My mom always had~~ a ~~huge impact on me~~ and although

physically gone, I try living a life as if she were

still here. Her presence will always be a part of who

I am now and who I will become.

DRAFT 2

Sudden Change

I was on my way home from a weekend spent with my
friends. Approaching my house, neighbors were
surprisingly gathered in my driveway. With the car
still running, I was instructed to hurry to the
hospital; My mom had suffered a heart attack. I tried
to stay as optimistic as possible, telling myself that
everything was going to be all right. One short block
away from the hospital, I was unexpectedly stopped by
my sister's boyfriend, Adam. The news he brought would
drastically change the rest of my life.

With tears in his eyes, Adam hesitantly approached
my car. In a compassionate voice and a startling look,
he muttered, "I'm really sorry." Those three
breathtaking words, along with his expression, were all
I needed to realize that my mom had died.

The remaining drive to the hospital was one of pure hell-
-I kept wondering how difficult my life would now be. Hoping
this was just a horrible nightmare and that I would soon
wake up, I hysterically rushed into the hospital. I
was brought to the area where my father was waiting. "We
lost her, Bud," was all he said as we grasped one another in
tears. The rest of the time spent there was a complete blur,
as I repeatedly broke down in disbelief and despair, realizing I was not dreaming.

The next two days were filled with funeral arrangements
and the facing of close friends and relatives. Needing back-

ground information on my mom, the pastor questioned my family. I remember telling him that my mom was very loving, always putting my needs and wants in front of her own. I shared a few examples like her missing work when I was sick, wearing old clothes so she could afford to buy me new ones, and staying up late to help me with my school work. Sharing and hearing images that my mom presented was very helpful in my coping with this tragic situation.

I had a great deal of dependence on my mom, and her death forced me to grow up a great deal, taking on bigger responsibilities. Things that seemed so simple before became more difficult without her around. She was always the mediator who would hold the family together with her rational thinking. Now problems take days to work out because of the lack of communication between my family. She was always there for me when I needed good advice. But, I was now in my first year of college, and was experiencing another change to go along with the ones college already presents. I saw this change as a challenge--the challenge of dealing with an adverse situation, one of many life throws at you.

People handle tough situations in many different ways. I feel character is developed by how a person deals with tough situations, life being full of them. Seeing this loss as a test of my character, I tried to think positive about the future and what it held. I keep thinking, when situations came up, "What would my mom want me to do?" My mom had a way of making me feel comfortable around her, always being a great listener and never holding a grudge. She will always be an inspiration to me and the way I go about helping people. She was always there to pick me up when I was feeling down and had a unique gift of making my problems disappear. I felt fortunate to have had nineteen years of her guidance and support.

This entire experience has made me develop as a person and notice a variety of things about life and myself. I realize how precious life is and how quickly it can be taken away. I find myself living for the day and not letting many opportunities pass by me. I involve myself in as many extracurricular activities as I can handle: baseball, intramural sports, and socializing to name a few. Also, I find myself expressing my feelings to others more frequently than in the past. My mom always had a huge impact on me and although she's physically gone, I try living a life as if she were still here. Her presence will always be a part of who I am now and who I will become.

Revising Draft 1

Whether or not you use a word processor, you will probably be reviewing your draft on paper. Without a hard copy of your draft, you may not be able to make decisions about what you have said and what you still need to say. Although revising can be a very individual process, with each of us going at it slightly differently, you nonetheless want to be systematic. In other words, you should have a process that you can turn to, regardless of the type of writing task assigned. It's hard to read your own essay and see what it needs. Because you know in your head what you are saying, you can read over parts that need work without noticing the problems. For this reason, you need to have a writing conference with yourself. Double-space your draft and leave ample margins. You need room to make notes and changes.

Marking the Text

Before addressing questions for revision, you need to have some tangible tools for revision. Keep in mind that revision is messy. Your draft will be slashed, circled, cut apart, and marked up in various ways. Here are some marks and methods to help you with this important process:

Carets	Carets (^) show where you want to insert a new word or phrase. Carets work best when you are adding a very small amount of information.
Arrows	Arrows (→) allow you to connect information, whether present in the draft or added, to the place where you want to insert it.

Asterisks	Asterisks (*) are good for marking the place where you want to insert big chunks of new information, something too large for a caret or arrow to accommodate. You may want to make a note next to the asterisk to identify the material you'll add.
Spider legs	Narrow strips of paper called spider legs are another method of adding information. You write new material on the spider leg and staple or clip the strip to your draft at the appropriate place. Keeping the strips narrow helps us avoid being too wordy.
Cut and paste	You can add, delete, or move part of your essay by cutting and pasting. Workable sections from an earlier draft can be retrieved and reattached to subsequent drafts. Scissors and staples or tape are your instruments here. If you are working with a word processor, a few commands will do the job. However, you should keep hard copies of everything. We never know when we may need to go back to an earlier draft and retrieve or revive a section of text. We can also inadvertently hit the wrong key and lose parts we wanted to save.
Circle in color	As noted earlier, circling in colored ink is a technique for reorganizing material. Using a fine-point colored pen, circle in one color all references to one topic; in another color, circle all references to another topic; and so on. On the next draft, combine all of the sections marked with a single color.
Circling	Circling is also a way to indicate the parts of your draft that you'll keep. This technique is especially useful if you hate crossing things out—and most of us do. After the time we spend generating and drafting a text, every word seems golden and necessary. Nonetheless, revision means deciding what stays and what goes.

HAVING A WRITING CONFERENCE WITH YOURSELF

You've generated information, written a discovery draft, and written another draft that is ready for revision. Although revision is very hard work, it can also be satisfying. With systematic questions and procedures, you will make progress that you can actually see. And that's a good feeling.

Asking Questions About the Heart of the Essay

1. Don't ask what's wrong with the draft. Rather, ask yourself where you want to head with it. A revision is not a matter of getting out the bad sentences, incorrect grammar, or spelling errors. It is a new "seeing" of the entire draft, its focus, content, and organization. Sometimes a draft will be pretty good but still need work to shape it into a better, far more interesting paper. Write down where you want to go with the draft: What strikes you as important to develop or refine? Keep in mind your purpose for this essay.

2. Ask yourself where the most important part of the draft is, the part that is most interesting, most exciting, most energetic—the heart of the essay? Identify it and mark it.

3. Ask yourself whether anyone would say, "So what?" after reading this essay? If the answer is yes, you haven't made clear why your experience is significant, why you chose to write this particular essay, or why anyone should care about what you have shared. Write down your response to the "So what?" question.

Asking Questions About the Development of the Essay

No matter how interesting your topic may be, too little or too much information will spoil the essay. Your reader may give up because there are too many blanks to fill in or too many details to plow through. Evaluate how well you have developed the essay by asking and answering the following questions:

1. Do I have enough information? Have I shown (not told) by using examples and illustrations? Have I told my thoughts and feelings at points where my reader will wonder about them? Have I described the scene, event, and people with enough detail so my reader can see them? Would dialogue help?

2. Is there any part that will confuse my reader? Have I explained each part well enough so that my reader will know what I mean, will not be thinking, "What's going on here?"

3. Have I assumed too much? Does my reader have the background or knowledge needed to understand this situation or event?

4. Do I have too much information? What parts really aren't needed—don't add anything important to my narrative?

5. What is this essay really about? Are there parts that are about something else? Can I delete them?

6. Do I have more than one story here? Which story is the one I want to tell?

7. Have I made this a dawn-to-dusk narrative, a 24-hour piece detailing everything, rather than focusing on the important part?

8. Have I added too many details and too much dialogue, made the piece very "fussy and busy"?

Use marking strategies to help you sort out what stays and what goes. Remember two basic questions: What am I trying to say in this piece of writing? Is there a point to this narrative? If you learn that you need more or better material, return to generating strategies.

Asking Questions About Organization and Unity

How easily your reader moves from point A to point B, from idea to idea, incident to incident, or detail to detail depends upon your organization of material. We can organize an essay in many different ways. Our purpose helps us decide which organization is best. In narratives, we most often move chronologically (time order) and spatially (movement from place to place, descriptively). In brief, we are asking, "How did I get from here to there?" A second question involves unity, whether everything in the essay actually belongs there, whether we have gotten "off the track" somehow. We have to ask if each part of the essay is related to its main idea, if each part contributes to development of the main idea.

1. How have I established a meaningful organization for my essay? Am I relating a single event (or person) within a certain time and space? Am I relating more than one event within a certain time and space?

2. How does each paragraph move the narration forward? Is each paragraph contributing to my main idea? Does each paragraph stick to one point or idea? To find out, try this process:

   a. Number each paragraph in the left-hand margin.

   b. Read each paragraph. In a word or phrase only, write down its main point or idea. What is this paragraph actually saying? If you find out that the paragraph has more than one point, and that you really can't reduce it to a few words, your narrative is off track.

    c. Now scan the paragraphs again. This time ask what each does for the essay as a whole. Why is that paragraph there? To insure that you write down what the paragraph *does* rather than what it says, use this sentence to guide you: "This paragraph is here because it _____." If you can't fill in the blank, you know that the paragraph needs attention.

3. How does each paragraph connect to or build upon the previous paragraph? Would more explicit connections (transition words) help readers to understand the flow of ideas better?

In narrative writing, transition words showing time relationships are very common:

    Order of events: *first, second, last*

    Beginning of an event: *before, at first*

    Middle of an event: *at the same time, meanwhile, next, then*

    End of an event: *finally, later, afterward*

    Time period of event: *during, briefly, periodically*

    Frequency of event: *often, rarely, frequently, sometimes*

    Specific time of event: *last year, the day before, now*

You'll ask questions about transition words again when you examine your essay for coherence, a word meaning "hangs together."

---

4. If you are still a bit shaky about organization and unity, make a scratch outline, nothing fancy but good enough to show you the main points, their order, and what support you have for them. You should be able to see rather quickly where you have too much, too little, or repetition.

Checking on Coherence

Coherence means that your reader can move easily from sentence to sentence and paragraph to paragraph. In the previous questions on organization, you were also checking on coherence to a certain degree—making sure that each paragraph related to the one before and after it. When an essay is coherent, the reader understands the relationship between what you have just said and what you are saying now. When an essay is incoherent, the reader becomes confused and, ultimately, irritated. When you are satisfied that the essay's content and organization are okay, check for coherence.

1. Are there enough transition words (e.g., *however, also, for example, because, although, additionally, furthermore, as a result,* etc.) to show relationships among sentences?

2. Are key words repeated in some appropriate way (e.g., synonyms)?

Be sensible about coherence: your essay is coherent if your readers know where they have been and where they are going as they read. You may not need many transitions in this particular essay, and sprinkling them throughout the piece may only clutter it up. More is not always better.

Checking Beginnings and Endings

Your opening paragraph can make or break the essay; a reader may immediately decide whether or not to continue. Consequently, you want your "lead" to be effective, to draw the reader in.

1. Ask if your opening paragraph, your lead, brings your reader right into the narrative, into the main idea or action.

2. Ask yourself where the narrative actually begins. Can you cut the first paragraph? The first two? The entire first page? That suggestion may seem extreme, but sometimes we "beat around the bush" a lot when we first get started on a piece of writing. Just getting started can be difficult, and rambling in the first paragraph or so is not unusual. However, you have to be rather brutal with yourself in assessing the worth of those opening paragraphs.

Your concluding paragraph is also critical. The reader will carry away a sense of the entire essay from your conclusion, so you want it to be a strong one, complete and memorable.

1. Ask if your conclusion just drops off, leaving the reader to wonder, "What's happening here?"

2. Ask if your conclusion rambles on, repeating and aimless.

3. Ask yourself how you want a reader to feel at the end of the narrative. Does the conclusion do it?

4. Ask yourself what you want a reader to know at the end of the narrative. Does the conclusion do it?

Considering the Title

Although your title may be unformed at this point, consider it another important element to be checked upon completion of the essay. When you have finished revising and editing, you'll need to add a title. Consider these questions: Does the title fit this essay, provide a glimpse of what it's all about? Does the title "grab" the reader, draw him or her into the essay?

Checking for Voice

When we speak, we carry an individual voice: tone, pacing, emphasis, rhythm, vocabulary. In effective writing, the reader gets this sense of the author; it is one of the distinguishing marks of an essay. Sometimes students think that academic writing is characterized by its lack of voice, by a dry, nondescript, very vacant author. It may be that years of reading textbooks have left that impression. But in truth, good academic writing carries a sense of the writer. If you reread the student writers in this chapter, you will find their voices to be both individual and important to the overall effect and success of the narrative. Although writing is *not* speech written down, it nonetheless conveys our individual voices through the way in which we use words and sentences.

Writing Activity

When you have completed the writing conference with yourself, write your next draft. Some of your classmates will read this draft, evaluating its development, organization, unity and coherence. For right now, don't worry about punctuation, grammar, and spelling.

Group Activity

In your group, take turns reading and responding to one another's drafts. Bring enough copies for your group, but hold onto them until you have completed reading your draft to the group.

A. **Read to the group.** Read slowly and clearly, adding no comments about your draft. Read the essay in its entirety. Comments and questions will come when you have completed the reading.

B. **Listen to a peer.** First, put your own draft aside and try to forget about it for a few minutes, which is understandably hard to do. Concentrate on the reader's ideas:

What part is most interesting to you? Why?

What was the most important point?

What would you like to know more about?

C. **Discuss each reading.** After each reading of a draft, discuss it orally, focusing on the content.

D. **Read the draft silently and individually.** Fill in the top of the peer response sheet (author's name, reader's name, date, and title of draft). Then respond briefly to the following questions. If you believe the essay was fine with regard to any question, say so rather than leave it blank. On the draft itself, note problems with items 2, 3, and 4.

1. What's at the heart of the essay, the "So what?" factor? If you are unsure, say so.

2. Where did you feel you needed more information, better details, examples, and so on?

3. Where did you feel you were getting too much information, getting bogged down, and the like?

4. Did you lose track of the story at any place, feel confused, or wonder how things fit together?

5. Did you have a sense of the writer's voice?

6. What did you like best? Why?

7. What specific suggestions do you have for improving the essay?

Writing Activity

Review the comments and questions arising from your small-group review. Allow yourself some time to absorb both the suggestions and your response to them. Incubating, allowing the ideas to sit on the brain for a short time, is just as effective in revising as it is in generating. Then, revise your draft once more. When you are satisfied that you have included what you want to say, in the order in which you want to say it, and that a reader would not suffer any jolts in following your narrative from start to finish, you're ready to look at the next level of revising: sentences.

REVISING SENTENCES

So far, you have been looking at sentences from one perspective: Are they grammatically complete? Now you'll look at them from another perspective: Are they effective? Sometimes we write sentences that are complete and technically correct but not very effective. Because our brains want to process information as quickly and efficiently as possible, we prefer that the information be packaged well. Whether we are consciously aware of it or not, we like variety in sentence length and construction. Sometimes, when students have learned how to write and punctuate a certain type of sentence, they use that type to the exclusion of all others. As a result, their writing stays far more childish than their intelligence and maturity deserve. When we have good ideas, we should be able to express them in intelligent and clear ways. Writing effective sentences has a great deal to do with that kind of expression.

We aren't just born with the ability to write effective sentences; like many other skills, it has to be developed. Time, effort, and sustained writing experience are needed. Another critical factor is care: We have to care whether or not our sentences work. If we value our ideas, if we value communicating those ideas clearly, then we should also care about whether our sentences work.

Group Activity

Before you meet with your group, read "Life As I Know It." As you read, put a plus (+) next to sentences which really work and a minus (−) next to sentences which don't (too long, too short, unclear in some way). Although there are other problems with the essay, just concentrate on sentences for now. You'll come across some fragmented sentences, but you may find they are used intentionally, to achieve a certain effect. You need to consider the sentences as they work within the paragraph. Do they balance one another (various lengths, different structures, etc.)?

LIFE AS I KNOW IT

"Mom, Greg saw me in my underwear!" "Daddy, Greg hit me really hard!" A typical day in the Douglas household. These are just a few of the many drawbacks in being the "older brother." Forget what you see on <u>The Cosby Show</u>. Forget about Alex and Jennifer's latest squabble on <u>Family Ties</u>. This is the real world and I am a kid dealing with real sibling rivalry!

Over the years I have learned actually more or less been forced to deal with my younger sister Ann. Since as far back as I can remember Ann has always gotten her way while I sat by watching in disgust. In matters such as money, the "family" car, nightly curfews, and the ever so popular teenage drinking, I have unavoidably paved the way for her. My parents have already been through all the normal teenage dilemmas with me. In their eyes I have done everything wrong, so with Ann they now expect it and deal with her teenage life in a more relaxed manner.

The best and most efficient way to illustrate my point is through examples. Although you will never be able to completely understand my situation, you will get a feel of the hell I have to go through every day being the older brother.

When I turned fourteen, everything changed for me. Mom and Dad stopped paying for things such as movies, junk food, and everything else that wasn't crucial to my survival as they saw it. I lived through this seventh grade only to see my sister three years later never have to deal with it. Every day Mom hands Ann a ten dollar bill just in case she might need it. Ann is now sixteen, and is still getting money from our parents every time she goes to the show or to the mall. Whenever I question them about this, they try to avoid an answer completely, or try to justify their actions by saying "she doesn't have enough money today" or "we just want her to be with her friends" which is usually followed by my sister informing me with a huge grin on her face that I have to drive her and her friends to the show.

Before my sister got her license, I was considered "Mr. Taxi Driver" whenever Ann needed to go somewhere I was her ride. I can remember once I worked the late shift from 10:30 PM to 6:30 AM. This meant I got home at 7:15 and slept between 8:00 and 4:00--or at least that was my original plan.

At about 9:30 I heard a pounding on my door. It was my sister exclaiming that she needed a ride to driving school at 11:00. Now you have to understand that 11:00 AM seemed like 3:00 AM to me. Since I realy had know choice in the matter I told her to wake me up when she was ready. The invevitable bellowing came just as Christy Brinkley and I were getting cozy on the sofa--in a manner of speaking the worst of it all was having until 12:30 to take Ann home. Sitting in the midst of a bunch of hyper fifteen year olds is not my idea of a good time. That night at work I was extremely tired but did anyone care how I felt--no. Ann's driving lessons finally paid off that spring, but things sure were different when she got her license than when I got mine.

When my friends and I got our drivers' licenses and started going out Mom began to worry. The dreaded curfew was now hung over my head. Every weekend through high school I would beg her to let me stay out, "Just a little bit longer," but I would always get an "I never fall asleep until you get home" answer. I really don't know what happened over the year. Maybe Mom just get tired of arguing and finally gave up because Ann is able to come home at a "reasonable hour" (as Mom puts it). Also because Ann learned from my mistakes and never argued with mom about when her curvew would be mom began to trust her. Mom no longer has a problem falling asleep. Ann is now able to sneak in at any hour without getting caught. I cannot believe what she gets away with. There was a time once when I thought to myself "ha--now she is going to get it!" (but as ususal Ann came out on top).

My family and I had planned a trip to Myrtle Beach. Ann didn't want to come along because her best friend was moving to Georgia soon and her boyfriend was leaving for college that week. After a long drawn out argument with our parents she managed to con them into letting her stay. Before we left Mom and Dad made sure Ann understood that she was not to have a party. This little talking-to meant absolutely nothing to Ann, but I wasn't going to tell my parents that.

Our fun-filled vacation ended a week later, at ten thirty in the morning when we turned on to our street. There as a line of cars all the way down the street! I immediately knew what was going on. I tired to warn my sister that we were back by honking the horn. My attempt was in vain I realized when I walked in the house to an unforgettable sight. There were at least twenty people passed out on the floor. Beer cans covered our new plush carpeting. The house smelled of beer, smoke and vomit.

After frantically searching the downstairs, they found my sister safely tucked away with her boyfriend. Everyone was kicked out of the house--needless to say, my parents were furious. Despite their anger all my sister had to do, after a long talk with my parents, was to clean the bathroom walls and carpet and pick up all the beer cans and cigarette butts. She also had to stay in for the rest of the day and think about what she had done.

When I was her age I was grounded for a week, when I lied to my parents. It was my friend's birthday and we had planned this for weeks. We told our friends that we were going to sleep over at his house. What we really did was Tom, Neil, Dave and I had a field party by ourselves. Our parents didn't even know that we all got so drunk that we passed out. Or about Neil crying because he thought Dave was dead. Or Tom coughing up blood and Jack Daniels all night. Or when the bottle blew up in the fire and caught Neil, and Tom's sleeping bag on fire when they were asleep. They didn't even know about the glass that got shot into Dave's arm. All they knew was that we weren't at Brent's that night, because she called to remind Neil of his dentist appointment. She called all the other parents and they all decided that we should be grounded for on week. Of course we were all the oldest in our families.

Now in my sister's case it was the first time she had been caught doing something of this nature and my parents didn't call any of the other parents to talk about punishment. She just simply made my sister clean the house and stay in for a day.

Now can you tell me that this is fair and the oldest don't get the worst of almost everything. We had to work for everything we got, but what we worked for our younger brothers and sisters are given. These examples should help you understand just some of the few times in our life when those little brats get the best of everything. Hopefully one day this will change and all children will be treated equally.

As a group, take each paragraph in turn and discuss any plus or minus sentences in it. Talk about why the sentence worked or didn't work for you as a reader:

1. Sentences that worked: easy to follow; vivid words; ideas clearly related; length appropriate (long or short) to the idea and context of the paragraph.

2. Sentences that didn't work: too short or too simple for the idea or context of the paragraph; too long, too many ideas in one structure; unclear, confusing, required reading several times.

3. How did the essay "sound": formal, informal, academic, funny, serious, chatty or conversational? How did the sentences contribute to the "sound" of the essay? Do you think you might recognize another piece of writing by this same student writer? Why?

4. What's the role of punctuation, specifically commas, in helping readers sort out ideas? Note some places where commas helped, hindered, or were needed.

Ways to Revise Sentences

We can revise sentences through one of two basic strategies: modify them in some way (add words, delete words, substitute words) or combine them. Refer to Part Two, "A Writer's Handbook," for examples.

Writing Partner Activity 1 _____

Together, choose a paragraph from "Life As I Know It" and revise the sentences that are unclear, awkward, or ineffective in some way. Discuss your reason for each revision: What made you decide to delete, add, or substitute words? What made you decide to combine two sentences?

Writing Partner Activity 2 _____

Return to your own personal-experience essay, exchange papers, and go through the very same process of marking sentences just completed with "Life As I Know It." Be sure to talk over the marks you make and reasons for them. Do not rewrite any sentences for one another. Sentences are rather like fingerprints: distinctively ours. What's more, we need to rework our own sentences if we want to improve our writing.

CHAPTER 5

Generating and Exploring Topics

You already know one powerful way in which we generate and explore ideas for writing—through responding to what we have read. There will be times, however, when you'll be asked to come up with your own academic topic. When that happens, you need to problem solve: generate your topic, explore it, and emerge with a workable idea. No matter what topic we choose, we all face a common set of questions once we begin to work on that problem:

✦ How do I get started?

✦ How can I keep my ideas going?

✦ How do I make sense out of all the ideas?

✦ Once I've decided on an idea, what then?

✦ What if I get stuck in the middle of my draft?

Although there are no formulas or single solutions for writing problems, we do have specific strategies to help us. Some work better than others, mainly because we have different styles of working and learning. To find out which are best for you, give each a fair tryout. You may find that some work well as study strategies or exam preparation too.

When we write, we often use more than one strategy to generate and explore topics and ideas. You'll work through these in this chapter:

Freewriting	Mapping
Looping	Directed reading
Listing	Cubing
Reporters' questions	Charts and outlines
Personal questions	

FREEWRITING

Freewriting might be considered "babbling on paper," a steady stream of thoughts on paper—thoughts that are often unrelated, disjointed, and incomplete. However, the very process of letting loose, of not censoring or editing out ideas, is valuable for writing. Too often, we stop ourselves, thinking, "Oh, this is stupid," or, "I don't know what I mean," rather than letting the words pour out. Since there is no discussion and no feedback on freewriting, there is no need to worry about how bizarre it might appear.

If you can freewrite at a computer, all the better. The physical ease of typing often helps stimulate ideas and allows for a more sustained writing period. It's important to write for at least five minutes nonstop. If you can't think of anything to say, simply say that: I can't think of anything. You'll find you can't shut down your brain, and pretty soon you'll find all kinds of words flowing again. Freewriting is a good strategy when you have no idea at all of what you want to write about.

LOOPING

Looping builds from freewriting. It's a strategy that helps us find a focus or a main idea for an essay.

1. At the top of a clean piece of paper, write a possible topic.

2. Now freewrite for at least five minutes on that topic. If you suddenly go "blank," write that you are "blank," and continue until something else pops up.

3. Stop and read what you have. Underline the most important part—it could be a word, a phrase, or a sentence.

4. Take that important idea and write a complete sentence about it. This sentence represents your best idea out of the first loop.

5. Take a short break.

Take a clean sheet of paper. Take your best idea from the first loop and write it at the top. Now repeat the looping process. Again find your best idea and write it out as a complete sentence. After a short break, repeat this process. For most people, three loops provide enough focus, allowing formulation of a good general statement for writing. If they don't, try another strategy.

LISTING

Listing is just what it sounds like: writing down words or phrases with no concern for order. Quantity is what counts here. Later, you will go back and sort out what's there; you'll see related ideas and can then begin to do some sorting and grouping. This strategy is used with a topic—putting down everything that comes to mind—and it is as useful when you are in the middle of an essay as when you are trying to get started on one. If you suddenly go blank in the middle of an essay, listing is a good way to get yourself back to writing.

Reading and Writing Activity

Before you read the following news articles on college students and cheating to get good grades, list your ideas about grades. Then as you read the three articles, highlight or underline the main points.

BIG LIES HAVE SMALL BEGINNINGS

Erma Bombeck

Michael Moore, a 24-year-old junior at Rutgers State University, thinks he is breaking new ground with his paperback, "Cheating 101: The Benefits and Fundamentals of Earning the Easy A."

His dream of elevating cheating to an art form offers such techniques as wearing a Walkman, using the stick-shift method (which indicates multiple choice directions) and being paged by a beeper during a test and getting answers from friends on an outside phone.

You call that creative? I knew people in college who cheated 30 years ago. They wrote answers on breath mints and ate the evidence, recorded answers on the ends of their fingernails and then bit them off. A few put notes on the soles of their shoes, and several rummaged through wastebaskets in the mimeograph room looking for master sheets.

But there is one glaring difference. The cheaters weren't the norm 30 years ago. They were the scum who were dishonest and brought shame and embarrassment to a university. Without integrity, they missed what education was all about. They were neither admired nor accepted, nor the stuff of which books were written.

According to Moore: "It's understood between students that cheating is a reality. You take it for granted that they have [cheated] in the past and will in the future." I want to be disgusted with Michael Moore, but he has to wait his turn. First I have to show my real contempt for politicians who lie and captains of industry who are consumed with greed, for plumbers who overcharge and lawyers dedicated to exploitation, for law enforcement officers who take advantage of people's trust and writers who accept Pulitzer Prizes for stories they invented.

They are the ones who paved the way for Michael Moore's book. Before any of us is too complacent about putting the blame on those mentioned above, look into your own lives. What kind of message are you sending to your children?

You can't break into a car, but it's OK to fish without a license.

You can't steal a bicycle, but it's all right to filch a few office supplies.

Don't lie to your mother, but you can tell the person at the box office you're big for 11.

The fall from integrity doesn't happen when you stub your toe over a large lie in your path. It's stumbling along a rough road mined with one decision after another of what is right and what is wrong. The important thing to remember is that a lot of books have been and will continue to be written on "cheating." Most of the authors, however, are serving time.

CHEATING MAY BE ON THE UPSWING AT UW–MADISON

Joe Schoenmann

She gets an A in cheating. She's so good that even when she got caught, the University of Wisconsin–Madison junior lied well enough to get out of it. "I could have done it without cheating, but I get nervous and I'm a very academic person and I really want to do well," she said, speaking on condition of anonymity.

It's not something she's very proud of—cheating in class to get A's—but the pressure to get grades is stiff, she said.

"And here, you can be anonymous in cheating because: So what? How many academic misconduct cases are there? Lots. And if you're caught, you can deny it. You can just say no."

During the 1988–89 school year, UW officials tracked 51 cases of cheating: 15 in the fall, 33 in spring and 3 in summer. The number rose to 71 cases in 1990–91, 27 in the fall and 44 in the spring. No cases were reported in the summer. This year, 28 cases were reported last fall. Most cases result in grade reductions (40 in 1988–89), followed by reprimands (13), expulsion (5), or additional work (2). Rarely do students appeal decisions (4 in 1988–89).

Peggy Miezio, assistant dean of students, keeps track of the numbers and usually deals personally with students who get caught. Over the years, she's found little change in the reasons students choose to cheat. "It's usually, 'It was stupid, I panicked, I wasn't prepared,'" Miezio said. But she's not sure if more students are cheating or more are getting caught.

Numbers might be up, she suggested, because of a UW code change four years ago that makes it easier for faculty to penalize those who violate academic conduct rules. That isn't exactly scaring the students. That won't happen, Miezio notes, until students feel more of an attachment to the institution. "Students don't see their own personal connection to the university. They'll say: Why does it matter? I'm just a number."

That's just what Rutgers University student Michael Moore says in his book, "Cheating 101." "Education is impersonal, and when we have professors that have other pressures on them—the publish or perish mentality—education becomes secondary," said Moore from his Hopewell, N.J., home. "Students pick up on these," he said. "They realize the professor really isn't interested in teaching, and they say to themselves, 'Why should I be interested in learning?' and they find shortcuts and take them."

Moore's book, an irreverent look at faculties and university systems, details methods of cheating. It caused a mild uproar when printed last fall. "I got good reactions from students and people with senses of humor and bad reactions from uptight administrators," he said.

REVIEW OF "CHEATING 101" (EXCERPTS)

Anthony Flint

Moore makes no excuses about the profits he reaps from the book, and acknowledges that he set out to make money. But he also considers "Cheating 101" to be a commentary on the shortcomings of higher education: ill-prepared professors more concerned with research, dreary required courses and the lack of training for real-world applications.

Rutgers officials, while praising Moore's entrepreneurial skills, have sharply criticized "Cheating 101" as a blatant violation of academic ethics.

But Moore denies that he's engaging in anything unethical. "I don't think people that are buying the book have never cheated before. They already know a lot of the methods. I'm not making a cheater out of anybody," he said, adding that he advises students not to cheat in their major or in nonrequired courses in which they really want to learn the material.

To see how your views compare with those of Bombeck and Moore, make a chart.

	Bombeck's Views	My Views
A.	_____	_____
B.	_____	_____
C.	_____	_____

	Moore's Views	My Views
A.	_____	_____
B.	_____	_____
C.	_____	_____

Even if you share some of Moore's views, do you have to draw the same conclusions as he does?

Group Activity

Bring your chart to small-group discussion. Do most of you have similar views? Why or why not? If you were to write an essay on this topic, what position would you take, and how would you support it?

Reach a consensus and bring a position statement, along with relevant support, to full-class discussion. Consensus, by the way, means that you can agree on the topic—but not that everyone agrees with the same degree of enthusiasm. Being able to reach a consensus is an important skill, not only in school but also in the workplace, the community, and one's home.

USING REPORTERS' QUESTIONS

Asking questions of a topic is another way of exploring it in a systematic way. From asking initial questions, you can move to asking more questions or formulating statements from the question.

Now read these two news articles on cheating, and use reporters' questions to sort out the information presented:

STUDY SHOWS HIGH SCHOOL, COLLEGE STUDENTS CHEAT, LIE

Marina Del Ray, Calif. (CPS)—College and high school students admitted to cheating, lying and stealing in a two-year national study on ethics, according to a report released this month.

The study, undertaken by the California-based Josephson Institute of Ethics, involved interviewing 8,965 young people nationwide and focused on ethics.

"There is a hole in the moral ozone and it is probably getting bigger," said Michael J. Josephson, president of the institute.

The report, he said, is indicative that the present 15-to-30-year-old generation is more likely to engage in dishonest and irresponsible behavior than other generations. Among the findings from the survey:

✦ Sixteen percent of college students and 33 percent of high school students admitted to shoplifting.

✦ Twenty-one percent of college students said they would falsify a report if necessary to keep a job.

✦ Sixty-one percent of high school students and 32 percent of college students admitted they cheated on an exam in the past year.

STRESSING SAT BRINGS CRIMINAL RESULTS

Lisa Baumann

When 19-year-old Lawrence Adler of Potomac, Md., paid his friend $200 to take the Scholastic Aptitude Test for him a year ago, he relieved himself of the anxiety and fear that can come with taking the test.

Adler probably experienced anxiety and fear at the highest level last month after a judge sentenced him to six months in jail for saying under oath that he took the SAT.

Adler not only paid off David Farmer, a freshman at the University of Virginia; he then lied to cover it up.

The case is believed to be the first criminal prosecution to stem from cheating on the SAT.

Criminal prosecution stemming from cheating on the SAT? Absurd.

Many students are required to take this test to apply to colleges. It's just another form of pressure put on teenagers. Don't they have enough to show from their years in school without the extra pressure?

Anyone who has taken a big test can relate. Students wait in a classroom, seated every other one in small desks. The atmosphere is tense and quiet, with students knowing that this test helps determine their future.

One test should not have such an effect on the life path.

FairTest, the National Center for Fair and Open Testing, has found the SAT to show inaccurate results based on biased context and format. Although the questions passed a sensitivity process, researcher Phyllis Rosser found that 40 questions on the SAT had extreme bias in favor of one gender or the other; 34 questions favored boys.

Should we prosecute the creators of the SAT because they claim it is unbiased and accurate?

We should take a step back and ask what these kinds of tests really prove. They show who is good at test-taking under pressure.

Test developers and users should throw out the SAT altogether. Then teens could concentrate on becoming well-rounded people.

Then Adler could concentrate on his studies, instead of paying someone else to do it for him.

At the top of a sheet of paper, write *cheating* and then write as many questions as you can addressing that topic:

Who?   Who cheats?   What kind of people cheat?

Why?

How?

Where?

What?

You can also pair questions?

How/Why?

Where/Why?

Who/Why?

What/Why?

QUESTIONS TO EXPLORE ONE'S VIEWS

Read Robert Samuelson's essay on young adults, their parents, school, and academic achievement. Highlight or underline Samuelson's major points. Note how he supports his ideas. How convincing is he? Why? When you finish the essay, respond through looping. At the conclusion of three loops, review what you have written and respond to the questions at the end of the essay.

TEEN-AGERS IN DREAMLAND

Robert J. Samuelson

Meet Carlos. He's a senior at American High School in Fremont, California. He's also a central character in a recent public television documentary on U.S. education. Carlos is big fellow with a crew cut and a friendly manner. We see him driving his pickup truck, strolling with a girlfriend and playing in a football game. "I don't want to graduate," he says at one point. "It's fun. I like it."

If you want to worry about our economic future, worry about Carlos and all those like him. It is the problem of adolescence in America. Our teen-agers are living in a dreamland. It's a curious and disorienting mixture of adult freedoms and childlike expectations. Hey, why work? Average high school students do less than an hour of daily homework. Naturally, they're not acquiring the skills they will need for their well-being and the nation's.

Don't mistake me: I'm not blaming today's teen-agers. They are simply the latest heirs of an adolescent subculture—we have all been part of it—that's been evolving for decades. American children are becoming more and more independent at an earlier and earlier age. By 17, two-fifths of Americans have their own car or truck. About 60 percent have their own telephones and television. Adult authority wanes, and teen-age power rises. It's precisely this development that has crippled our schools.

The difference, Coleman concluded, lies with parents. "Parents [of public school students] do not exercise as much authority over their high-school-aged students as they once did," he recently told a conference at the Manhattan Institute. Since the 1960s, public schools have become less demanding—in discipline, required course work and homework—because they can't enforce stiffer demands. By contrast, parents of parochial school students impose more control. "The schools therefore [are] able to operate under a different set of ground rules," Coleman said.

There are obviously many good public schools and hard-working students. But the basic trends are well-established and have been altered only slightly by recent "reforms." Change comes slowly because stricter academic standards collide with adolescent reality. In the TV documentary, Tony—a pal of Carlos—is asked why he doesn't take tougher math courses to prepare him as a computer technician, which is what he wants to be. "It's my senior year," he says, "and I think I'm going to relax."

Adolescent autonomy continues to increase. "Teens have changed so dramatically in the past decade that more advertisers . . . are targeting 'adults' as 15-plus or 13-plus rather than the typical 18-plus," notes Teenage Research Unlimited, a market research firm. It estimates that the average 16-to-17-year-old has nearly $60 a week in spending money from jobs and allowances. By junior year, more than 40 percent of high school students have jobs.

These demanding school-time jobs are held predominantly by middle-class students. Popular wisdom asserts that early work promotes responsibility, but the actual effect may be harmful. In a powerful book (*When Teenagers Work*), psychologists Ellen Greenberger of the University of California (Irvine) and Laurence Steinberg of Temple University show that jobs hurt academic performance and do not provide needed family income. Rather, they simply establish teen-agers as independent consumers better able to satisfy their own wants. Jobs often encourage drug use.

Our style of adolescence reflects prosperity and our values. We can afford it. In the 19th century, children worked to ensure family survival; the same is true today in many developing countries. Our culture stresses freedom, individuality and choice. Everyone has "rights." Authority is to be questioned. Self-expression is encouraged. These attitudes take root early. My 4-year-old daughter recently announced her philosophy of life: "I should be able to do anything I want to do."

Parental guilt also plays a role. The American premise is that the young ought to be able to enjoy their youth. Schools should spoil it, as if an hour and a half of daily homework (well above the average) would mean misery for teen-agers. Finally more divorce and more families with two wage-earners mean that teen-agers are increasingly left to themselves. They often assume some family responsibilities—shopping or caring for younger children. Many teen-agers feel harried and confused, but the conflicts among all these roles (student, worker, child and adult) are overwhelming.

Americans, young and old, delude themselves about the results of these changes. A recent study of 13-year-olds in six countries placed Americans last in mathematics and Koreans first. But when students were asked whether they were "good at mathematics," 68 percent of the Americans said yes (the highest) compared with only 23 percent of the Koreans (the lowest).

This was no quirk. Psychologist Harold Stevenson of the University of Michigan, who has studied American and Asian students for years, finds the same relationship. Americans score lower in achievement, but, along with their parents, are more satisfied with their performance. "If children believe they are already doing well—and their parents agree with them— what is the purpose of studying harder?" he writes.

Good question. No one should be surprised the U.S. businesses complain about workers with poor skills, or that a high school diploma no longer guarantees a well-paying job. More school spending or new educational "theories" won't magically give students knowledge or skills. It takes work. Our style of adolescence is something of a national curse. Americans are growing up faster, but they may not be growing up better.

Respond to Samuelson's ideas *after* you've completed a looping exercise. Review what you've written and apply these questions.

1. What am I saying? Is this a reflection of something I really believe or merely a mood right now?

2. Am I consistent? Do I always feel this way? Does what I have expressed here match my opinions? If not, how different? Why might I have expressed different views or opinions?

3. What's shaped my opinion or feeling on this topic? What experiences or observations have led me to my current opinion?

4. Where does this opinion, feeling, or belief lead? What does it suggest about me? About the world I live in? What, if anything, am I trying to say about my personal vision of the world?

If you were going to write an essay on this topic, how would these questions have helped you?

MAPPING

Mapping, sometimes called clustering, is one of the most visual strategies we have for exploring a writing topic. We store a great deal of information in the brain, often forgetting we have it until something

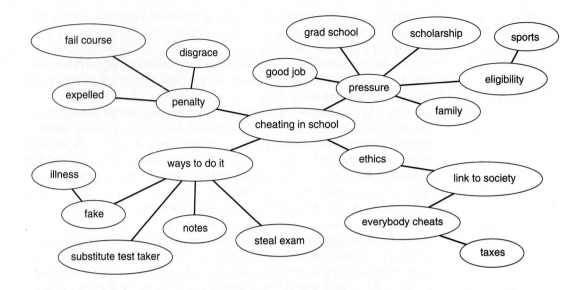

calls it into consciousness. So if we can call up one piece of information or memory, we may be tapping into a wealth of information. Because it is graphic and concrete, mapping can help the brain make the connections. For this reason, mapping is an excellent study technique as well.

Start the process by writing the subject or general topic in the center of a clean piece of paper. Draw a circle around it. Then, write down every word or phrase that pops into your head as you look at the subject. When you have a number of words or phrases, circle them, review them, and join related ones by lines, as shown in the following example:

Because the map shows the relationship among ideas, you can quickly see which area holds the most potential for development. The map also suggests major points for such development. For example, the general area of *pressure* to cheat suggests five major reasons: maintaining athletic eligibility, raising a grade point to ensure admission into graduate school or a strong application for a top job, maintaining or applying for a scholarship, and family expectations or continued financial support. These offer plenty of material for writing an essay.

Now review your map and choose one area that interests you or that you believe might be best for further exploration and development. Make a scratch outline indicating what your purpose and major points would be.

READING TO EXPLORE OUR IDEAS

Each of us approaches a written text with a personal frame of reference. We are influenced by our past experiences as well as by our current situation. We are also influenced by our gender, ethnicity, and age. Even people with similar backgrounds and ages will nonetheless interpret what they read somewhat differently. Something happens when we read: a weaving of personal sensations, images, and responses—some logical and some purely emotional. Therefore, you need to trust your responses. The meaning of that written text is not in the teacher. Nor is the meaning totally in those marks on a page or solely in you. It evolves from the dynamic interaction between you and what you read.

You can use this interaction consciously. It will help you better understand both what you read and your response to it. At the same time, this process can help you to develop topics for writing. Using Diane Ravitch's essay, you'll systematically explore the ideas and your immediate response to them through the following activities:

Summarize the Main Idea

Before you read the entire article, read the first and final paragraphs. Then, skim the entire article, looking only for main ideas, underlining or highlighting them as you come across them. Ask yourself, How did Ravitch get from her major point in the introduction to her conclusion? Now read slowly and carefully. When you complete the reading, write down Ravitch's main idea.

Argue with the Author

In the margins, note when you agree or disagree with the points being made, the ideas being presented. Also note why you agree or disagree. Imagine the author sitting across the table from you. What would you say to her? What would you want to know?

BACK TO THE BASICS: TEST SCORES DON'T LIE

Diane Ravitch

When I was in public high school in Texas in the 1950s, one of the last things a girl wanted was a reputation as a good student. Girls who got good grades were "brains," and brains were socially handicapped. Most girls strived to cultivate the June Allyson image: a follower, not a leader; cute and not too smart; or at least not so smart that the guys felt threatened. Apparently—despite the women's movement and the presence of significant numbers of successful women as role models—it is still considered inappropriate in most schools and colleges for girls to seem "smart." As a female student at Hunter High School in New York City recently explained: "I make straight A's, but I never talk about it. . . . It's cool to do really badly. If you are interested in school and show it, you're a nerd." In elite institutions where students are chosen for their academic ability, girls are more willing to challenge the boys academically than they are in nonselective schools and colleges. But with the demise of most single-sex girls' schools and colleges, there are now even fewer institutions where girls can be leaders and achievers without feeling like freaks. The popular culture—through television, movies, magazines, and video—incessantly drums in the message to young women that it is better to be popular, sexy, and "cool" than to be intelligent, accomplished, and outspoken: Madonna has replaced June Allyson.

In 1986 researchers Signithia Fordham and John U. Ogbu found a similar antiacademic ethos among both male and female students in an all-black high school in Washington, D.C. They noted that able students faced strong peer pressure not to succeed in school. If they did well in their studies, they might be accused of "acting white." Fordham and Ogbu observed that "peer group pressures against academic striving take many forms, including labeling (e.g., 'brainiac' for students who receive good grades in their courses), exclusion from peer activities or ostracism, and physical assault."

These attitudes, whether expressed by boys or girls, blacks or whites, discourage academic achievement. If boys or girls who study are derided as "goobs" and "dweebs"—two of the many pejorative terms for good students catalogued in a recent *New York Times* survey of teenage slang—then most boys and girls are going to avoid studying. Permissive parents and permissive educators don't help the situation by leaving adolescents adrift in a culture shaped largely by mass media. A national mathematics assessment released in 1988 revealed that American teenagers know the basics taught in elementary school, but their academic performance trails off as they get older and peer pressures begin to take effect. Only half of all 17-year-olds "reached a level of proficiency associated with material taught in junior high school mathematics."

Unfortunately, outside the cultural bubble inhabited by Madonnas and dweebs lies a real world, and in that world poor academic achievement is not without consequences. Last March, a comparison of students in 17 nations reported that our fifth-graders ranked eighth out of the 17; our ninth-graders ranked 16 out of 17 (beating out Hong Kong only); and our 12th-graders ranked last in biology, third from the last in chemistry, and fourth from the last in physics. Just a few weeks ago another international test of mathematics and science was released by the Educational Testing Service, with the same dismal results. Compared to 13-year-old students in Ireland, South Korea, Spain, the United Kingdom, and four provinces in Canada, our students scored last in mathematics and well below the mean [average] in science.

There is a growing real world correspondence between our declining test results and our declining economic prowess. Those countries that promote hard work and self-discipline in school have surged ahead, eroding the technological edge that we once enjoyed. According to the *New York Times,* Japan's annual share of American patents grew over the past 15 years from 4 percent to 19 percent, while our own share dropped from 73 percent to 54 percent. Experts point to the lack of a well-educated labor force as one of the prime causes of our diminishing economic position. Government policy is partially responsible, as are inadequate levels of savings and investment. But we have wounded ourselves, socially and economically, by failing to nurture scientists, engineers, inventors, and, in fact, a general citizenry who can read, write, compute, and adeptly use technology. In the 17-nation science study, the bottom quarter in the ninth grade of U.S. schools is described as "scientifically illiterate."

So what are we doing about it? Among the nations that regularly lead the world in international competitions, like Korea and Japan, there is a strong core curriculum that begins in elementary school. U.S. educators should be demanding that all future teachers get a solid liberal education, one that includes math, science, history, literature, and foreign language; and some educators are. Educators and concerned citizens should also be insisting that all children learn science and mathematics and history and literature and a foreign language in every grade from elementary school onward; but few educators are, because they either don't believe in doing so or know there aren't enough qualified teachers to offer such a rich curriculum.

What we shouldn't be doing is denying that a problem exists, or jettisoning objective measures that reveal our educational shortcomings. . . . [Ravitch argues that rather than use the SAT as a college admission test, schools should measure what students have actually studied in science, history, literature, mathmatics, and foreign language—an achievement test which, she believes, would force high schools to teach subjects that matter.]

But no matter what kind of test is used, we will continue to have serious cultural problems undermining educational achievement: the negative attitudes of parents who urge their sons to strive and achieve but not their daughters; and the negative attitude of educators who accept the destructive peer culture, not acknowledging their responsibility to establish a climate in which academic achievement, hard work, and brain power are honored. . . . We will continue to lose ground and squander our educational resources until teenagers and their parents come to recognize that academic achievement requires the same motivation and active involvement as achievement in sports or music.

Question Yourself

What wasn't clear to you? Think in terms of asking the author what she means. Fill in the blank:

I don't understand _____.

I wasn't ready for _____.

I was surprised when I read _____.

Connect with Your Experience

What did you think of as you read? What other issues came to mind? Do your observations and experience lead you to agree with Ravitch or oppose her?

Establish the Point of View

To whom do you believe Ravitch is writing? What seems to be her attitude toward students? Toward parents? Toward teachers? Toward society in general? How do you know?

Keeping Your Reading Journal at Hand

Earlier, we talked about maintaining a reading journal as a way of understanding what you read and generating possible writing topics. The questions and statements in the preceding activities are merely an expansion of that idea. If you apply them consistently, they will lead you to the issues and to your ideas about those issues.

Group Activity

As you discuss the following questions, be sure to allow each person enough time to express his or her views. Take notes on anything you find interesting or might want to explore further. Ask questions when you don't understand someone's views.

1. What does Ravitch mean when she writes about the *destructive peer culture?* What evidence does she provide to back up her use of *destructive?* Do you agree with her view?

2. Who or what does Ravitch blame for what she believes is a terrible situation in American education? Does your personal experience or observation lead you to agree or disagree with her point of view?

3. According to Ravitch, everyone in America should be concerned about the state of public education. What case does she make for this point? How do you think she would respond to people who have no children in school and say, "Why should I care what goes on there?"

4. "So what are we going to do about it [the problem]?" asks Ravitch. What does she suggest as possible solutions? Evaluate her solutions: What are they? What would each require and from whom? Is each solution workable? Would it be supported by parents? Educators? Taxpayers?

5. Compare Robert Samuelson's ideas with those of Ravitch. Both writers address American teenagers, schools, and problems with attitudes. Both are exploring a serious issue for the 1990s. If they make the same point, do they use the same examples or reasons to support it? Do you find one writer more convincing than the other? If so, why?

Writing Activity

Ravitch argues that "the popular culture—through television, movies, magazines, and video—incessantly drums in the message to young women that it is better to be popular, sexy, and 'cool' than to be intelligent, accomplished, and outspoken." Samuelson argues that "Americans are growing up faster, but they may not be growing up better."

Choose one of these statements as your topic. Then use at least two different strategies to generate and explore your ideas on that topic.

Save your work, you may use it for a later writing assignment.

CUBING

Cubing, named for the six-sided perspective of a cube, is a powerful strategy and especially well-suited for academic writing. Through it, we can systematically examine a subject from multiple points of view: six angles, six different perspectives. Like freewriting and looping, cubing depends upon sticking with it for 3–5 minutes of writing on each angle.

1. **Description:**   What something looks like; its general characteristics, physical qualities; facts and figures that help us see it; defining features.

2. **Comparison:**   How something is similar to or different from something else.

3. **Association:**   What memories something stirs in us; personal connections; thoughts, examples, experiences.

4. **Analysis:**   What something's made of, the parts; reasons why something happens; controversies, investigations, supporting evidence.

5. **Application:**   How something's used, what it can do; what problem is solved or created.

6. **Argumentation:**   Opinions, conclusions, recommendations for or against; criticism.

Using an idea from Samuelson's essay, that today's high school students lack self-discipline and serious work habits, we can see how cubing works.

1. **Description:**   What characterizes today's high school students? lazy? who says so? evidence of? bored? how know? what's the racial mix of students? does that make any difference? family structures of students? important? urban kids, suburban kids, rural kids—all the same? bright? turned off? why? defiant? talented? caring? self-centered?

2. **Comparison:**   Males/females; Caucasian, black American, Hispanic-American, Asian-American, Native American; achievement in science/math vs. humanities; U.S.A. vs. Japan or Germany; students in 1950s vs. students in 1990s.

3. **Association:**   Not working in math, working hard in social studies, hating physics; giving Sara a tough time because she did all the assigned work; nobody really caring about what I had to say; dumb questions in textbooks; English teacher = robot; even when interested, didn't want to look like it.

4. **Analysis:** Causes for lack of school work—assignments seem dumb and boring, unrelated to life; family not care if kids do them or not; working too many hours outside of school; sports more important; never had to work around home or have any responsibility; have too many home responsibilities, no energy left; disruptive family; teachers not demanding quality work.

5. **Application:** Problems created by lack of self-discipline—never get sense of satisfaction of doing a job well; habit that stays around in adult life; can get into serious trouble; when decide want to work, get a particular job, etc., not be able to prove can do it.

6. **Argumentation:** Revolution in curriculum—make pertinent for 21st century and kids will tune in and work harder; many kids have serious family problems that affect school and work habits—get at the family problems first; get rid of so much TV watching; create better homework assignments and structure classwork for active participation.

> Which perspective or angle do you like best? If you were going to write an essay on this general topic, which perspective might you use and why?

Writing Activity

Pick a topic, perhaps one you've been exploring already, and try the cubing exercise. You should spend about 30 minutes on it. When you have finished with the exercise, choose one of your cubing perspectives. Formulate a statement that could be the basis for an essay. How would you support this statement? Now choose a different perspective and formulate a statement. How would your essay be different? Has your purpose for writing changed?

Developing a Controlling Idea for an Essay

You've been exploring the topic of students cheating. Now you'll try out two different topics, ones with added complexity: American families and the American homeless. Consider this complexity as you try out ideas and learn how to develop a good controlling idea for your essays.

Just as a topic sentence guides the development and content of a paragraph, a controlling idea guides the development of an entire essay. In academic writing, the controlling idea is usually stated rather than implied; an explicit statement is generally found within the first paragraphs. It tells us what the essay is about, what major point the writer will develop. It may also tell us the writer's opinion or judgment on the subject, as in this example:

> Due to more economic freedom for women, marital relationships today are significantly different from those of a generation ago.

What would you expect the writer to develop? What information is promised to the reader? Chances are you would expect to know just what "economic freedom" means. Then you would expect to learn how this freedom has brought about a change, and just what that change entails. You would need the contrast between women of your mother's generation and your own. The writer is promising you an illustration of "significantly different."

Here's another example:

> Domestic relationships today are more stressful than those of my parents' generation.

Again, what would you expect to learn? First, you would expect the writer to define or limit what is meant by domestic relationships. Some relationships might carry more stress than normal, simply because they are more nontraditional. Second, you would expect to learn what the writer considers to be stressful. And you'd expect to see the comparison between two generations laid out clearly for you to evaluate. The writer is making an assertion, that relationships today are more stressful. As a reader, you have every right to expect that the writer can "prove it," or at the very least, convince you that the point is valid.

There are various ways in which a writer states a controlling idea, each carrying a promise to the reader. If the general topic were American families, the following offer possibilities:

Descriptive   American families today look different from those of a generation ago (would describe the various configurations of single-parent families, lesbian and gay families, cross-cultural families).

Explanatory   Childless couples searching for adoptable white infants have found eastern Europe a new resource (would explore this new baby market, perhaps provide readers with information on how to proceed).

Analytical   Statistics show that the American family continues to shrink, and polls state that economics is the major factor (would analyze the economic reasons for a reduction in family size).

Evaluative   Until families provide more stability, many children will fail to develop their learning potential (clearly the writer's opinion, a judgment that will need support).

Sometimes these categories overlap. With a controlling idea such as "serial marriages are commonplace today," our writing would be both descriptive and explanatory. Our readers would expect to learn just what serial marriages are and how and why they came to exist. We might also analyze the situation. However, there is no hint of evaluation, of judgment, present. If we stated that "serial marriages are destructive" or "serial marriages make good sense," we have changed to an evaluative controlling idea. However, we would need to be descriptive as well, to explain just what we mean by the term "serial marriage." It's important to state a clear controlling idea. Your reader wants to understand your purpose for writing the essay "up front."

Using Strategies to Develop Controlling Ideas

People have a tendency to respond quickly to some issues, perhaps out of a strong emotional feeling about them. However, quick responses are often superficial, reducing a complex issue to a simple one. Using a generating strategy will help you avoid this situation.

Topic: the homeless in America

Because this topic is a fairly complex one, cubing might be a good way to generate more ideas for exploration and writing.

Description.   What things look like, characteristics, definitions.

Who are the homeless? Where are they living? What is a shelter? What is the life of a homeless person? Homeless men—characteristics; homeless women—characteristics; ethnicity of homeless; new homeless—blue-collar worker of the 1980s and 90s; children of the new homeless.

Comparison. How is something or someone like or different from . . . ?

Homeless in America vs. homeless in _____; male vs. female homeless; difference between a home and a shelter; are all shelters the same? Do different states have different rules and regulations regarding the homeless; are all private agencies alike?

Association. Personal connections; memories, experiences.

Homeless in Boston and Cambridge, sleeping on bench on Brattle Street; homeless in Berkeley, sleeping on lawn across from dorm; police; women with grocery carts laden with junk, belongings; sleeping in subways, doorways; mentally unstable, singing and talking to self, personal uneasiness.

Analysis. Reasons, controversies, investigations.

Why an increase in homeless; why more families homeless; why more women homeless; economics, tearing down affordable housing, letting people out of institutions, lack of affordable mental health care, lack of jobs, lack of job training, losing jobs, drugs, alcoholism, family abuse; who's educating the children of the new homeless?

Application. Problem solving, social implications, economic implications, what can be done?

State and federal assistance; new definition of equality; health care; renovation of inner city, expansion of low-cost housing; job training; new vision of jobs for the 90s.

Argumentation. Opinions, recommendations, criticism, conclusions.

Renovate inner city, affordable housing; national health care; job training; change economic policies that created recession; better rehabilitation; tougher laws on drug and alcohol abuse; tougher laws on family abuse (wife beating); stop forcing people into shelters—issue of personal freedom; literacy/education.

Cubing provided many ideas that could be worked into a controlling idea:

✦ Female homeless represent a new and growing problem for American cities.

✦ Economic policies of the 1980s are responsible for the increase in homelessness.

✦ A new definition of homeless in America, blue-collar workers.

✦ Renovate the inner city.

✦ Redefine jobs and job training for the 1990s.

✦ Develop a national health care plan.

✦ Children of the homeless, lost to illiteracy, ill health, maintaining the cycle of poverty and hopelessness.

✦ Redistribute some foreign aid into American cities.

We can try out a couple of these ideas and see what might develop as a controlling ideas and major points:

Controlling idea: The female homeless represent a new and growing problem for American cities.

Who are they?

Why an increase?

✦ Family abuse and desertion

✦ Welfare cutbacks

✦ Letting mentally ill out of institutions

✦ Cutbacks in social welfare programs

✦ Eliminating cheap housing

Controlling idea: The economic policies of the 1980s are responsible for the increase in homelessness in America.

What were these policies?

How did they contribute to homelessness?

✦ Loss of jobs

✦ Loss of affordable housing

✦ Values, attitudes of Reagan and Bush administrations

✦ Failure of Congress/political partisanship

✦ Widening gap between wealth and poverty

✦ Cutbacks on social welfare programs

✦ Recession

Group Activity

Statistics from the U.S. Department of Housing and Urban Development say that more than 25 percent of the homeless are children and that 40 percent of the homeless are families (*USA Today,* March 18, 1992, p. 1A). Using "children of the homeless" as your topic, develop at least two controlling ideas. Follow the model that has been presented, asking questions and listing potential material for development of major points.

INFORMAL OUTLINING AND ORGANIZING

Scratch Outline

When people hear the word "outline," they often get a mental picture of a complicated system involving different types of numbers and alphabet letters—a very formal presentation of major points and subpoints. That kind of outline is a useful reading guide, helping us see at a glance what the text is all about. For writing, however, a very brief, informal outline is more useful. It's not necessary to use any numbers or letters, only some indentations or titles to indicate the difference between the major point and its support points. For example:

Controlling idea: The female homeless represent a new and growing problem in America.

Who are the female homeless?

+ Age, race, unemployed, uneducated

Why on street now?

+ Leaving abusive homes
+ Lack of social programs to assist
+ Lack of inexpensive housing
+ Letting mentally ill out of hospitals
+ Cutback on welfare benefits

Why should anyone care?

From this initial outline, we can do more refined planning and make changes that are needed. An outline good enough to guide our writing, a plan, is all that is needed. We don't want something so refined, so complete that we are reluctant to make changes. *An outline good enough to help us and not too good to throw away is best.*

Comparative Outline

Informal organizational plans can also help us determine our controlling idea.

Topic: The new homeless in America, a result of economic policies of the 1980s

Economic Policies of 1970s	Economic Policies of 1980s
_____	_____
_____	_____
_____	_____
_____	_____

Alike: _____

_____

Different: _____

_____

What conclusions can I draw?

_____

_____

_____

What point do I want to make?

_____

_____

_____

Possible controlling ideas?

_____

_____

_____

Cause and Effect Relationships

A controlling idea can be a cause and its effects, as in this example:

Topic   Children of the homeless
Cause   Family on the street
Effects At risk—educationally
               medically
               emotionally
               physically

Or there might be a causal chain, one cause or effect leading to the next step:

cause→effect→cause→effect→

recession→job lost→home lost→family on street/homeless

Children at risk—educationally
                  medically
                  emotionally
                  physically

What conclusions can I draw?

_____

_____

_____

What point do I want to make?

_____

_____

_____

Possible controlling ideas?

_____

_____

_____

Comparison and Contrast Chart

Yet another graphic way of looking at a topic can help us see the similarities and differences quickly:

TOPIC: CHILDREN AT RISK		
	1970s	**1990s**
Similar	Immigrant children Migrant workers' children Below poverty line	
Different		Gangs and gunfire Crack babies AIDS babies Working-class children Breakup of family Lack of immunization

What conclusions can I draw?

_____

_____

_____

What point do I want to make?

_____

_____

_____

Do I want to go further, investigate reasons for similarities or differences?

_____

_____

_____

Controlling idea: An increase in violence has put city children at risk in the 1990s.

Why? In what ways?

_____

_____

_____

What would be my purpose in writing?

_____

_____

_____

New controlling idea: Children are born at risk in the 1990s.

Now what is my purpose?

_____

_____

_____

New controlling idea: The breakdown of the American family in the past 20 years has left more children at risk.

What would be my purpose in writing?

_____

_____

_____

Opinion Chart

A chart such as the one on the next page can help us lay out ideas for a position paper or some sort of argumentative essay, a common writing assignment in college classes.

My Opinion: _____

_____

Headings: _____   _____   _____

Why: **Reason/Evidence**   **Reason/Evidence**   **Reason/Evidence**

_____   _____   _____

_____   _____   _____

Details/Examples   **Details/Examples**   **Details/Examples**

_____   _____   _____

_____   _____   _____

My Conclusion: _____

_____

After you read Allan Bloom's thoughts on college students in the following excerpt from *The Closing of the American Mind,* study the two responses worked out in chart form.

SELF-CENTEREDNESS

Allan Bloom

Students these days are, in general, nice. I choose the word carefully. They are not particularly moral or noble. Such niceness is a facet of democratic character when times are good. Neither war nor tyranny nor want has hardened them or made demands on them. The wounds and rivalries caused by class distinctions have disappeared along with any strong sense of class (as it once existed in universities in America and as it still does, poisonously, in England). Students are free of most constraints, and their families make sacrifices for them without asking for much in the way of obedience or response. Religion and national origin have almost no noticeable effect on their social life or their career prospects. Although few really believe in "the system," they do not have any burning sentiment that injustice is being done to them. The drugs and sex once thought to be forbidden are available in the quantities required for sensible use. A few radical feminists still feel the old-time religion, but most of the women are comfortably assured that not much stands in the way of their careers. . . . Students these days are pleasant, friendly, and if not great-souled, at least not particularly mean-spirited. Their primary occupation is themselves, understood in the narrowest sense. . . .

There is, indeed, a certain listlessness about them, an absence of a broad view of the future. . . .

But the great majority of students, although they as much as anyone want to think well of themselves, are aware that they are busy with their own careers and their relationships.

RESPONSE 1

My Opinion: Most women are not "comfortably assured" that there are no barriers in the way of their careers.

Headings: Business   Medicine   Education

Why:

Reason/Evidence	Reason/Evidence	Reason/Evidence
Few top women in top management jobs	Women medical students/M.D.s harassed	Few women administrators
	Discouraged in surgery specialty	Few rank as professors

Details/Examples	Details/Examples	Details/Examples
Fortune 500 Co.	Stanford U.	1 of 10 in local university
Local businesses	harassment incident	1 of 8 in high school
	Local clinics	Only 4% prof. female

My conclusion: Although women have made some career gains, they still don't have the same access as men. Women students can't assume entry into the career they want.

RESPONSE 2

My Opinion: *Students are not free of most constraints.*

Headings: *Economic*   *Sexual*   *Family*

Why:	**Reason/Evidence**	**Reason/Evidence**	**Reason/Evidence**
	Lack of money	*Awareness of*	*Responsibility*
		disease	*for others*

Details/Examples	**Details/Examples**	**Details/Examples**
Piling up	*Fear of AIDS*	*Nontraditional*
student loans	*Other sexually*	*students*
Working 1 or 2	*transmitted*	*Single parent*
jobs	*diseases*	
Recession/inflation		
Parents not able to		
support student		

My conclusion: *Professor Bloom might have found students at the U. Chicago in the late 1980s to be free of constraints, but that's not the situation of students today.*

Writing Activity

Using information from Joan Beck's essay "Why America's Students Are Falling Behind" or Susan Chira's "Some Challenge Notion That U.S. Schools Are Failing," prepare an opinion chart. Use your own ideas, observations, experience, and discussion notes, as well as what is presented in the article. You may take either side of the issue, but in either case, be reasonable and logical in your choice of evidence.

WHY AMERICA'S STUDENTS ARE FALLING BEHIND

Joan Beck

It's worrisome enough that the Japanese can build better cars and more TV sets than Americans. But that they are producing smarter students should be of far greater concern. Why are Japanese—and Chinese—children doing better academically than American youngsters?

There is no doubt American elementary students lag seriously behind comparable Asian children. Long-term, cross-cultural studies, taking into account socioeconomic status, language differences and cultural factors confirm the disparities.

The reason is not because Asian children are innately more intelligent than their American counterparts, says a new book, *The Learning Gap*. It's because of crucial differences in how Asian schools are run, the amount of time Asian and American youngsters spend on academics and the attitudes toward school and achievement youngsters absorb from their parents and their culture.

The book suggests several changes in American schooling, some of them surprising, some of them in conflict with prevailing wisdom. Harold W. Stevenson and James W. Stigler, who wrote *The Learning Gap*, did much of the extensive, long-term research that documents the problem. Both are professors of psychology, Stevenson at the University of Michigan and Stigler at the University of California, Los Angeles.

The studies on which this book is based involve large, representative samplings of same-age children in Minneapolis, suburban Chicago, Sendai (Japan), Taipei (Taiwan), and Beijing (China). The tests were painstakingly constructed to be culturally fair and comparable.

Asian children not only spend much more time in school—longer schools days, half-day classes on Saturday, less vacation time—but they do more homework, even during vacations. Asian families make the home more conducive to studying than do American families. No matter how cramped the home or how poor the parents, most Asian children have their own study space and desk.

Asian parents believe—and their children are expected to understand—that academic learning is their primary responsibility. They spend less time in play and organized sports than American youngsters and do fewer household chores because their parents don't want to interfere with studying.

American parents and teachers are likely to assume that innate abilities play a major role in how well children do in school. But Chinese and Japanese parents think achievement is directly related to hard work and effort. The difference has far-reaching consequences in how children behave, how schools are set up and how school and home interact.

American children who see their success or failure directly related to innate factors have little reason to work hard, the book notes. Asian youngsters who are taught the hours they invest in school work will pay off in achievement and that low marks indicate insufficient effort, try harder at their studies.

American parents are more likely than Asian parents to be satisfied with their children's academic performance and to think they are doing well, when international comparisons show that they are not. So they underestimate what their youngsters are capable of doing and the children see no reason to work harder.

The problem may get worse, with the growing emphasis on teaching children to have self-esteem and to feel good about themselves, regardless of their achievements. Such attitudes rob youngsters of motivation and limit what they accomplish, Stevenson and Sigler suggest.

Many American parents fear that raising expectations for their children will create harmful stress. But Stevenson and Stigler say there is no evidence to support such fear. "Meeting reasonable challenges enhances self-confidence and self-esteem," they point out. "Lack of challenge accomplishes little. Americans accept this precept in athletic achievement—surely the same principles apply to academic achievement."

More money alone won't solve this country's education problems, say Stevenson and Stigler. The United States already spends more money per student than almost every other nation in the world, including Japan, Taiwan, China—and a larger percentage of its gross national product.

Based on observations of successful schools in Asia, Stevenson and Stigler urge teachers be given smaller course loads and more time for preparation. They see no problem with increasing class sizes. And they urge more whole-class instruction rather than in-class grouping or tracking by ability.

American children often feel isolated and lonely because they do so much school work independently, even in the classroom, the researchers say. That may be a major reason they are less enthusiastic about school than their Asian counterparts, they suggest.

The book also advocates more challenging and interesting textbooks, more recess breaks during the day so children can work off energy and socialize, more opportunities for professional development for teachers, more interaction between home and school and a national educational policy to clarify the mission of the schools.

"The belief in the importance of hard work is not alien to Americans," the book points out. The problem is we have become reluctant to teach our children its value. As a result we—and they—are losing out competitively in far more important areas than cars and TVs.

SOME CHALLENGE NOTION THAT U.S. SCHOOLS ARE FAILING

Susan Chira

Forget all the bad news about American schools. There is no crisis in American education, say a number of renegade researchers whose ideas have touched off a bitter debate with broad implications for education policy in an election year.

By falsely claiming all American schools are failing, these critics charge, the Bush administration and others divert attention and money from the real crisis: poor inner-city and rural schools.

The debate itself reveals how little Americans know about their schools' performance and how far away the country is from defining just how good its schools should be.

The defenders of American education wave a batch of surprising statistics: test scores and drop-out rates have held steady for at least 15 years, the percentage of top-scoring students is roughly the same as it was 15 years ago, and comparisons that show American students trailing those in nearly every other country are distorted by faulty methodology.

"Most schools in America are better than they were in 1981," said Harold Hodgkinson, director of the Center for Demographic Policy, a research organization in Washington. "I'm interested in a focus on the worst kids in the worst schools. Given the fact that everyone agrees that the bottom third of our kids are awful, [sic] they get very little spent on them."

But the purveyors of bad news are regrouping, charging the renegades with complacency, and fighting them statistic by statistic. Even if schools over all are not much worse than they were 15 years ago, they say, they are nowhere near good enough and they still trail America's competitors.

"The critics are wrong in saying the schools are just as good as they ever were," said Diane Ravitch, an assistant secretary of education. "That is deeply damaging; it inspires complacency and a false sense of self-esteem. To say we do as well today as we did 20 years ago—our kids are not going to be competing with their parents but with children being educated in other countries." . . .

[Defenders of American education] believe that whatever declines do exist have occurred because schools now, unlike those of a generation or two ago, are trying to educate everybody—more immigrants, more minorities, most students who once would have dropped out and gotten good jobs on the assembly line. And they say international comparisons are flawed because American students as a whole are being compared to other countries' elite. . . .

Moreover, children are scoring at about the same level on the most reliable standardized test—the federally financed National Assessment of Educational Progress, widely known among educators as the nation's report card.

Reading scores are about the same as they were 20 years ago. Math scores have held steady since 1973. Science scores are somewhat lower than they were in 1969, but scores of 9- and 17-year olds have improved steadily during the 1980s. Both these tests and SAT tests show that scores for minority students have also risen. . . . Average scores on tests required to attend business schools also rose. The percentage of students scoring above 600 points (out of 800) on the SAT math and verbal scores fell until 1975 but has held steady since.

Yet for virtually every statistic the researchers produce, critics of American schools offer a rebuttal. Scores on the "nation's report card" tests may have stayed about the same for 20 years, but they are stuck at low levels, according to the National Center for Education Statistics, part of the Department of Education. . . . While American schools still produce some brilliant students, Ravitch argues that even at the top there is reason to fear. The percentage of students who scored above 600 on the verbal SAT may have stabilized since 1975, she says, but go back only three years, to 1972, and the numbers show a drop of 35% in the last 20 years.

Many scholars argue that the researchers are right to say that schools have not gone downhill, but are drawing the wrong conclusions. "It's true, but it's irrelevant," says Marc Tucker, president of the National Center on Education and Economy, a Rochester, N.Y., research center. "Doing as well or slightly better than we used to do is doing appallingly badly relative to the rest of the world."

Group Activity

Compare your opinion charts. Determine a single controlling idea (in this case, one that states an opinion). Pool all ideas that would support your controlling idea, and choose the best supporting material for it. Then, create an informal outline, just as though you were going to write the essay.

Writing Activity

Review all the writing topics you've explored in this chapter. Choose one topic to develop into brief essay.

CHAPTER 6

Writing to Inform, Writing to Analyze

Expository writing, writing whose purpose is to inform or explain, is the type of writing found most often in school, the workplace, and the community. It differs from narration in that the writer's emphasis is on the subject matter in exposition. And where narration is often in chronological order, expository writing uses many different patterns of organization, including chronological. Comparing and contrasting information or exploring a cause and effect relationship, for example, will lead us to a specific organization pattern or strategy. Expository writing often seems very utilitarian: it helps us get the job done or it helps us understand some issue or situation. Expository writing is characterized by a controlling idea or thesis that is then developed through facts, reasons, examples, and illustrations. Expository writing is also characterized by analysis, which means the writer has broken down the information, studied its parts, and then commented on the significance of that information. We'll work with analysis a little later in this chapter.

Reports are a common expository writing task, one that is important to most businesses. Essays, on the other hand, are more common in academic settings. These two forms of writing differ in their purpose. Reports present accumulated information but, generally, do not contain the writer's opinion on that information. Essays, by contrast, incorporate the writer's personal point of view or opinion on the information presented. Quite often, however, writing tasks are a mix of report and essay. The writer may provide the information common to reports but accompany it with analysis that reveals a personal perspective or opinion.

Although we tend to think of such writing tasks as school work, a discussion with business people will quickly reveal the importance of informing and analyzing in the workplace. Hundreds of daily decisions depend upon information and thoughtful analysis, accurately and clearly presented. This important skill is also needed in our personal lives. Buying a car, for example, demands thoughtful analysis, at least if we want to get the best car for our budget. Although it's true that we can depend upon "experts" to provide analysis for us, on everything from the best brand of athletic shoes to the most able politician, we really need to rely on ourselves.

ORGANIZING EXPOSITORY WRITING

At the heart of expository writing is a general organizational pattern:

Introduction or lead

The hook—something to get the reader's attention

Background or context—something the reader needs to know in order to follow or appreciate your points; the importance of your topic

Thesis or controlling idea—of the entire essay

Development of first major point

Topic sentence—main idea of this paragraph

Explanation of the main idea

Concluding sentence or a lead into the next paragraph

Development of second major point

Development of third major point (and so on)

Conclusion

Summary—sometimes provided, a brief review of all major points just presented in essay

Significance—usually provided, a brief statement of why readers should be concerned

Implications—usually provided, a brief statement of what may or may not occur

Read Eric Betthauser's expository essay on the video generation. What was Eric's purpose? What was the significance of his essay? Why is Eric's topic a good one for informing and analyzing? How did Eric organize his essay?

Super Mario: A Member of the Family

If you happen to meet a child who spends more time with Super Mario than his or her father, don't be too surprised. This is the generation of Pac-Mania, of "my score is higher than yours," of kids with frazzled hair and glazed eyeballs. It is the video game generation, and the more time children spend with Donkey Kong, that ape of video game fame, the less time they spend with real people.

It's a phenomenon that begins before children can even read. They go for the glory of the high score of their favorite VG, a score that wins approval of peers, or maybe even a shot on a video game TV show! Parents rarely share the enthusiasm.

Even so, parents are often to blame. They dump off their children at the arcades, especially when the folks are out for Tuesday night bowling. Parents give their young ones a roll of quarters: "Go amuse yourselves." They later wonder why they're caving in to buying a Nintendo for the kids.

Once that Nintendo is bought, look out! Children somehow metamorphasize to blank-faced, jittery video warriors often complaining of "fire-button thumb." As soon as school ends--zoom! Right in front of the screen they go. Taking a short break for dinner, they continue the battle in early evening. "I've got to get to level six," they are often quoted as saying. The dinner conversation, incidentally, is not how English was, but how we killed the vampire on level three.

All night the battle in videoland drags on. Once bedtime comes, these children are not read a book before slumber; rather, they are lulled to sleep by the memory of little beeps indicating that the hero has conquered yet another foe. When the day comes, the same cycle repeats itself. The games often last most of the day on weekends.

As these children grow older, many have thoughts that turn to love, which can mean dating. Not the video children; they'd rather master Tetris. Spending time with their parents when they were younger wouldn't drag them away, so why should members of the opposite sex? Read a book? Play a school sport? Nope, they're content in front of their video screen.

This behavior, of course, has to result in something. Quicker reflexes? Maybe, but these people also spend no time developing social skills or family ties. They live in a fantasy world with few friends besides other VG maniacs. They've spent so little time with their families that they barely know each other. In times of trouble, they have almost nowhere to turn for support, and if they do, they don't know how to interact. Technology, such as in video games, often yields great results. It can also cause us to forget ourselves and those around us.

Eric Betthauser

Eric was interested in a cause, video games, and their effects on children and families. Skim Eric's essay and fill in the effects he attributes to video games.

Cause   Children playing video games excessively

Effect 1   _____

Effect 2   _____

Effect 3   _____

How did Eric organize and support his main points?

Development/major point 1 _____

    Support _____

Development/major point 2 _____

    Support _____

Development/major point 3 _____

    Support _____

Now examine Eric's introductory paragraph or lead:

Hook _____

Background _____

Thesis or controlling idea _____

_____

Examine his concluding paragraph:

Summary _____

Significance _____

Implications _____

In addition to figuring out his general organization, Eric also had to develop adequate support. What kind we use depends a great deal on our audience and our purpose, as well as on the main idea we're presenting and whether or not we are using research or other outside sources. Eric was not required to use outside sources for this assignment. Consider the following list and decide what Eric used as support.

Ways to Support Ideas

Personal experience, anecdotes, observation
Examples
Reasons
Effects
Description/specific details
Step-by-step explanation
Reference to authorities or expert opinion
Facts and statistics

What other support might have been helpful in Eric's essay? Why? Would expert opinion be available? If so, where would you advise Eric to look for it?

Selecting supporting material for an expository essay involves two other important questions: (1) Is this material relevant, on the topic, and to the point? (2) Is there enough information? If you've ever read something and a voice in your head was saying, "Get on with it!" you know the meaning of relevant. Sometimes we get a sense of "beating around the bush" when writers get off the topic or fail to make the point efficiently. As readers, we get pretty annoyed when information isn't relevant to the point being made.

As readers, we expect *unity;* we expect everything to be relevant, on the topic, and appropriate to the point being made. Whether we refer to the entire essay or a single paragraph within it, unity is critical to the success of that writing.

Is Eric's essay unified? Does he present relevant supporting material? Does he provide sufficient material? If a voice in your head was saying, "This isn't complete enough," or, "I need more information," the writer has failed to provide you with sufficient material. Rather than being annoyed, we may simply stop reading altogether.

The aspects of writing that we have been looking at thus far are somewhat mechanical; that is, we can go back to the essay, pick them out, and display them graphically. There are two other aspects, however, that don't lend themselves to that type of display: the writer's voice and the significance of the piece of writing. You were concerned with voice and significance when you wrote your narrative essay; they were at the heart of your personal-experience writing.

They are similarly important in expository writing. Despite the emphasis being placed on the subject matter, we want a sense of the writer to come through. We want the feeling that one human is talking to another. In short, we want *voice.* And without a sense of significance, the entire point of the writing is lost. As readers, we need to feel that our time, as well as that of the writer's, was well spent on this piece of writing. We want to come away thinking, "That was interesting," or, "I learned something."

Did you get a sense of Eric in the video games essay? If you did, how did he manage to connect with you? What was the significance of his essay? Why should we be concerned with his topic? How has his analysis of the effects of video games expanded our knowledge or enhanced our thinking?

In the next student example, Tom McDonald, because he was interested in exploring two different comic book eras, used a different organizational pattern. As you read Tom's expository essay, think about the significance of what he is saying. How does he link comic books with a much larger issue?

Comic Books: Then and Now

Early in its life, the comic book was a simple, somewhat mindless creation to keep children happy on family
trips, in the backs of cars, and during other occasions
when they should be seen and not heard. Now, comic books
have an adult audience, with intricate plots, less than
super heroes, and portrayals of graphic violence.

Comic books--before the 1980s--consisted of characters
like Daffy Duck and Batman. Although entertaining, these
fictional subjects were hardly realistic, having no real
life problems. Batman was never drunk, never sad, and
basically never anything less than superb. All Daffy was
meant to do was make us laugh, taking us away momentar-
ily from the drudgery of our daily lives. Batman was
equally simple, never having any question of purpose of
motivation. He was the perfect patriot, the perfect white,
middle-western, middle-class, heterosexual gentleman, and a
perfect scholar, knowing a good deal about everything.

The art of this old breed of comic book fit its message, simplistic and clear-cut. The reader isn't made to
work or interpret this production line art at all. That's
the way artist teams did things, and the reader had no
choice but to accept it. Now, a very different picture is
painted.

In the graphic novel <u>The Dark Knight Returns</u>,
Batman is portrayed as an over-the-hill alcoholic,
haunted by his past. With violent crime in Gotham
City in a frenzy, the aged Bruce Wayne dons his black
cloak again, not by his own choice, but driven by
some mysterious dark force he cannot control. Ultimately, the Dark Knight has become so sickened by
this new crime wave in Gotham that he has become violent. This time it's kill or be killed and Mr. Wayne
chooses the former, victimizing street gangs with an
extremely physical edge. Finally, it seems, the authors are trying to confront the fact that the world
isn't a bowl of cherries.

The writers of this new breed of comic book are educated, thinking men who manage to throw political and social commentary into their twisting, dancing story line. A current issue of Spiderman deals exclusively with the issue of cruelty to animals, making a powerful point to the reader that we may be wrong to torture these animals in the name of science. In today's comic book, it's not uncommon to see Shakespeare quoted. For example, in a recent issue of <u>X-Men</u>, Storm, the leader of the renegade gang of mutants known as the X-Men, quoted MacBeth in her dialogue in which she grieved over the loss of an innocent man by her own hands. The readers of this new comic are actually made to think, and demanding thought is often a characteristic of a productive, useful piece of fiction.

The art in this thoughtful new creation surpasses its writing in the provocation of thought. Awarded for its imagery and artistry, <u>The Dark Knight Returns</u> portrayed a macabre vision of the same Gotham City that had earlier been shown to us through rose-colored glasses. No longer was Batman slim and trim--his new portrayal can only be described as a demonic heap of brutish flesh. Again the simplicity and wholesomeness of the comic book of yesterday is made into something complex and sometimes lurid. This change isn't to shock the audience; it's to urge them to look beyond the black and white outline that we're presented with so often in everyday life.

Finally, the change in comic books can be seen in the vocabulary used. The words used for description went from "BIFF, BAMM, WHAMMO" to somewhat intellectually stirring words and phrases, worthy of Hemingway, like "adamant," "boisterous," or "deviously."

As you can see, the world of comic books has undergone a certain Renaissance or rebirth, changing in script and illustrations from idealistic to realistic, simple to complex and thought-provoking. It could, in fact, be argued that comic books are a mirror to society's change and will continue to parallel our lives.

Tom McDonald

Tom used comparison and contrast as the organizing strategy for his essay. Before you look back to see just how Tom used this strategy to explore his topic, examine the following chart. Then, as you skim Tom's essay, decide which of the three options he used.

Method 1	Method 2	Method 3
Introduction	Introduction	Introduction
Discuss A	Show likenesses between A and B	Discuss A and B on one point or topic
Discuss B	Show differences between A and B	Discuss A and B on second point or
Conclusion	Conclusion	Conclusion

Your topic and thesis or controlling idea will determine which of these patterns is best for you. For example, if it's important to emphasize the individual points, as is often the case with a more complex topic, Method 3 will be best. If you are interested in a general, overall comparison, then Method 1 or 2 is best. Sometimes, writers mix these patterns.

When you use comparison and contrast as a way to explore and analyze your topic, you need a strong controlling idea or thesis and careful organization. You have two subject areas instead of one, and you must have a point beyond mere comparison/contrast. If you omit your point, the reader will wonder why you are doing the comparison/contrast in the first place. Tom McDonald, for example, used comic books to make a point about changes in our society, and by implication, changes in today's kids.

In addition to deciding that comparison and contrast would be his organizational strategy, Tom also had to decide how to arrange his support material in each paragraph.

Arrangement

Topic sentence
   Example (and/or)
   Fact (and/or)
   Personal experience (and/or)
   Illustration (and/or)
   Reason (and/or)
   Expert opinion .

Topic sentence
   Example (and/or), etc.

After grouping material for each paragraph, Tom had to make a few more decisions. What point and material should be first? Last? And why? The following are typical ways we arrange the overall order in the essay:

Least important to most important: We build momentum and leave our reader with the most powerful point and material.

Most important to least important: We get the reader's attention immediately. In essay exams, we need to use this order, or we might run out of time before getting to the most important point. Newspapers and business reports use this order, mainly as a time saver for busy readers.

Known to unknown: In most learning situations, we need to move from what we know to what we need to learn. In writing, we also may need to establish a common ground, things our readers know, before presenting new material. The "known" then provides the context and foundation for new material.

Accepted to controversial: Again, establishing a common ground with our readers allows us to pursue new, debatable material.

Step by step: Sometimes, our material can be explained only through a chronological order. Everything from how-to books to historical accounts relies on this order.

Spatial: When we describe things or people, we rely on spatial order; we move from a set point to another set point. In biology labs, as well as art studios, we are often confronted with the need to order observations spatially.

Return to Tom's essay and note how he arranged his essay. Then skim Eric's essay and note his arrangement. Did they use the same arrangement? Were they limited to certain arrangements because of their subject matter?

WRITING INTRODUCTIONS AND CONCLUSIONS

Students often report that the most difficult part of their writing task is the introduction or the conclusion. For this reason, they are sometimes advised to leave the formal introduction until last, until they can review their entire paper and write an introduction that matches it. Conclusions can also be troublesome, mainly because we want to leave the reader with our main point and yet not repeat what we just said in the body of the paper. Fortunately, we have some strategies to help us with this writing.

Introductions

Introductions, also called leads, are critical to the success of the essay. Effective introductions do two things immediately: focus our attention on the subject and provoke our curiosity or interest.

Group Activity

Select a favorite magazine or newspaper, read through several articles, and then, from separate articles, choose two leads that interest you and two that you find boring. Bring them to class.

In your group, read your leads and discuss their effect—positive or negative—and why. As a group, choose one that you agree upon as effective, and be prepared to discuss your lead in whole-class discussion. As a class, list characteristics of effective leads.

Strategies for Introductions

Quotation: An appropriate quotation is a common strategy for introducing academic essays. The quotation may come from an expert on the subject you are exploring, an "ordinary" person with related experience, or any number of well-known sources (e.g., literature, religious or philosophical writings) or well-known people (e.g., educators, scientists, journalists, politicians). The quotation helps focus the reader on your subject. For some topics, music lyrics may provide a wonderful introduction to your subject and point of view.

Illustration: An example illustrating your topic may give the reader a sense of "being there." Allowing people to sense the situation or issue (showing rather than telling) may be essential in drawing them into the points you will explore or argue.

Anecdote: Providing a brief story is a good way to raise interest in your topic. If you are the main character in the story, you might also be showing your reader why this topic is important to you. Your relationship to the topic becomes immediately clear.

Historical background: Sometimes, a topic needs a bit of background in order for readers to understand why things are as they are or why a problem occurred.

News stories: If your topic is on a current or controversial subject, you may find a local or regional newspaper article that can serve as an introduction to your discussion.

Statistics: Facts and figures may surprise your reader and gain interest in the topic. For example, many people associate homelessness with single, older males. Current statistics, however, show families comprising 40 percent of the homeless.

Questions: Asking a question or a series of questions in the introduction may draw the reader into the main text, where you will answer those questions.

Controversial statement: Saying something shocking is another way of getting readers into your discussion. You have to use good judgment, of course, as to the degree of shock value.

You may use several of the strategies at the same time, especially if the essay will be somewhat lengthy. And you may end up writing your introduction after the essay is completed. Don't feel that you have to get the introduction "right" before you can go on with the essay. In fact, learning to let go of the introduction is important. In early drafts, you may end up with false introductions, a fair amount of text that should be crossed out. All of us repeat and spin wheels as we try to get into the subject. All writers, no matter how experienced, generally end up throwing out many paragraphs of false introductions.

Some strategies for writing the introduction:

✦ Find your favorite line or lines from the body of the essay, write it at the top of page 1.

✦ Consider once more your purpose, your audience, and your own personality.

✦ Then review the strategies, and pick one that appears to be the best match with your purpose, audience, and personality.

✦ Try at least four potential introductions using that strategy.

✦ If nothing works or appeals to you, pick a different strategy and repeat the process.

Conclusions

Students often report that writing a conclusion, however short, is nearly as difficult as writing an introduction. They know that the conclusion is supposed to leave a lasting impression on the reader. However, they also know that just repeating the main idea has been overworked as a strategy. What are the options then? In some cases, the same strategies used in introductions also work well in conclusions. There are other strategies that are particularly well suited for conclusions, however.

Strategies for Conclusions

Question: Posing a question for further consideration on the topic can be very effective.

Quotation: Sometimes, the right quotation acts as a summary statement of the discussion.

Image: Leaving the reader with a physical image, a picture, is another way of reinforcing our main point.

Back to lead: When writers refer back to something in the introduction, they bring the reader "full circle." The entire discussion has then been framed by opening and closing statements focused on the very same words or image.

Resolution: The writer can answer the question posed or problem raised in the introduction.

Summary: This strategy must be used sparingly. A summary is a restatement of the main points. Since the writer has just presented these points, the reader might be turned off by a restatement, especially in a short essay. Unless the essay is very long, it's better to avoid anything that even hints at "This is what I have just told you."

Return to the two student essays and evaluate the introductions and conclusions. What strategies did Eric and Tom use? What other strategies might have strengthened their essays?

Group Activity

Evaluate another of Tom McDonald's essays, "In Search of a Good Scare."

✦ Is his purpose clear?

✦ Does he show awareness of his audience?

- ✦ Is his controlling idea clearly stated?
- ✦ Is his material well organized?
- ✦ Does he provide enough material?
- ✦ How does he support his points?
- ✦ Are the transitions appropriate?
- ✦ Does his voice come through?
- ✦ Are the lead and final paragraphs strong?
- ✦ What is the significance of his essay?
- ✦ Why is this an expository essay?

In Search of a Good Scare

Despite some popular misconceptions about fear, America thrives on it. From movies to amusement parks or skydiving to ghost stories, fear is a need for many of us that demands to be fulfilled.

Freddy Krueger. His name is as common to us as Superman. In A Nightmare on Elm Street, parts one through five, Freddy can be found viciously and sadistically murdering teenagers, plucking them from their slumbers and ruling their dream worlds. And in the end, the newly petrified moviegoer is horrified to find that Freddy is far from finished. Often, that viewer is so petrified that sleep for the next few weeks is either unattainable or very restless. However, when the next one comes out, save our petrified viewer a spot somewhere near the front.

Many people have fond memories of days spent at amusement parks. Perhaps a more appropriate label for these places would be "Please scare the hell out of me" parks. The longest lines are invariably for the biggest, fastest, scariest roller coasters in the park. Every time the rider starts out, part of them is screaming, "I don't want to do this! Please, please make it stop!" But when the ride is over the terror-stricken participant goes inexplicably to the back of the line to ride this nightmare once more.

Somebody . . . anybody . . . please tell me what is fun about jumping out of an airplane! As the plane ascends and the ground is just a memory, second thoughts abound. As the parachutist approaches the door he will soon fling himself out of, his heart is hammering in his chest, ready to explode. Yet the thrill seeker still jumps. WOW!

Finally, our taste for fear can be shown in the infamous ghost stories told in the dark or around a campfire. With hearts beating and imaginations running wild, the listener wants to cover his or her ears, but is afraid to miss the next eye-watering plot twist. Why do we submit ourselves to this torture?

When we are scared in certain ways, our minds and bodies react electrically. The adrenalin "kicks in" and we feel alive and excited. It's almost like a natural high. And we like the feeling. So, we overcome our fear to feel its effects, and the rush we feel becomes almost addictive. Ultimately, fear is a whirlwind of excitement that we often willingly take part in for the sake of its surging, powerful effects.

Tom McDonald

The next student essay needs work. Although the writer had some good ideas, she had trouble trying to clarify, organize, and develop them. Consequently, as readers we are left to piece things together. In addition, we are distracted by sentence, punctuation, and spelling errors. Read through the essay quickly, to get an overall idea of its content and intended purpose. Then, go through it slowly, evaluating it as you go. How would you help the writer turn this into an acceptable essay? Be specific and constructive in your advice.

Movies

There are basically three types of movies which attract the viewers attention, in other words its purposes and effects: crime, horror, and comical.

Crime movies have a way of capturing our interest to focus on the exciting detective aspect of catching the criminal. The cops and detectives seem to go through a lot of greif and frustration at the lose of more victums when the evidence is thin. Nevertheless, the good guys always finish off bad guys whether or not it's a shoot out to the end or a sentence of death or life imprisoned. This was the adventurous purpose of crime movies. The educational part shows viewers that crime doesn't pay and sooner or later the truth will come out, and justice will punish the wrong. Crime movies also have fast paced action when the presure begins and at the climax of the solution. For example, "Lethal Weapon" was about two cops, vets, who were after the main mafia men, were selling drugs laced with poison. These cops were tortured and still they hung on. To make a long story short, the cops beat the mafia at their own game and shut them down. Another case, "The Godfather" the mafia takes the law into thier own power.

A horror movies purpose is to thrill and frighten the veiwer with scary, gruesome scenes and exaggerated sounds. It is intensified by a stalking of some crazy person or thing, which keeps coming back to life for series after series. To illustrate, "Halloween I, II, III", "Friday The 13, I, II, III, etc., "Jaws", "The Shining", and "Nightmare on Elm Street I, II, III".

Comical movies are for entertainment, moreover, enjoyment. Since we all have a serious side to ourselves, the effects of a comical movie can help us maintain our sense of humor about life. laughter is good for the body and mind. Some examples are "Private Benjamin" starring Goldie Hawn, "The Glass Bottom Boat" with Doris Day, and Rod Sterling, and a musical comady by Walt Disney "The Sound of Music" of the Vantamp Family.

In conclusion, the purpose and effects that crime, horror, and comical movies have on veiwers depends on what attracts them in the first place. Each movie has a way of exaggerating its characters somewhat to emphasize a point.

For his expository essay, Stephan Severson explored similarities between two of his favorite television shows, *The Flintstones* and *The Honeymooners*. Note the changes Stephan made between his first two drafts:

Revision   Changes in content

Changes in organization

Changes in sentences

Editing   Complete sentences

Punctuation

Spelling

Read through each draft quickly to get an overall sense of each. Then read through each draft slowly, noting the changes he made. Comparing paragraph to paragraph might help you see how the changes improved or, in some cases, didn't improve Stephan's essay. Did he eliminate good material from his first draft? Did he add material that is essentially irrelevant to his point? Be specific in your response to changes he made and changes he might have made.

Stephan had a good expository subject. What suggestions do you have for taking better advantage of the subject, for improving it, and for making a significant statement about it?

DRAFT 1

Copycat

Have you ever noticed how much two television shows can seem alike. Growing up with television I have witnessed this many times before. But there are two shows that compliment each other The Flintstones and The Honeymooners. The main reason why these two shows seem identical is because of the main characters, Fred Flintstone from the Flintstones and Ralph Cramden from the Honeymooners.

First of all, Fred's and Ralph's attitudes are very similar. They both have an explosive temper always using it to its full potential. Both of these characters have best friends (Fred's being Barney Rubel, and Ralph's being Ed Norton) Which they always seem to say that their friends are no longer welcome in their house. Ralph always using the trade mark "out, get out!" and Fred using insulting swear words such as "fricking reckun runbk ruk."

Another aspect of this relationship is that both characters share an enormous figure, which distinctly alientes them from the crowd. In each episode the boys are always being put down because of their weight. It doesn't help the fact that Alice and Wilma slave to prepare a hardy meal for their hard working husbands. Guest appearances always seem to poke fun a Fred and Ralph, usually ending up in some sort of trouble. Along with the weight issue comes their mothers-in-law, both women have no time for their sons-in-law. These women really know how to get a rise out of Fred and Ralph. During the end of the season the boys are always in a conflict where their mother-in-law is visiting and has to stay overnight, which leads to both Fred and Ralph's humble temperment.

Adding to the list of likenesses is the fact that both men in the show always find a way to get into an excessive amount of trouble, later having to explain the whole story to their loving wives. Wilma Flinstone and Alice Cramden. Usually every show is dedicated to the mayhem revolving around Fred and Ralph's interaction with trouble, always bringing Ed and Barney into the picture. Usually the trouble takes place outside the homestead, in a pool hool or when the boys go bowling.

Finally Fred and Ralph always find a way of entertaining the audience, even though to very distinct age groups. When saying this I mean that the Flinstones is a cartoon, and the Honeymooners is a classic black and white. After watching both of these great shows I have come to a conclusion. The Flintstones was created in regard to the Honeymooners success.

DRAFT 2

Copycat

Have you ever noticed how much two television shows can seem alike? Growing up with television I have witnessed this before. When saying this, two shows come to mind: the Flintstones and the Honeymooners. These two shows compliment each other with the uncanny mannerisms of the characters. There is distinctly one main reason why the two shows seem identical: the characters.

After watching both the Honeymooners and the Flintstones, I sense that the main characters from the Flintstones are identical to those in the Honeymooners. Fred Flintstone, for example, is much like the character Ralph Cramden. They both possess violent tempers that explode like blood-gushing volcanoes. Also they both have a pretty big frame of a body, due to their voracious appetites. Another quality that brings Fred and Ralph closer together is their mothers in law. Fred and Ralph are always in some kind of trouble when these women appear. This interaction with their mothers-in-law creates another quality in Fred and Ralph: the famous out burst. Fred's outburst is "frikn rakun ruchin...", and Ralph's famous outburst, "to the moon."

One of the biggest similarities of the shows is Fred and Ralph's best friends, Barney Rubbel from the Flint-stones and Ed Norton from the Honeymooners. Both Barney and Ed share qualities of zany humor, brainless ideas, and countless hours of tormenting Fred and Ralph. This has been displayed by both shows whenever Fred and Barney, or Ed and Ralph, participate in bowling, pool, or attend a boxing match. Plus Barney and Ed are always an accomplice to whatever mischief Fred and Ralph create.

Another aspect of similarity in character is the women in both shows--Fred's wife, Wilma and Ralph's wife, Alice. Both Alice and Wilma slave for their husbands throughout each entertaining show. Cooking and cleaning are a must for these women; neither one has a job. The Flintstones and the Honeymooners both had episodes in which Wilma and Alice insisted that they have jobs. But according to Fred and Ralph, the women were to stay at home.

Not only do Fred and Ralph have similar wives, but so do Ed and Barney. Their names are Betty Rubbel and Trixie Norton, but neither woman has a very big role. The only time these two women can be seen is when Alice or Wilma is the focus of the episode. The only other time that Betty and Trixie are involved is when all four characters are need for an special occasion such as going out to eat.

After watching both shows, the viewer can draw only one conclusion, that the Flintstones was created because of the Honeymooners success. In no way is this a rip on either show; my personal belief is that the television industry was looking to created a successful show with a general plot that would have an enormous effect on a diverse audience.

Stephan Severson

Apply the evaluation criteria to Stephan's second draft:

✦   Is his purpose clear?

✦   Does he show awareness of his audience?

✦   Is his controlling idea clearly stated?

✦   Does he provide enough support for his points?

✦   Does he provide good support?

✦   Is his material well organized?

✦   Are his transitions appropriate?

✦   Are the lead and final paragraph strong?

✦   Is the significance (the "So what?" factor) clear?

✦   Does his voice come through?

✦   Are his sentences clear, effective?

✦   Do grammar and mechanics (punctuation, spelling) conform to Standard Written English?

You may have already touched on some of these criteria, but going through them point by point provides a clearer view of the essay's strengths and weaknesses.

Writing Activity

Using one or several generating strategies, explore potential topics for an expository essay. Then, choose one and write a discovery draft. Remember: your purpose is to inform or explain. Your readers will expect to learn something about your chosen topic, and your emphasis is on that topic—not on you! Your instructor will provide a timetable for subsequent drafts and peer response.

ANALYZING

When we analyze, we are really asking many questions: What's going on here? What is this all about? How did this occur? Why did it occur? Who's involved? What's involved? We are interested in examining the parts that make up the issue, situation, or problem. Our analysis will lead us back to consideration of the whole once more, its overall meaning or function. If you watched the news during the Persian Gulf War, you no doubt heard many military analysts. They would comment on the progress of the war by looking at the various parts of it: what the armed forces were doing, what military commanders were saying, and what the Secretary of Defense was saying, for example. From these various points of view, the analysts would study the war, draw conclusions about its progress, or speculate about future action. Their task was to present viewers with, presumably, a coherent statement or picture of what was happening at that time. Suggesting or stating the significance of the event or issue is the logical outcome of analysis.

During national political campaigns, we are surrounded by political analysts who seem to have analyzed everything that moves. They listen to the candidates, the campaign staffs, and people across America. Like military analysts, they then analyze all the parts and present their view of the situation. During the 1992 presidential election, some television stations and newspapers analyzed political ads in an effort to let voters know whether or not a candidate was being honest. And most of us have listened to sports analyses by ex-athletes, some on national television and some in the local coffee shop or corner bar. Analysis, then, is a familiar way of dealing with our world.

Analysis Project

The Gallup Organization undertook a poll for *Life* magazine between March 30 and April 5, 1992. Data were collected from telephone interviews with 614 women and 608 men (age 18 or older) in order to learn how people would respond to questions focused on women running America. The margin of error in the poll was 3 percent in either direction; direct comparisons between men and women could result in an error as high as 6 percent. Lisa Grunwald then wrote "If Women Ran America," to accompany the poll results.

Read through the poll results carefully. At the conclusion of your reading, you will be asked to analyze them: What differences emerge between men and women, between generations, and so on? Why might one group favor a certain proposal? Even though you might have strong personal reactions to some topics, keep in mind that your first task is to analyze the information—not argue with it.

IF WOMEN RAN AMERICA . . .

Lisa Grunwald

FAMILY

If women ran America, would child care be more available and maternity leave guaranteed?

A majority of Americans—but more women than men—favor government support of programs that help working parents. The greatest gender gap exists between younger women (ages 18–45) and older men (46 and up). Eighty-four percent of younger women favored paid maternity leave; just half of the older men agree. And 86% of the same women want the government to help develop childcare programs; only 58% of the men concur.

POVERTY

If women ran America, would government be more attentive to the needy?

Fifty percent more women than men (44% vs. 29%) believe the double-edged problem of poverty and homelessness should be an "extremely important" government priority. But neither women nor men condone a free ride. Since 88% overall support laws requiring welfare recipients to work if they can, it's no surprise that 91% of men and women favor increased spending for child care so parents on welfare can work or attend school.

CRIME

If women ran America, would there be stricter gun control?

Seven out of 10 women favor making it harder to buy firearms; half the men agree. The verdict on capital punishment is less clear. Women more than men choose life imprisonment for murders (40% vs. 33%), while more men than women prefer the death penalty (54% vs. 46%). Three out of five people believe that addressing social problems is a better way to reduce crime than beefed-up law enforcement, but women believe it more strongly than men.

VIOLENCE

If women ran America, would they be tougher on crime?

Twenty percent more women than men (55% vs. 46%) say the government should make fighting crime and violence an "extremely important" priority. More women than men say the system is "not tough enough" on drug dealing, rape and sexual assault, and wife abuse. A sizable gender gap relates to drunk driving: 76% of women as opposed to 58% of men say that the criminal justice system should be tougher on offenders.

WORKPLACE

If women ran America, would there be greater equality for working women?

Women take workplace equality issues more seriously than men do. Unequal pay for equal work, sexual harassment, discrimination in hiring and promotions, child care—all are rated by more women than men to be "very serious problems" for women. Men are more likely to label most of these issues "somewhat serious." Women's top concern? Pay inequity. Two thirds rate it a very serious problem; half the men agree.

ABORTION

If women ran America, would abortion be legal?

Judging from the poll, the legal status of abortion would be no different if the reins of government were in the hands of either women or men. It would be legal—with some restrictions. Overall men are slightly more supportive of legal abortion than are women. Age—rather than sex—is a telling factor and could change the politics of abortion in the future: 53% of younger women, ages 18–45, favor access to legal abortions "always" or in "most" circumstances, while just 36% of the women over age 45 agree.

PRESIDENT

If women ran America, would America be a better place?

Nearly six in 10 people say it would not make much difference whether men or women ran the government. Still, about one out of three believe government would be better if women were in charge. (Says one woman: "Men have been in so long, let's see what the gals can do.") Sixty-one percent hope to see a woman elected President in their lifetime. More women than men hope for a woman President (young women are especially intent on this), but more men than women believe they'll see it happen.

Note: At the time this poll was taken, there were only two women in the United States Senate, only three states with female governors, and only one female Supreme Court justice. In the 1992 elections, 186 women declared their candidacies for congressional offices. As a result of the 1992 national election, 6 percent of the U.S. Senate and 11 percent of the House of Representatives are women; however, 54 percent of the American population are women. (Statistics from the Center for American Women and Politics, Rutgers University)

Your Analysis of Poll Results

A. Which issues are women most committed to? Why do you think this is so? Men? Why?

B. Which issues appear to be rather evenly supported by both men and women? Why?

C. Which issues have an "age gap," where the age of the respondents made a difference in their views? Why?

GRUNWALD'S CONCLUSION

It is no surprise in a year that saw vexing recession, unacceptable scholastic test scores, unaffordable health insurance and the breakup of the Soviet Union, to find men and women agreeing that the economy and health care should come before foreign affairs . . . but where women's views differ from men's, those views seem to lend particular insight into what the agenda of women in power would be. [p. 41]

A. Based on your reading of the polls, what do you think this agenda might be?
B. Does this suggest that American men don't care about these issues?
C. Or does it only suggest women care more?
D. How can you be fair in your analysis?

Lisa Grunwald's Analysis of Poll Results. As you read Grunwald, notice how she presents her analysis. She draws conclusions from her reading of the polls, but she neither says nor implies that hers are the only conclusions. She adds to our knowledge without insisting that her analysis is the only one to interpret the polls. Notice how she uses questions in her analysis.

FURTHER EXCERPTS FROM GRUNWALD

Women, for example, are far more committed than men to cushioning the hard corners of the country, to making it simply a safer place. Women want stricter law enforcement against drunk driving and firearms and drug dealing, which may be another way of saying that they want to keep their children alive. It's not that men don't care about these issues. It's simply that women care more. Is it because womanhood has never been measured by the length of a pistol? Because manhood and cars and risk taking have so often gone hand-in-hand? Or is it because, as any woman who's carried and borne or cared for a child will tell you, the act of mothering takes a little more time than the act of fathering? . . .

Motherhood may be one way to explain why a woman's world would be crisscrossed with safer streets, but there is a less lovely reason as well, which is women's history as victims. . . . In 1990 an estimated 683,000 American women were raped; at least two million are abused each year by husbands and boyfriends. . . ."Even those of us who have not been victimized by crime are often victimized by the fear of crime," says former Dukakis campaign manager Susan Esterich. "It limits our lives—limits our choices, limits where we work, and when we go out, and where we live."

Safety first. But fairness also, especially for women at work. Not so long ago, prospective female employees were regularly asked to promise they wouldn't get pregnant. In 1990 women who worked full-time were still earning an average of 71 cents per male-earned dollar. [pp. 41–42]

[Regarding the workplace], as Colorado Rep. Patricia Schroeder puts it, "The most stressful thing is that we have a workplace where people are not allowed to mention their caregiver role. We tolerate a car breaking down more than a sick child at home." Only 3% of the nation's businesses offer day care.

Eighty-five percent [of the women] say they would approve of a law requiring businesses to allow employees an unpaid, 12 week family medical leave. . . . Behind that number are dying parents, spouses in surgery, new babies, sick children. Of those who support family leave, nearly 30 percent more women than men want it available for gay couples too; behind that number are the slow and awful ravages of AIDS. [pp. 42–43]

As she concludes her analysis, Grunwald focuses on an important question: If women ran America, if they had power, would they really be any different from the men who run America? As you read her commentary, note how she challenges us to think about this question.

If women ran America . . . they would not just run the Congress; they would run the special interests as well. Is there any reason to think that a female head of an insurance company would lobby any less vigorously than a man against a national health plan? Women would hold the federal purse strings and would have to decide if a peace dividend was worth laying off the thousands of workers who feed their families by making B2s. And with women having most of the power, they would have most of power's temptations: not just the perks of higher office, but also the lust to maintain those perks. Would women, once they had left behind their status as outsiders, really be able to defy not only the stereotypes about themselves but also the stereotypes about power?

Then, Grunwald responds to her own question, suggesting that perhaps women are different from men:

One way to answer the question is to admit—as feminist groups of two decades ago were not inclined to do—that there is something inherent to women's experience that makes them different from men. [pp. 44–45]

Examining Other Sources

If you were interested in pursuing Grunwald's question about women and power, you would need to search out other sources.

Read the excerpt from Carol Gilligan, whose research examines psychological differences between males and females. How does Gilligan add to our knowledge?

IN A DIFFERENT VOICE

Carol Gilligan

Sensitivity to the needs of others and the assumption of responsibility for taking care lead women to attend to voices other than their own and to include in their judgment other points of view. [p. 16]

Thus women not only define themselves differently in a context of human relationships but also judge themselves in terms of the ability to care. Women's place in man's life cycle has been that of nurturer, caretaker, and helpmate, the weaver of those relationships on which she in turn relies. [p. 17]

The discovery now being celebrated by men in mid-life of the importance of intimacy, relationships, and care is something women have known from the beginning. [p. 17]

How is Gilligan's research reflected in the poll results? In Lisa Grunwald's analysis? How does a writer benefit from his or her ability to search out relevant research?

If you were interested in pursuing the question of why there have been so few women "running America," you might find some material from "20/20" helpful as a starting point. On May 29, 1992, ABC News correspondent John Stossel reported on the research of Harvard University educator Carol Gilligan and others: Girls confident at age 11 end up confused and unsure of themselves at age 16. Researchers concluded that hormonal changes in adolescence may be generally positive for males and less so for females. That is, males become bigger, stronger, and more confident as a result of the physical changes they undergo. Girls, by contrast, become less confident as they pass through the many physical and emotional changes characteristic of early adolescence.

Stossel also reported on the work of Catherine Krupnick, another Harvard researcher: Teachers call on boys more than they do girls. Boys are generally more noisy and aggressive, vie for attention, and get it. As a result, girls end up in a "silence ghetto" within the classroom.

Stossel visited a classroom of five-year-olds where he found the research "acted out" in front of him. The boys cared little for responding in an orderly fashion, often shouting out answers without being called on. When Stossel asked the girls why they thought the boys did that, one little girl told him, "Because they don't care if they know the answer or not. They just like to talk."

The following readings might also be useful to you in analyzing the situation of women in American society.

BACK TO THE BASICS: TEST SCORES DON'T LIE

Diane Ravitch

When I was in public high school in Texas in the 1950s, one of the last things a girl wanted was a reputation as a good student. Girls who got good grades were "brains," and brains were socially handicapped. Most girls strived to cultivate the June Allyson image: a follower, not a leader; cute and not too smart; or at least not so smart that the guys felt threatened.

Apparently—despite the women's movement and the presence of significant numbers of successful women as role models—it is still considered inappropriate in most schools and colleges for girls to seem "smart." As a female student at Hunter High School in New York City recently explained, "I make straight A's but I never talk about it. . . . It's cool to do really badly. If you are interested in school and show it, you're a nerd." In elite institutions where students are chosen for their academic ability, girls are more willing to challenge the boys academically than they are in nonselective schools and colleges. But with the demise of most single-sex girls' schools and colleges, there are now even fewer institutions where girls can be leaders and achievers without feeling like freaks. The popular culture—through television, movies, magazines, and videos—incessantly drums in the message to young women that it is better to be popular, sexy and "cool" than to be intelligent, accomplished, and outspoken: Madonna has replaced June Allyson.

AUTHOR SAYS GIRLS LOSE SENSE OF SELF

Los Angeles—At 7 going on 8, Lacy Bird likes baseball and ballet and riding bikes with her best friend, Whitney. School is fun; reading is her best subject.

Boys are barely a blip on the radar screen.

And Lacy knows just what she wants to be when she grows up.

"I think about being a doctor and a waitress and a linguist," she says without hesitation.

The contradictions in the list don't make a difference to the suburban Simi Valley second-grader. It's what she wants and, for now, she believes she can have it.

Hang onto these memories—life won't always be so sweet, says Emily Hancock, a psychologist whose work at Harvard University led to her book, "The Girl Within" (Fawcett; $10). The clear thought and solid sense of self present in 9-year-old girls often erode at adolescence, her book suggests.

At puberty, the girls swap their blue jeans for a skirt and their independence for a more clearly defined female role, Hancock said. In fact, the Berkeley resident says she believes that a woman's best years may be over by the time she is 11 or 12 years old.

"Girls get buried. The loss of their sense of self doesn't depend on adolescence—it happens before then," Hancock said. "As girls get bigger, they get taken out of the tree house and asked to come inside. You lose something essential when you're no longer an adventurer pursuing your own interests."

Hancock stumbled on her theory while researching grown women's reactions to their own adult development. In studying 20 women, she found that each participant's true identity emerged when she remembered who she had been at age 7, 8 or 9.

"By reaching back to the girl within, the women were on their way to reclaiming their independence," Hancock said. Once that girl is unearthed, Hancock believes a woman can recover her true identity.

Independent research backs up the theory. A study by the American Association of University Women, a national organization of college students and graduates that promotes equity in education for women and girls, found that girls' self-esteem erodes dramatically between fourth grade, when they are 8 or 9, and the time they enter junior high school.

"AAUW did a study in the fall of 1990 . . . showing that girls' self-esteem drops off two times as much as boys' in adolescence," said Sharon Schuster, president of the organization. "Boys' self-esteem falls off some, but not nearly as much as the girls'."

The information parallels prior findings in the organization's acclaimed study about how girls fare in American classrooms.

How might Stossel's television news report contribute to our understanding and interpretation of the poll results? Ravitch's? Hancock's? AAUW's?

Group Activity

Study the two graphs carefully. When you are familiar with the factual information presented there, analyze what it might mean for American society as a whole. Why are people interested in family changes and family values? What impact do they have on economics, education, and other areas? Think in these terms: What's going on? Why? What might happen? Why?

Changing Families

The facts of family life today mean fewer children live with two parents; 25.5 percent live with just one, usually their mother. And while married-with-children remains a prominent living arrangement, a growing number are blended stepfamilies.

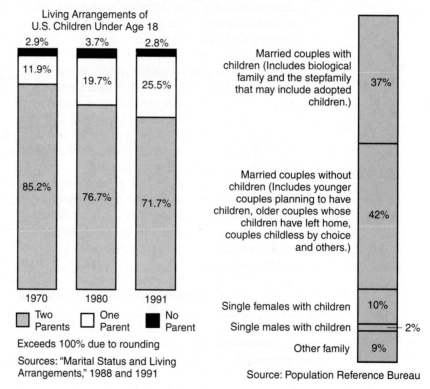

Living Arrangements of U.S. Children Under Age 18

	2.9%	3.7%	2.8%
11.9%		19.7%	25.5%
85.2%		76.7%	71.7%
1970	1980	1991

☐ Two Parents   ☐ One Parent   ■ No Parent

Exceeds 100% due to rounding

Sources: "Marital Status and Living Arrangements," 1988 and 1991

Married couples with children (Includes biological family and the stepfamily that may include adopted children.)   37%

Married couples without children (Includes younger couples planning to have children, older couples whose children have left home, couples childless by choice and others.)   42%

Single females with children   10%

Single males with children   2%

Other family   9%

Source: Population Reference Bureau

America's Family Values

Study after study suggests that Americans still cherish the nuclear ideal, a model of family life that stretches back generations. People long for a sense of commitment to community and family ties.

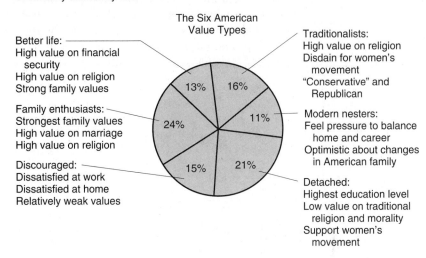

The Six American Value Types

Better life:
High value on financial
    security
High value on religion
Strong family values

Family enthusiasts:
Strongest family values
High value on marriage
High value on religion

Discouraged:
Dissatisfied at work
Dissatisfied at home
Relatively weak values

Traditionalists:
High value on religion
Disdain for women's
    movement
"Conservative" and
    Republican

Modern nesters:
Feel pressure to balance
    home and career
Optimistic about changes
    in American family

Detached:
Highest education level
Low value on traditional
    religion and morality
Support women's
    movement

America's Most Important Values

Rank order of 10 values on three different questions	How important	Learned in family	A "family value"
Being responsible	1	1	1
Emotional support	2	2	3
Respect for others	3	3	2
Happy marriage	4	5*	4
Faith in God	5	8	5
Live up to potential	6	5*	7
Follow moral code	7	4	6
Earn good living	8	5*	8
Help community	9	9	9
Being free	10	10	10

*Three values were tied for fifth place ranking in the proportion who say they learned the value in their family.

Writing Activity

Write a brief expository piece in which you analyze information from *one* graph on American families. Follow the process you went through in working with "If Women Ran America." Use the information in the graph as your starting point. For example, if the graph shows an increase in single-parent families, you could analyze possible causes or possible effects or both.

CHAPTER 7

Reading and Responding to Arguments

In both school and the workplace, we face issues to be studied and addressed. And even though we often give oral responses, we are just as often required to present our opinion in writing. Consequently, writing a position statement or paper is a fairly common writing task. This type of writing requires us to analyze the issue, formulate a clear statement of our position, and defend that position with support that is both relevant and adequate. Responding to an issue also requires that we write somewhat dispassionately, regardless of how passionately we may feel. We may argue fiercely in our homes or the student union, but for academic or business purposes, we are required to remove some of the emotion and replace it with logic.

With its emphasis on logic, the position paper requires a careful structuring of information as we build a case. However, we can't merely state our view and expect that a reader will accept it. We must provide both solid evidence and sound reasoning. An important part of that reasoning includes figuring out what the opposition would say, and either accommodating or refuting that view. This practice does not weaken the position paper; rather, it strengthens it. We want to appear reasonable, and agreeing with reasonable arguments from the opposite side is one way of doing so. Counterarguments that we can't accept have to be refuted, that is, have to be shown as wrong, illogical, or unreasonable. Similarly, because we want our readers to take us seriously, we must write with a tone that is likely to gain the reader's respect. If you have ever observed an argument in which people are shouting at one another, you know what happens when tone and language are ignored. You don't want someone mad; you want someone listening. One of the real advantages to writing rather than speaking is our increased ability to control the tone and remain reasonable.

Before you write a position paper, you'll explore some pieces that confront and analyze an issue. As you work your way through these pieces, you'll be discovering strategies that will help you with your own writing.

TO HUNT OR NOT TO HUNT

The following student essays illustrate two views on deer hunting. Even if hunting is not part of your world, you no doubt have views on conservation of the environment, firearms, and rituals associated with growing up. Read through both essays for an overall, first response. Then, read slowly and carefully, and respond to the questions that follow the essays. These are first-draft, unrevised student essays.

ESSAY 1

Many people believe that deer hunting is a mindless slaughter but in reality it is a challenging sport and is necessary for the preservation of the species.

A deer has many advantages over a hunter in the woods. For example, their senses are much keener than that of the hunter. A deer may smell a hunter before he even gets close. The deer can then walk around the hunter and the hunter will never see the deer. The deer also have a sharp sense of hearing so the hunter has to be very quiet or the deer will hear him and flee from him. Their sense of sight is poor and they cannot define colors, so they rely on being able to see movement well. So the hunter must remain motionless while hunting.

A natural camouflage and speed are also advantages the deer has. A deer is very difficult to spot in the woods due to its natural grayish brown fur that blends very well with the trees and fallen leaves. A deer is also very swift and quiet. For example it can be there one second and gone the next and the hunter never saw or heard him. Once spooked, a deer can run for miles through the thickest forest so quick you will never see him.

With all these advantages that the deer has over the hunter, it makes it a fair sport for the hunter to get his deer. If a hunter is lucky enough to shoot a deer he may be killing a deer but allowing for a chance for more to live. It's like a harvest, by taking a few you allow many more to live. If you didn't harvest the population, it would grow and there would be a lack of food. Because of the lack of food many many more would starve to death over the long winter months, which seems more cruel and mindless than killing them instantly with a bullet. This may not follow the rule of nature, that only the strong survive, but it allows for many more of the species to survive the winter months.

Essay 2

The deer hunters are at it again. I know for a fact that a certain percentage of deerhunters only stalk these animals because they perceive it as the "manly" thing to do. I find it amazing to think of these guys trudging through the forest, feet freezing, frustrated, toting an expensive, accurate, high-power rifle that they could scarcely hit the broad side of a barn with. These are the men who carry semiautomatic rifles that will pound out projectiles of hot lead as fast as you can pull the trigger. Sometimes they even kill a deer with one, but usually just a sapling or their self-esteem fall prey.

These men are not hunters, they are one of the boys paying their dues for acceptance or self-assurance. They are not marksmen these sportsmen. They are not hunters, they are laborers. They most often don't even like venison, they merely think they do because "men are meateaters Men like venison." The semiautomatic rifles are a real farce. If you don't hit a deer with one shot, it is only by sheer luck that you will hit it with a rapid succession of shots to follow. All the good marksmen I know hunt with a bolt-action rifle, they are unlikely to get a second shot. Also, these involuntary hunters I have mentioned seldom butcher their own deer, but rely on a locker to do all the cutting because they don't know how and don't want to know how.

These guys are a rather small minority I'm sure, but they are not out to enjoy a sport and obtain a greatly prized foodstuff. They ae out to prove something to themselves and their friends and family. I sound like I'm condemning this practice but I'm not. I am, perhaps, making fun of it but I know people who deer hunt for the reason's I've mentioned. They have as much right to be out there, it's just sad to see them gauge manhood by what you do, not what you are.

Responding to the Arguments

State the position taken:

Essay 1 _____

Essay 2 _____

Although these two writers are not directly arguing with one another, each does present a different point of view: (1) Deer hunting is not only a sport, but also a necessary conservation effort. (2) Deer hunting is not a sport but rather a male ego trip or ritual.

How did each writer support his position? Consider the strategies each used: examples, expert testimony, pointing out consequences or important implication, responding to opposition.

Put a check mark next to each strategy used:

Strategy	Essay 1	Essay 2
Examples	_____	_____
Expert testimony	_____	_____
Consequences or implication	_____	_____
Responding to opposition	_____	_____

Examples. Examine the examples that the writer of Essay 1 used: What were they supposed to prove? Did they work? Even if you know nothing of deer hunting, could you relate to them?

Examine the examples used by the writer of Essay 2: Why is the type of rifle an issue? What's the implication of semiautomatic rifles? Did this writer use examples or present reasons? Look at the descriptive words for the rifle in paragraph 1. Why did the writer choose these particular words? What is he implying?

Expert Testimony.   Neither writer used expert testimony. Could each have done so? Would expert opinion strengthen Essay 1? Where would you bolster the argument with expert opinion? Where would you turn to find the right kind of experts for this essay?

Would expert testimony strengthen Essay 2? How and where would you suggest it? Where would you find experts to strengthen this essay?

Consequences.   What consequences or implications did Essay 1 note? Did you find them effective? Could the writer have made a stronger case for conservation and animal control?

In Essay 2, does it make any difference whether or not these hunters eat venison? Does it make any difference whether or not these hunters hunt because they like to or because they think they must? What is the implication suggested by "gauging manhood"? Could the writer have made a stronger case?

Responding to the Opposition.   In Essay 1, the writer is sensitive to the charge that hunting isn't a sport, precisely for the reason brought out in Essay 2: weapons used today may give hunters the edge. Should he have been clearer in his defense of the rifle or addressed the various types of rifles available and used? The second point addresses "mindless slaughter," refuting it by saying that hunting is a conservation measure and that it is humane in the face of starvation. The writer also notes that starvation "seems more cruel and mindless than killing them instantly with a bullet," even if this act goes against a law of nature that only the strong survive. Was this an effective point to include? Why?

In Essay 2, does the writer make any concessions to the opposition? Is he clear about it? In other words, would most readers understand that he is not condemning all hunters?

Group Activity

These essays were very early drafts, unpolished but clear enough in the positions taken. What specific suggestions would you have for each writer as he continues drafting and revising?

Examples (add or subtract): _____

_____

Expert opinion (add): _____

_____

Important consequences or implications of position: _____

_____

Response to opposition: _____

_____

Organization of major points: _____

_____

Tone/language: _____

_____

Group Writing Activity _____

Even if you know nothing about deer hunting, you can respond to one of these essays, mainly because they touch on larger issues:

+ Conservation and management of wildlife
+ The definition of what's sporting
+ The definition of manliness (with a side issue of females who hunt)
+ Rituals of growing up and being accepted
+ Family tradition

Discuss these issues, reach a consensus, and formulate a thesis statement that clearly states the position you will defend. Then state your major points and how you would support each. Formulate your response to the opposition. Where do you think you would place it: first, woven into your major points, or last? Why?

PSYCHOANALYZING LITTLE ARTISTS

The next student essay makes a link to a larger societal issue more directly. Marge Harnden, an art major, responded to a television program with "A Sign of the Times."

A Sign of the Times

di Over Easter vacation, I happened to catch a show on TV that was featuring children's art in our major museums. The work was being displayed because children have the unique freedom to express themselves in any way they see fit. They don't have the limitations and control adult artists do. Children needn't follow the "rules" to making good art, such as color, coordination, perspective, subject material and imagery. Adult artists (to be taken seriously) must follow such "rules"; children draw however and whatever they fancy to draw.

Near the end of this interesting program, a prominant museum director walked along the walls of work, pointing out different pieces. To my surprise and dismay, she began to analyze the work! "The children must have used blue here to convey their feelings of peacefulness. And this one used gray very effectively to exaggerate the bleakness of his city scene. The bright yellow sun, however, symbolizes hope for a better world."

EXCUSE ME? I have yet to see such a symbolic six year old. Why was this woman applying adult concepts to a child's simple (and beautiful) drawing? Hadn't the whole show just said this stuff was great because it contained no hidden messages, no limitations? Maybe the little girl used blue because she liked that color, maybe she couldn't find the green crayon, and settled for second best. How could the museum director even know?

This woman was not viewing art. She was practicing psychology, analyzing and picking the work apart to discover the how and why. In the adult world, we are all guilty of such senselessness. There always needs to be a deeper meaning, the conveyance of some ingenious (and usually social) idea within the work of art, or it is written off as merely "illustration." Adults cannot enjoy the freedom children have in art because we don't let ourselves.

Perhaps it is reflection of our society. Haven't we built ourselves a complicated world, one where the reason we do things is almost as important as what we do? (Inquiring minds want to know!) How many millions of dollars does corporate America spend in marketing research, delving into such things as why one may prefer the blue over the green? Our adult world is self-analyzing and critical. The calculating, controlled environment we have created has taken away the wonderful spontaneity we admire in almost everything children do.

Perhaps we have much to learn from those children. Maybe if we could just learn to accept things for what they are and resist our urge to analyze life, our world would be a much less complicated, more free and enjoyable one.

Marjorie Harnden

Responding to the Arguments

Summarize (present the main points only of) Harnden's argument:

_____

_____

_____

What strategies did she use to present her position?

_____

_____

_____

What was her most convincing point and why?

_____

_____

What was her least convincing point and why?

_____

_____

If you disagree with Harnden's position, offer a contradiction through one or more of the following:

Fact _____

Observation _____

Statistics _____

Explanation _____

Causes or effects _____

If you agree with her position, provide additional support through one or more of the following:

Example _____

Explanation/reason _____

IDEOLOGY OF A CHILD'S PROGRAM

When we deal with issues, we have to pay close attention to the language used and whether the writer was appealing to logic or to emotions. In academic writing, we need to appeal to logic rather than to emotions. Does this mean we have no emotion about the issue? No, of course not. But it does mean we hold strong emotions in check when we respond. Certain ideas or words strike us emotionally, and are meant to, and therefore we have to be on guard. Most American adults, for example, grew up with "Communism is bad." The following student essay was written during the cold war era when the United States desired to contain communism. As you read, pay particular attention to the major points, support, and logic (or lack of it). Although you may be tempted to believe the writer was merely having fun, consider the essay as a serious one. The degree to which television influences young children is a serious issue.

Smurfs--Innocent Entertainment?

Smurfs are the latest craze to sweep through America. They can be found everywhere: on television, on toy store shelves, even on breakfast cereal. A serious problem is arising from this, and it must be faced. America has smurf mania. The group of Americans who have been overwhelmingly grasped by smurfs is the children. Kids are becoming addicted to the smurfs. Children watch the smurfs every week without fail. They've even memorized the smurf characters' names. These smurfs, however, are not all that they appear to be. The smurfs carry an evil subliminal message and are indoctrinating America's youth with communism.

Color imagery is the first step used to indoctrinate the children. The smurfs are drawn in flamboyant colors. These colors are used to catch a child's attention at a glance. Once a child is watching intently, a subtle message is immediately carried to the young, impressionable viewer. The only smurf who is not dressed in blue and white is Papa Smurf, who is the aged, but sovereign dictator over the other smurfs. Papa Smurf is clad in bright, communist red. His specific coloring is important in constructing the apparent dominance of red over the other colors. This inference of domination is carried over to the supposed domination of the Reds over other nations. Imagery, depicted through the use of color, is first used to grasp the child's attention and then to infer a red dominance to the youth. The color imagery, however, cannot only be viewed in a procommunist manner.

The colors when seen all together are a vivid red, white and blue. These colors do not connotate procommunist feelings at all. They give rise, instead, to nationalistic feelings for the American youth. So not everything about the coloring of the smurfs can be considered to be spreading procommunists feelings. The lifestyles of the smurfs, however, cannot be denied.

The procommunist lifestyle depicted is easy to analyze. The smurfs live on a commune. All that is accomplished by any individual smurf is done for the sole benefit of the society. There is no personal gain or advancement for any smurf. There is no such thing as personal wealth. Papa Smurf, the old gent, is the dictator over the smurf commune. His word is law. Individualism is attacked by the smurfs. Great cooperation is stressed. Because the smurfs live in cartoonland, everything turns out favorably for their communal society. Never do the smurfs have a poor harvest as often occurs in communist nations; nor are there any insurrections. The smurfs manage to maintain a tremendously high morale simply by singing the jolly little verse (which any American child can sing for you if you ask). All of these examples of a model communist culture can hardly do anything but impress children with the simplicity and superiority of communism. Lifestyle is probably the most obvious of the areas that the smurfs tread on, though there is a flaw in their communist lifestyle.

The main fault in the procommunist lifestyle of the smurfs is their noninvolvement in the affairs going on around them in the forest. The smurfs appear to be content with the holdings. They show no designs to conquer the rest of the forest, to "liberate" the forest's proletariat. Not everything about the smurf lifestyle can be considered to be boosting communism. Another area, however, in which there are irrefutable points of procommunism is that of symbolism, political symbolism to be specific.

Gargamel, the arch enemy of the smurfs, is a wizard. He is a lower wizard, rock bottom would probably be closer. In the world of smurfs, Gargamel presents an evil representation of capitalism. Gargamel is always attempting to capture the smurfs. When smurfs are boiled, they turn to gold. So, Gargamel is hoping to get rich. Gargamel is also an individualist, his only companion being his cat. Gargamel epitomizes the great American capitalistic dreams of rags to riches. Not only would he gain wealth from boiling the smurfs, but he would also rise considerably in the eyes of the other wizards. Gargamel is clad in an outfit worn by Catholic monks in the Middle Ages. His outfit associates religion to capitalism, thereby implying that religion is evil (another communist doctrine). The icing on the cake concerning Gargamel is that he always loses. Not once has he captured a smurf long enough to boil it. This reiterates a subliminal theme of the smurfs that communists always triumph over capitalists.

The smurfs may be cute, colorful Saturday morning cartoon characters, and many wrongly believe them to be innocent, but they are an evil craze among the children of America. It is high time that the parents take a closer look at what their children are watching, because right under their noses, the smurfs are indoctrinating America's youth with communism.

Responding to the Arguments

A. Briefly summarize (list only the main points of) the writer's position:

_____

_____

_____

B. If we think about the larger issue, the effect of children's television programs, specifically cartoons, is this an issue of importance? Why?

_____

_____

C. What strategies did the writer use? On a separate sheet of paper, list each major point and the strategy used to support it.

    Examples   Explanation/reasons
    Facts   Observations
    Statistics   Expert Opinion

D. How would you rate the effectiveness of the support?

_____

_____

E. What kind of support would you use if you were trying to convince parents that some cartoons may be dangerous?

_____

_____

_____

F. Acknowledging the opposition:

Major Points	Opposition Would Say
_____	_____
_____	_____
_____	_____

G. Addressing the opposition is an important aspect of dealing with issues and arguments. However, one can go too far. How did this writer destroy his own position in the process?

_____

_____

_____

H. Examine the logic of these comparisons:

Color imagery/red dominance _____

Lifestyle/commune _____

Gargamel/capitalism _____

Gargamel/religion _____

How has the writer gone astray in these?

I. Language is critical when we discuss issues. How would most Americans respond to the word *communism,* rationally or emotionally? What about words like *evil* and *innocent?* Are these neutral?

_____

_____

What about phrases which are so absolute that "it's this way only"?

"Communists always triumph over capitalists"

_____

"America has smurf mania"

_____

"indoctrinating"

_____

"Once a child is watching intently, a subtle message is immediately carried"

_____

And what is inferred when the writer states:

> "the jolly little verse (which any American child can sing for you if you ask)"

_____

> "Gargamel is also an individualist, his only companion being his cat"

_____

Does the logic—if this is so, then this must be so—hold up? What flaws can you note in this line of thinking?

J. Is this a topic where expert opinion and library research would benefit the writer's opinion? Where would you turn to get information on this topic?

_____

_____

_____

K. Structure of the essay: Briefly note how the writer presented information.

Intro _____

Body paragraph 1 _____

Body paragraph 2 _____

Body paragraph 3 _____

Body paragraph 4 _____

Body paragraph 5 _____

Body paragraph 6 _____

Conclusion _____

Where and how does the writer address the opposition?

_____

_____

What's the advantage of presenting your view and the opposing view at the same time?

_____

_____

Why might you address the opposing view in the introduction?

_____

_____

Why might you address the opposing view in the conclusion?

_____

_____

Group Activity _____

Discuss various cartoon shows you watched as children or that children currently watch. What examples can you provide in defense of the program? Why? In opposition to the program? Why? Would you use one show or several in your support? Who is your audience? What do you know about them? What assumptions can you make? What must you be careful of? List both arguments and counterarguments as you discuss this topic.

When you have generated enough information and formulated a position for or against children's cartoons, develop a rough outline for your essay. Include each major point and its support (example, facts, stats, experts, etc.). Be sure to note where you would put in any concessions that you would make to the opposition.

Be prepared to discuss your thesis and outline in class.

THE BEAUTY QUEEN

You're probably smiling at Sally's question and her naïveté. However, anyone who's grown up in America knows there's no (or few) "fairly, kind of, you know, cute queen." Beauty in America is big business. The issue is: who benefits?

The next student position paper is more sophisticated than that of the Smurfs. Before reading the essay, record your responses to the following statements:

1. Beauty pageants are _____.

2. Beauty pageants provide a useful function.

    _____

3. Beauty pageants degrade women.

    _____

As you read Kevin Piper's essay, respond in the margins to the ideas being presented. Note your response to various words and phrases that may strike you as particularly vivid or abrasive.

Atlantic City, Again

"The greatest spectator sport in America is not football or baseball. It's watching pretty girls and that
won't change." So says Albert Marks, chairman of the 1984
Miss America Pageant, and he's probably right. An estimated one-third of the nation's population--three quarters
women--watched the 58th annual event this past Saturday.
Some 75,000 smaller but similar contests involving millions of women are held each year. There can be no doubt
about the popularity of such events, but what does all
this say about our culture's view of women?

It is time to recognize the Miss America Pageant for
what it is--a commercial and prurient exhibition of women as
sex objects. It remains an enduring symbol of chivalry that
by rights should have died years ago. The pageant degrades
the collective female identity, perpetuates popularly held
myths about sex roles, and maintains normative standards of
women that have no place in the twentieth century.

From its beginnings in 1921 when Atlantic City business interests wanted a way to lengthen the tourist season, the annual Miss America Pageant has operated from the
central premise that a woman's value in this world is
directly proportionate to her proportions. Keeping in mind
the massive commercial event the contest has become, I
find little to distinguish it from pornography. Both
industries view women as objects of sexual art, and both
know that, simply put, sex sells. The only difference
seems to be that pageantland prefers virgins, while the
pornographers prefer experienced subjects.

The event sends a clear message to men, women, and children: attractive women are valuable property to be possessed, manipulated, and exploited. (God help those who, by
reason of genetics or grooming, are designated as unattrac-
tive.) Nothing could be more ridiculous than the Miss
America tradition of parading around in swimsuit and high
heels. But the tradition exists to prove a point. The same
kind of point was made at slave auctions not too long ago. A
full viewing was necessary to properly evaluate the merchandise. We are just more legal and dignified about it today.

Pageant defenders maintain that the event is a non-
commercial scholarship competition and not a beauty con-

test. True, the pageant itself is a nonprofit operation and has developed into the largest source of scholarship money for women. Yet, one would have to be blind not to notice the incredible commercialism involved. The promotional value of these contests is well tested. Seemingly every commodity and tourist trap in the republic has its own beauty queen. You name it and cleavage can sell it-- and does.

On the issue of beauty versus intellect, it is clear that modern contestants must have both formal education and talent (usually singing ability) to survive the long journey to Atlantic City. A certain foundation of self-accomplishment has become an informal standard. However, half the competition still directly revolves around silently posing in swimsuit or evening gown. It's hard for me to see how this posing can be mistaken for academic promise. The reality is that if the posing events were dropped, nobody would watch and the whole process would become just a long "Gong Show." That is, if it hasn't already.

Finally, pageant officials and most contestants vehemently deny that participants are being exploited. They say they voluntarily choose the rugged, painful, and expensive road to the top of glitter world. This is true. What's more, these young women are not nitwits. They are bright individuals with firm ideas of where they want to go. Nonetheless, I can't help but feel that they are participating in a crass game which demands a price from all women. The offerings of cash, prizes, and publicity notwithstanding, these women owe their sex more respect than this. And society owes these women more recognition and opportunity than a flesh show can justly provide.

No longer can any of us tolerate the moral and social cost of these institutionalized pageants. Affording (supposedly) women equal legal rights while at the same time allowing indignities like the Miss America exhibition to continue is hypocritical. The battleground for human dignity goes beyond statute books and courtrooms. It's time that people wake up and realize that the Miss America Pageant went out with the chastity belt.

Kevin Piper

Responding to the Arguments

Summarize Piper's position:

_____

_____

_____

List the strategies (e.g., examples, facts, expert opinion, statistics, reasons) used to support his position:

_____

_____

_____

Piper also uses analogy, a strategy that compares one thing to another, in this case a very negative comparison bound to cause an emotional reaction in many readers. List it and then comment on whether or not he may have gone too far and risked alienating his readers.

_____

_____

List his responses to the opposition:

_____

_____

_____

How did he then turn the responses to opposition into his points once more:

_____

_____

_____

List at least one point that would require more substantial evidence before most readers would accept the point.

_____

_____

Comment on the tone of this essay.

_____

_____

List specific words or phrases that you believe are "loaded," emotionally charged, and perhaps risky in terms of alienating the reader.

_____

_____

Group Activity _____

Formulate a response to Piper's essay. Divide up the writing task so that each person in the group has a specific point to make and write up. You may choose to agree or disagree with his point of view. Before deciding, read these articles pertaining to the 1992 Miss America Pageant. Use any information that is available and appropriate to support your response.

NO DUMMIES: MISS AMERICA HOPEFULS SMASH STEREOTYPES

Terry Mulcher

Atlantic City, NJ—The Miss America Pageant is a durable slice of Americana and probably will be as long as it survives its critics. The feminist movement calls it demoralization of the "second sex." The contest's sponsors defend it as a scholarship program that will award more than $10 million to about 80,000 women this year. No matter a person's opinion of the pageant, the contestants—at least this year's lot—smash the stereotype of the blond bimbo who smiles sensuously and shows a little cleavage in hope of winning the rhinestone crown, $35,000 and a little red sports car.

Many of the contestants are intelligent, articulate women with top-flight credentials. For example, Miss Wisconsin Stephanie Ann Klett is pursuing a master of fine arts degree from Moray House College in Scotland. Klett is a member of the National Organization for Women, describes herself as an "ardent feminist" and plans to push an AIDS platform if crowned. Carrie Lee Davis is a South Carolina doctor who has delivered 35 children, set up clinics and taught preventive medicine in rural South Carolina communities. Leah Hulan, Miss Tennessee, is a commissioned officer in the army, who has done undercover intelligence work in Panama. Patricia Ann Northrup, Miss California, is a graduating senior at California Polytechnic State University studying aeronautical engineering and music composition.

Why would they use duct or graffer's tape to push their breasts to the center to create cleavage? Why would they use a hemorrhoidal ointment to reduce swelling under their eyes, or glue their swimsuits to their buttocks for the strut down the runway in a pair of high-heeled shoes? Why would two contestants approach Davis, the doctor, and ask her to write prescriptions for diuretics which help them shed water weight? Even after she said no and stressed the dangers of diuretics, the women still wanted them. Contest promoters say one of the aspects of a "wholesome" woman is that she stays in shape physically.

Women's advocacy groups say the pageant forces women to fit a certain mold and to believe that to be successful, she must grow up to be thin, blond and beautiful. David Schleicher of the Anti-Sexist Mens' [sic] Network in New York calls the contest a meat market. "We all know it's really a forum to continue the whole brutality and sexual objectification process against women that reaches its culmination in forums like Playboy and Penthouse," Schleicher said.

• • •

LETTERS FROM "USA TODAY," SEPTEMBER 25, 1992

CHANGING IMAGE

As the executive director of a local preliminary pageant to Miss Amer-ica, I have been trying to change what people think about pageants. With the Miss America program, the emphasis is placed on intelligence (interview is 30% of total score) and talent (40% of total score). Yes, beauty of the face and figure is part of it, but a small part.

—Sherrie L. Cottom, Centerville, OH

SENDS WRONG MESSAGE

Beauty pageants give a terrible messge to little girls. I have two daughters, 9 and 11. They think you have to grow up and be a Barbie doll with a thin waist. I totally disapprove of these pageants.

—Nancy Smith, Tulsa, OK

WOMEN AS OBJECTS

Being a former contestant in the system, I have run across pageants where over three-quarters of the women had breast implants or reductions. The message the pageants continue to send out is that women are viewed as objects.

—Debra Grady, Notre Dame, IN

JUDGE DISAGREES

As a judge for last week's Miss America pageant, I disagree with your editorial which stated that "pageants shout that a woman's measurements matter most." For the record, as judges, we were never given contestants' measurements, let alone asked to judge them. The qualities we assessed were: intelligence, ability to inspire others, achievements, leadership, communication skills, confident presence and commitment to volunteerism. Let's not forget that the most impressive "figure" in the Miss America pageant is the $10 million in scholarships. Any program which empowers women with $10 million in scholarships gets my vote.

—Ann-Marie Bivans, Miami, FL

BUILDS CONFIDENCE

I never could have been what I am today without pageants. I participated at the local level and did a lot of preliminary pageants. I met a lot of friends, and it gave me a lot of confidence. Pageants are what you make out of them: helpful or not so helpful. If looked at realistically and allowed to help in educational pursuits, they can be very positive for young women today.

—Kim Huffman, Starksville, MS

HASN'T HELPED HER

I am a veteran of different pageants. In the long run, even though they claim that you gain poise and confidence, it can be defeating in today's society. I won several pageants. In the long run, it hasn't helped me in any job choices. In fact, I think it's been a deterrent. I don't even tell people anymore that I competed because they look at you like an airhead instead of looking at your degrees. It's irritating to see certain lines still be touted so highly, with a majority of women in society today still not getting the education they deserve.

—Layla Bryant, Kansas City, MO

MISS AMERICA PAGEANT, NBC SEPTEMBER 19, 1992

The following information was obtained from the live broadcast of the Miss America Pageant.

Jobs and Majors. Included in this year's group are the following majors or professions:

Professions	**Graduate School**
Police officer	Law (3 contestants)
Physician	Counseling
Sports broadcaster	Marketing (2 contestants)
	Music
Undergraduate Majors	Sports medicine
Aeronautical engineering	Biology
Communication	Communication
(16 contestants)	Central and
Music and theater	South American Affairs
Education	Chemistry
Business	Business
Psychology	
Advertising	
Political science and prelaw	
Public management	

Judging. The criteria for the preliminary judging included talent, swimsuit, evening gowns, and interview. Finalists were judged on talent (30% of total score), swimsuit (15%), evening gown (15%), and interview (40%). The swimsuit category was noted as stressing "athletic ability, fitness, and nutrition." However, the contestants wore spike heels. Miss South Carolina, a doctor, won the swimsuit competition.

Commercialism. The 1992 Miss America introduced commercials for Loving Care Hair Color, Vaseline Intensive Care Lotion, and Ultra Slim Fast throughout the television broadcast.

ON YOUR OWN

Judith Christ's position paper deals with censorship and warning labels in the music industry. Before you read, jot down your ideas about placing warning labels on records and tapes. As you read, make marginal notes of your responses to Christ's arguments.

Stop the Labels

For the past five years, censorship has been brought up in the music industry. Parents have been wondering what exactly their children are listening to and the meaning behind it. People have gathered together to join an organization called the Parents' Music Resource Center (PMRC). This organization consists of twelve members who originated the idea of warning labels. I feel warning labels should not be placed on records and tapes.

My reason is because warning labels are simply too expensive. It costs money to have the labels printed and the cost of having someone apply them. In today's world, the cost of printing thousands of adhesive stickers would be quite high. Besides the printing process, many hours would be spent having an individual put on the stickers or purchasing a machine to apply them. Even with an automated machine, a person would have to stand nearby to prevent machine malfunctions. From my experience, I have found that working with a labeling machine and putting on stickers by hand takes many hours of hard, tiring work.

Also, who should have the power to make the decision? I feel the answer is no one. Record companies and recording artists are too close to the product to pass unbiased judgments. Organizations such as PMRC should not have the right because their decisions are merely personal opinions. Basically, it comes down to the fact that no one or no group will be able to satisfy all people involved. Personal decisions will not work. One person can not determine what all others see as "offensive." What one person may call a crude statue of a naked body may be considered art by another person. It is simply not right for an invidual to decide what is right for others.

The PMRC and similar organizations are simply concerned aabout what children are listening to for entertainment these days. It is safe to say that there are many performers around who have put out some rather outrageous material. Parents have the right to worry about what their children are taking in, and it is nice to see some are concerned. However, if parents are truly doing everything they can to help their sons and daughters, they will not need the music industry to babysit. If parents are really communicating, they will know what their children are listening to and can talk to them about it. We should let record companies conduct their business and let the consumers decide if they want to purchase their products or not. A good parent will make it a point to be at least a small part of that decision.

Judith Christ

Writing Activity

Using strategies you have practiced in this chapter, analyze Judith Christ's position. Then, before you decide whether to support Christ's position or argue against it, try the following strategies:

1. In your journal, freewrite on what you've read. Allow yourself the freedom to respond and develop your own ideas.

2. Next, fill in the following outline:

Christ argues _____

_____

because _____

_____

Christ's Major Points	Your Response
_____	_____
_____	_____
_____	_____

Christ's Support/Evidence	Your Response
_____	_____
_____	_____
_____	_____

3. Finally, determine whether you will support her position or not. If you agree with Christ, offer additional support material. If you disagree, formulate opposing evidence.

Remember, no matter what position you take, you must defend it through logic, facts and reasons, statistics, or expert opinion. Add information gained from your own observations, firsthand experience, and reading. Concede valid points to the opposition. Keep your tone logical, rational, and calm. Do not go on the attack and risk losing your audience.

Developing and Organizing Your Response. The following suggestion is only one way in which writers respond to issues. Your teacher may provide you with others or ask that you follow a different form.

Introduction.   Provide a brief summary of Christ's position, and then state your own position (agree or disagree). Use thesis format to show your position of agreement or disagreement; that is, don't say "I agree" or "I disagree." The thesis should make your position perfectly clear.

Paragraph 1.   Discuss Christ's first point, reminding your reader what Christ said, and then respond with your own point.

Paragraph 2.   Discuss Christ's second point, and so on. Follow this process for all the points you wish to present and discuss.

Conclusion.   Very briefly, remind the reader of your position and why you hold it. Be careful not to introduce any new material or unrelated issue in the conclusion.

Adding the opposition's Valid Points.   You must decide where to place opposing views. Sometimes, it is advantageous to add them in the introduction; for example, if you suspect that many readers will disagree with your position, it may be better to concede their valid points immediately. At other times, the conclusion is the most likely place for them, especially if you know most of your readers will agree with you. And, at still other times, writers intertwine them in the body paragraphs, as Kevin Piper did. If the issue is particularly complex or controversial, placing the point and counterpoint together helps readers.

Peer Response

As you respond to one another's essays, follow this process:

1. State the writer's position.
2. List the main points, with support and evidence.
3. Disagree with the points—even if you agree with the writer, list counterpoints or arguments.
4. Note any problem with organization.
5. List any words or phrases that strike you as "loaded."

CHAPTER 8

Analyzing and Writing Arguments

In the previous chapter, you may have found yourself defending your opinion quite often, and just as often, listening intently to an opposing point of view. One of the most interesting things about our world is its variety of people and opinions. Reasonable people can and do disagree on many issues, everything from the best way to provide health care to the most efficient use of a limited tax base. In fact, disagreement is one of the ways through which people expand their world. In considering positions other than our own, we learn something more about a complex issue or situation. This skill is a useful one, whether we are at school, work, or home.

Acquiring this skill requires us to put our emotions aside and rely on logic. Sometimes it is quite difficult to do so. For example, as you read each of the following statements, note your immediate response in your journal:

1. Abortion is murder.
2. Immigration is ruining America.
3. Welfare breeds lazy people.
4. Prayer belongs in public schools.
5. Gun sales should be outlawed.

Now think about why you responded as you did. Chances are your emotions took over. These statements go back to strongly held beliefs arising out of years of family and religious training. Consequently, when we face such issues we tend to respond emotionally rather than logically. Where personal moral and ethical beliefs are concerned, we simply believe we are right. However, when we construct academic arguments, we must set aside the strong emotions that accompany such beliefs and rely on logic to prove our point. This task, of course, is easier said than done.

PROBLEMS OF REASONING

We have already explored ways in which writers support their position in reasoned and logical ways, but we also need to take a closer look at problems of reasoning. People who disagree with our position are quick to point out where our reasoning falls apart or violates some principle of logic. What's more, in an academic setting, some teachers may be more interested in how you presented your argument than in the position you took. It's important, then, that you avoid the most common flaws in this type of academic writing:

✦ Oversimplification

✦ Generalization without evidence

✦ Exaggeration or distortion

✦ Faulty logic

✦ Slippery slope

✦ Inappropriate expert opinion

✦ Out-of-date material

✦ Emotionally charged vocabulary

✦ Attacking the person rather than the issue

Oversimplification

Oversimplification means that a complex issue or situation has been presented as though it were a simple one. For example:

A lack of education is responsible for inner-city riots.

Inner-city riots are a complex problem, and a lack of education for inner-city youth is only part of that problem. Jobs, the lack of economic opportunity, and family stability are just as important. The availability of drugs and weapons, as well as the growth of neighborhood gangs, also contribute to the problem. To place the responsibility on a single factor, education, is simplistic. As a result, the writer of this statement appears ignorant, incapable of analyzing a complex issue for relevant, supportable causes for this tragedy. To say money is the solution to this complex problem is equally simplistic. Economics is one part, but only one part of many.

Another form of oversimplification is the "either/or" proposal. You may have seen bumper stickers such as "America: Love it or leave it," a statement which denies any middle ground. Further, just because someone disagrees with some government policies or actions doesn't mean he or she doesn't love the country. Writers who make an either/or statement are trying to make the reader believe there are a very limited number of ways to look at an issue or situation. In the 1992 presidential election, some environmental issues were presented as an either/or choice: save the spotted owl and destroy jobs. The reality is somewhere in between, and environmental and economic issues are certainly more complex than either/or. Either/or sounds good emotionally, though, and that's why we run into it.

Generalizations

In constructing an argument, you will need to generalize from facts, examples, statistics, or other means of support. However, when you generalize, you must be very careful not to exaggerate the meaning of those facts, examples, or statistics. That is, you must have the evidence to back up your generalization. For example, if you have observed that married students appear to be better students, you cannot generalize that *all* married students are better students. You could investigate studies of married students, their achievements and grade point average, and you might find support for your observation. But if you then say that students would be better off to marry while in college, you're in logic trouble. You would have made a sweeping generalization and jumped to a conclusion that isn't valid. Some students cannot function with competing demands from a marriage and college work. Other students end up failing because their marital relationship is in trouble. Without evidence, then, you simply cannot make such a generalization.

Even with evidence, you might do well to use some qualification or limitation on your generalizations.

Unsupported/sweeping generalization:

Married students are better students.

Supported:

Of the ten married couples in my classes, seven are honor students. A recent college survey shows over 50 percent of the married students have a GPA of at least 3.00.

Qualified:

Many married students appear to be top students.

Marriage seems to agree with some college students; many are honor students.

Exaggeration or Distortion

An exaggeration or distortion of the facts is another way in which writers destroy their own credibility. For example, if you observed that a couple of students regularly cheated in your math class and then reported that cheating was widespread, you would be guilty of exaggeration. Although it's possible that cheating was widespread, without solid evidence you cannot make the claim.

Faulty Logic

Arguing in a circle is a way in which writers can be illogical. For example: "Football players are unintelligent which is why they are football players." Besides being a ridiculous generalization, this statement is circular and proves nothing at all. The cause and effect simply don't work.

Irrelevant examples are also illogical. Whatever evidence you use must be clearly related to your position. For example:

Women demand equal pay, but they still want to be taken out to dinner. Therefore, they really don't want to be equal.

These two issues have nothing to do with each other. Equal pay is an economic and work issue; a dating practice is a social one. And even though one might argue dating does involve economics, in this case, the writer cannot make the leap from equal pay to going out to eat.

Another type of flaw is called a *non sequitur*, a Latin phrase meaning the conclusion simply doesn't follow from the evidence presented. For example:

> A student fell asleep in class twice this week. The class is obviously boring, and that teacher should be fired.

There's no logical connection between these two sentences. The student may have fallen asleep because of working late, illness, drinking too much the night before, or a host of other reasons. There is no evidence that the class is boring, let alone that a teacher should be fired because a student fell asleep.

A similar flaw called *post hoc* occurs when a writer says one event causes another simply because it happened first. Sometimes people jokingly say something like: "Of course it rained; I just finished washing my car." The two events have nothing to do with one another: we can wash our cars all we want, and not assure anxious gardeners or farmers of rain. In writing, this flaw in logic is serious.

> Since MTV has been on television, the number of teenage pregnancies has increased. It is obvious that MTV is responsible for increased sexual activity and the resulting increase in illegitimate children.

There is no evidence that MTV is responsible for either increased sexual activity or pregancies among teenagers. Without scientific studies linking increased sexual activity and pregnancies to MTV, no one can make this claim.

Slippery Slope

Yet another flaw is the "slippery slope." It occurs when a writer assumes that one problem inevitably leads to more and more serious problems. For example: "If we don't fight communism in Central America, it will spread to all of South America." There's no proof that communism in a Central American country would lead to communism in South America.

Inappropriate Experts

We've seen advertisements on television in which some celebrity tells us that we should drive a certain car or drink a certain soft drink. However, unless that celebrity also happens to be an expert on cars or soft drinks, there is no reason why we should pay any attention to his or her claims. When writers use expert opinion, they are calling upon someone's demonstrated excellence in a field. It's critical that someone we cite as "expert" really is, and what's more, that we are using that expert appropriately. An astronaut, for example, is an expert in engineering, but why listen when he or she tells us to drink a certain brand of orange juice?

Out-of-Date Information

In addition to making sure experts are experts, academic writers also have to use current facts in their defense of a position. In some fields, such as psychology, sociology, and chemistry, the use of outdated material might destroy the argument. Checking sources to ensure they provide the latest available information is an important part of defending a position.

Emotionally Charged Words

Some words can be counted upon to produce irrational reactions: *welfare, drugs, abortion, capital punishment,* and *patriotism,* to name just a few. In an academic argument, however, we do not want to produce an irrational, emotional reaction in the reader. Rather, we want to appeal to logic. Choosing words that are neither negatively or positively charged is important to your defense.

Attacking the Person

Ad hominem is Latin for "to the man." It means the writer is guilty of attacking someone's character rather than the issue itself. For example, the mayor opposes building a new sports arena because he believes the costs are simply too high for the present tax base to support. Sport enthusiasts might charge that the mayor is a "wimp," never made an athletic team, and dislikes sports; therefore, he doesn't want the arena built. Personal attacks appear mean-spirited and most often turn people off.

Group Activity

Read Mike Royko's piece on legalizing marijuana and decide

1. what his principal arguments are.
2. whether he uses logic or emotion.
3. if he violates any principles of logic.
4. how he supports his arguments.
5. if he addresses his opposition.

Then, defend the legalization of marijuana by citing arguments not used by Royko or by expanding (not just repeating) those he does use. When you have completed the defense, argue against the legalization of marijuana by responding to Royko's and your own arguments in favor of it. Be prepared to share your work in whole-class discussion.

Royko, incidentally, is a Chicago journalist. His column appears in papers nationwide, and he is best known for his biting commentary on American politics and lifestyles.

LEGAL MARIJUANA—A POT OF GOLD

Mike Royko

I've been playing around with a fascinating number—14,000 tons. That's the amount of marijuana—foreign and domestic—that's said to be consumed each year in this country. Actually, the federal narcs think it might be even higher. A recent raid in northern Mexico turned up 10,000 tons. The narcs were stunned because they thought that Mexico produced only one fourth that amount. But for this column's purpose, let's stay with the 14,000-ton figure.

If you break that down, it comes to 448 million ounces. I'm told that one ounce of marijuana will produce between 20 to 40 joints, depending upon whether you are frugal and make skinny ones, or are self-indulgent and make them stogie-sized. There's also a waste factor—seeds, twigs, bugs, spillage and so on. So let's be conservative and figure 20 joints an ounce. That's just under 10 billion joints a year. If you divide that by the population of this country, it comes to about 40 joints for every man, woman and child.

Now, we can assume that millions of little toddlers and preschoolers don't smoke it. We can even assume that most of the kids in elementary school don't, since most of them don't have the purchase price. And we can assume that millions of old codgers in nursing homes or two-room flats don't use it.

So who's doing all this grass-smoking? Recent studies say that teenagers are smoking less and less pot. So the biggest users are the age groups that range from young adults to middle-agers. And they're a huge part of the population. If they aren't the majority, they're not far from it. That tells us something obvious: There's a great demand in this country for marijuana.

As any Harvard economist—or dry goods salesman—will tell you, when there's a great demand for something that isn't hard to supply, somebody is going to supply it. Obviously, that's happening. Whether you live in a big city, a suburb, or a small town, you can easily buy marijuana. If you aren't sure where to get it, just ask the nearest teenager.

So I have a simple question: If so many Americans want and use marijuana, if they are already getting it so easily, if they insist on spending billions of dollars a year on it, why are we screaming at Mexico, why are hordes of narcotics agents floundering around in futile attempts to find it, why are the police and courts wasting time and money trying to put dealers in jail for selling it?

It ought to be obvious by now that the politicians in Washington can talk all they want about stamping it out, but they can't do it. It has become one of this country's biggest cash crops. It's a big part of Mexico's economy. So maybe it's time to give up trying to stamp it out, and consider legalizing it, thereby controlling it.

It would allow the narcs to stop wasting their time trying to stop it, which they can't do, and would let them concentrate on chasing far more harmful drugs, such as heroin and cocaine. And, best of all, it could be taxed. A $10- or $20-an ounce federal tax would bring in more than $5 billion or $10 billion a year. And every local government could slap on a little tax of its own.

Who would sell it? Private enterprise, I suppose. The day it became legal, we'd see nationwide pot franchises springing up. And we could stop feuding with Mexico, since our own needy farmers could grow enough to meet all local demands. Why, they would probably end up dealing in marijuana futures on the Board of Trade.

The sale could be regulated just as we now regulate the sale of booze. TV and radio advertising of pot would be banned, just as we've banned the advertising for liquor and cigarettes. Minimum age limits would be set. Sure, it would be impossible to enforce the laws 100 percent. But the fact that teenagers find ways to buy beer doesn't prevent the rest of us from drinking it.

And, yes, I'm aware that marijuana isn't good for us, although scientists still aren't sure what the effects really are. However, the scientists do know a lot more about the effects of even the finest scotches, the most elegant gins, the most regal cognacs. Even if you pay $5 a shot and tip the bartender a deuce, they will still quiver your liver and strain your brain.

So it might be time for us to stop pretending that we can do something to stop marijuana from being sold and consumed. In a country where the citizens—and even illegal aliens—have unlimited freedom of movement, and where there is almost no control of its own borders, we can't do it. Then why not try to at least regulate it and let our own farmers and businessmen make a buck.

Are we ready for a McJoint?

CONSTRUCTING A POSITION PAPER

Approaches

There are various ways in which we can construct a position paper. One way is to state our position and then defend and explain it point by point. This is a *deductive* approach. But we might also approach it in the opposite way: present and defend the points and then present our position as the conclusion. This approach is *inductive*.

DEDUCTIVE APPROACH

I believe or feel this way because of

this, this, and this.

You state your position in the introduction and then present the evidence which supports your position.

Children should not play competitive sports—because of—physical injury, emotional trauma—lasting effects, on both child and family.

Introduction: Anecdote, background information, thesis stated:

Children should not play competitive sports because of the threat of serious physical injury and emotional trauma.

Body: Evidence to support (facts, statistics, examples, expert opinion):

Serious physical injuries—what are they, how often they occur, lifelong effects, etc.

Emotional trauma—what is it, how often it occurs, effects on child and family, etc.

Conclusion

INDUCTIVE APPROACH

Because of this, this, and this

I believe or feel this.

We present the evidence and lead up to our position, to our conclusion based on that evidence.

Introduction: Anecdote or background information. No thesis here.

Body: Evidence to support your position:

Serious physical injuries—what are they, why are they serious, lasting effects, etc.

Emotional trauma—what is it, how does it occur, lasting effects on child and family.

Conclusion: Statement of thesis:

Because of the very real threat of serious physical and emotional trauma, young children shouldn't participate in competitive sports.

Expectations

Readers have certain expectations when they read an argumentative essay or position paper. One of these is recognition of the opposite point of view. Where you place the opposition's point of view is up to you, but readers look for it. You also have a choice as to whether you will simply admit the strength of an opposing point, allow it, and move on, or refute it. Both of these strategies work in your favor; both indicate that you have carefully considered the evidence on both sides of the issue.

Another expectation is that of appropriate background or history. Readers want a context for the issue or problem, so we have to provide them with it, even if we believe they already know something about the subject. A strong, clearly stated thesis is another expectation. Sometimes, we merely suggest our opinion, but in a position paper it is explicitly stated—leaving no doubt about which side of the issue we are on.

Group Activity _____

A. Refer back to the essays on the Smurfs and the Miss America Pageant. How did these students deal with the reader's expectations relative to an opposing point of view? Now refer to Royko's editorial on legalizing marijuana. How did he deal with the opposition? In your opinion, which was most effective in addressing the opposition? Why?

B. How did Royko provide the reader with background information on marijuana? Was this an effective opening? Did the writer of the Smurfs essay provide an effective context for his argument? And what of the Miss America argument? Do readers understand why this issue is important or a problem?

C. Do readers get a clear, well-stated thesis in these three pieces?

A Basic Format

Your instructor may provide you with other formats, and the following may be adapted. For example, you may decide to present your position before addressing the opposition. Or you may decide to present both your points and the opposing ones at the same time. Consider your audience. If you believe they might be hostile to your position, you might want to grant them the allowable points right away. You'd be saying, "These are valid and reasonable, and I accept them," thereby gaining some good will. Or you might decide to refute their points immediately. This strategy might stop the reader from arguing with you along the way. You want readers to think about *your* point of view. You can probably remember times in a verbal disagreement when instead of listening to the opposition, you were mentally on the defensive, conjuring up your argument and not fully listening to what the opposition was saying. In any case, your consideration of the audience and their likely response should guide your decision.

I. Introduction

A. Gain reader's attention and interest (e.g., a brief story, startling statistic, quotation)

B. Establish context, background for the reader (e.g., history of problem, how issues developed)

    C. Provide thesis, direct statement

II. Address Opposition

    A. Grant allowable points

    B. State and reply to unallowable points

       Show they are

         untrue

         illogical

         dishonest

         absurd

         ambiguous (not clear, not defined)

III. Present Your Position

    A. Present evidence

       Support through

         facts

         reasons

         statistics

         expert opinion

         examples

         analogy

    B. Use order of increasing interest or importance

IV. Conclusion

Checking Resources

Often we choose to defend a particular point of view because we have already thought about the issue. Before consulting library or human resources, check the present status of your personal information:

✦ What do you already know about the issue?

✦ Why are you convinced of the truth of your position?

✦ What information do you have from firsthand experience?

✦ What have you observed that supports your claim?

✦ What have you read that supports your claim?

✦ What examples do you have to support your claim?

✦ Whom do you know that might be able to provide you with expert opinion?

Testing Evidence

In conversations, we can sometimes get by without offering substantial evidence for our opinions. When we write, however, we are expected not only to provide evidence but to ensure that such evidence is trustworthy. Test your evidence by asking the following questions of it:

✦   Is it accurate? It is your responsibility to verify that what you use is both accurate and up to date. You also need to check for bias.

✦   Is it reliable? Evaluate your evidence by comparing different sources. They all should say the same thing.

✦   Is it to the point, relevant? You must back up the exact claim you have made.

✦   Is it representative? The examples you provide should be very typical for the situation.

✦   Is it sufficient? You need to provide enough evidence.

EVALUATING A STUDENT POSITION PAPER

For your first reading of Lorie Hilson's paper, read rather quickly to get an overall sense of her position. Then write a few sentences indicating your initial reaction. Were you interested in this issue? What is your personal opinion of it? What was most convincing in the essay? Least convincing?

When you have finished your initial notations on Hilson's essay, read the draft again, this time slowly. Then respond to the questions that follow the essay.

FINAL VERSION

Wanting Winners

This boy of nine is up to bat, and his parents are in the stands watching. He strikes at the first ball that is pitched. His father yells, "How many times do I have to tell you to let the first ball go by?" We are in a generation where fun has been taken out of kids' sports because parents want winners.

According to what I have observed at ball games, parents want winners for their own selfish reasons. One of these reasons is so they can brag to friends and neighbors what a great team their child is on. Also another reason is that some parents feel a child's performance is a reflection on themselves. These kinds of attitudes leave little room for the child to just enjoy the sport for the fun of it.

When winning becomes more important than the fun of the game, young children get serious injuries. Most of these injuries don't have a lasting effect; however, once in a while they may cause permanent damage to the muscle or bone tissues of a young girl or boy. Take, for instance, a young boy I know who was playing basketball when he fell, damaging his elbow and upper right arm. Now at the tender age of fifteen he can only run track. Another example is of a young boy whose father wanted him to be on the winning baseball team; therefore, he taught him to throw curve balls at too young of an age. Now the boy's right arm hurts him to a point that he no longer plays any type of ball. Was the sacrifice of the son's arm worth it so the father could say he had a winner? The answer is no.

Besides the physical injuries that kids get, they experience emotional pain that is caused by what parents say to them. Sometimes emotional pain is more harmful than physical pain ever could be. Once at a wrestling match, a boy of nine was wrestling out on the mat. Afterward his mother told him he could have done better; his tears started flowing down his cheeks like big raindrops. His mother had just taken the fun out of wrestling for him. I wonder if we as parents realize how important our approval is to a child.

There ought to be a class for adults only on how to lose gracefully. A kid, however, would have to teach this class because kids have an inborn grace for losing. We as adults lost our ability to accept losing somewhere in the process of growing up. I think we should just go to kids' sports and watch children play, and then maybe we could learn how to put the fun back into their sports. Then as parents we could say, "We had fun," instead of saying, "We have winners."

Lorie Hilson

Defining the Issue

Has Hilson provided enough information for the reader to understand both the issue and its importance? What questions still need to be addressed or answered? Is the issue really arguable (that is, can reasonable people have opposing views on it)?

Forming a Clear Thesis

Find Hilson's thesis. Is it appropriately stated? Should it be qualified in any way? Does she fill out her thesis promise? Stray from it? Add anything not covered in her thesis or introductory material?

Supporting the Thesis

Find Hilson's reasons for her claim and number them. Then consider each in terms of its evidence. How is it explained or supported? How clear or convincing is each? Have any important reasons been left out? Has she overemphasized weak reasons?

Check Hilson's reasoning. Has she made broad, unsupported generalizations or oversimplified anything, for example?

Handling Counterarguments

Has Hilson addressed the opposing view? If not, where and how would you deal with counterarguments: Where might be areas of potential agreement? Where would you anticipate objections? Why? How would you refute them? Be certain to think through the counterarguments, being careful to include some of the strongest and not just the weakest. Presenting only the opposition's weakest points weakens your own position.

Being Reasonable

Does Hilson maintain a reasonable tone? Note places where the tone appears thoughtful, believable, and trustworthy. Are there places where the tone becomes too emotional, sarcastic, and the like?

Organizing Effectively

Reread the opening and final paragraphs and evaluate their effectiveness. Does the opening give a good preview of the argument to follow and provide a context for why it is an important issue? Does the conclusion leave one with a good sense of the importance of the issue?

Now reread the major points and determine if they should be reordered. Also check if any evidence is misplaced. Note topic sentences, transitions, and summaries, and determine if some should be added or changed for greater effectiveness.

Evaluating Overall

What is the strongest part of Hilson's essay? Why? What is the weakest part, the most in need of further thought and revision? What would you suggest for revision?

Look at Hilson's earlier draft of "Wanting Winners" and note the changes she made between it and her final draft on pages 229–230. How did Hilson strengthen her essay?

DRAFT 1

Wanting Winners

Kids sports are a common sight. *W*e see them out on

1   football and base ball fields, in swimming pools, on

tennis courts and basket ball courts, and *on* parallel bars

just to list a few sports.

for children

When I go to a base ball game and hear a father call

out to his son or daughter because of an error that

has been made   *child*
they make. I stop to reflect ~~on~~ if the ~~kid~~ is out for

fun or were they told that winning was the whole idea

2
of the game. I know this kind of action by either

parent is an (embarrassment) to the child, for I have

asked my own children about how they would feel if they
                         this
were in ~~that~~ kind of situation.

I feel that there ought to be a class on how to

lose gracefully for adults only. We are the ones who

remove the fun out of kids sports by wanting our
                      winning
children on the best team ~~or the winning team which-~~

~~ever you prefer.~~ Children have this inborn grace on how
          we
to lose, ~~us~~ as parents have a habit of destroying it.

My feelings are based on experiences that I have

encountered over the last year or two. For an example,

at a base ball game one, in perticular comes to mind.

This boy is up to bat his parents are in the stands

watching he strikes at the first ball that is pitched.

3
His father stands up and yells "How many times do I

have to tell you to let the first ball ~~pitched~~ go by".

The boy is nine or ten years old, scared of the ball

hitting him the way it is, without his father adding to

it. The fun has just left the game for this boy.

When winning becomes more important then the fun of the game or sport, we have young children getting serious injuries. Most of the time these injuries don't leave a lasting effect on the young girl or boy, but once in a great while the injury my last a life time. Take for instance a young boy I know was playing basketball, the boy fell damaging his elbow and (uper) arm, he

5 now can only run track, at the tender age of fifteen. Another instance that I know of is a young boy who father wanted him to be on a winning base ball team, so he taught the boy how to throw curve balls, now that boys right arm hurts him to a point that he no longer can play any type of ball. Was it worth the sacrifice of his son so he could say his son was on a winning team? To that question in my opinion the answer is a (defiant) no.

When at a wrestling match this last winter with my oldest boy. I told my son that no matter what placing he recived, I would still be proud of him. This is how all parents should feel I thought, boy did I get my mind changed in a hurry that day. The lady sitting next

4 to me also had a boy wrestling that day, as she sat

there watching her child wrestle, she started to use

such language that I was (ashame) to be sitting by this lady.

~~When did~~ winning ∧ become so important that we as
W   has

parents seem to misplace the (emphasizes) on the whole

? concept of kids sports. (More and more children are

6 starting to enter sports at a much younger age then

ten years ago.) This points out ∧ that ~~the~~ parents ~~what~~
to me   as   we want

~~there~~ children to be ~~the best~~. It's no longer left to
winners

the child to decide if he or she is out for fun but

whether she or he is the best.

Lorie Hilson

Writing Activity

Write a response to Hilson. You may either agree or disagree with her position. If you agree with her, provide additional support (not repeating her points). If you disagree with her, either take her points and refute them or develop an opposing point of view. Be sure to go through the list of resource questions for yourself (since you won't use library research or outside resources for this writing task) and test the evidence you supply.

ON YOUR OWN

You have been responding to positions taken by others. Now you'll support your own position on some issue that interests you. You won't be using library sources for this essay, so you need to limit yourself to an issue where you feel confident about your firsthand knowledge or experience. For example:

Should college sports be dropped?

Should college students hold jobs?

Should day care be available on campus?

Should all students be required to take a common set of courses?

Should first-year courses be pass/fail?

Should first-year students be required to live on campus?

Should the student union be a smoke-free building?

Should extracurricular activities be dropped?

Should the library change its hours?

As you choose an issue, be sure it is one on which reasonable people might disagree; that is, there must be two sides to it.

Exploring the Issue

Freewrite on your topic for at least five minutes: what it is, who's involved, and so on. If you believe you have enough to write an essay on this topic, apply one or two of the generating strategies from Chapter 4. Since you have to deal with both sides of the issue, some sort of chart would probably work well. Even if you are already certain which side of the issue you will defend, laying both out will help you define the issue.

For	Against

Formulate the position you'll take in a very tentative, rough thesis statement:

State the purpose of your essay:

_____

Consider your audience: How would your readers define this issue? What assumptions would readers be likely to share with you? What kind of support would be likely to work with your readers?

_____

_____

_____

_____

Group Activity

Run your topics by one another. Help one another decide if you can write on this issue, and just as important, if you really want to.

Developing Reasons

When you're sure that you have a good topic, list every reason you can think of by using a base statement something like one of these:

I think this because _____

My position is this because _____

When you have as many reasons as you can think of, read through them with your reader's eye. Which of your reasons are the strongest? If you come to the conclusion that none of them is, perhaps you should find another topic.

When you have some strong reasons, brainstorm on each one. The brainstorming should turn up some good support. If it doesn't, move to the next reason.

Anticipating the Opposition

Take each of your reasons and list every opposing reason or point you can think of. Then review them and decide which you'll respond to. Use this format to help you think about it:

I'll respond to:

Opposing point: _____

_____

I'll respond to it because _____

I'll concede it because _____

I'll refute it _____

Now take each point you intend to refute. Brainstorm on each point and note for yourself why you are able to refute it: distorted, absurd, irrelevant, illogical, and so on.

I'll refute it because _____

_____

Before you begin to draft your essay, you might want to restate your thesis. Has the work you have done thus far led you to qualifying or changing your tentative thesis?

Organizing

One of the major decisions you make is organization. For this type of writing, preparing a scratch outline may save you time and energy later. The outline should be considered tentative, good enough to show what you plan, but not so good that you would be unwilling to throw it out. For example:

Introduction

Thesis: Student union needs a fast-food franchise.

Body

    Major Point: Cafeteria inefficient

    Support: At noon, 20-minute wait in line for food

               Another 10-minute wait at checkout

               Result: miss class or bolt food

               Result: food often cold

    Major Point: Cafeteria expensive

    Support: Burger, fries, coke in cafeteria $3

               Burger, fries, coke in franchise $2.25

               Salad in cafeteria $1.75

               Salad in franchise $1.25

               Result: can add extra $5 per week

    Opposition: Fast food has fewer food options

    Refute: Depends on which franchise one gets

    Support: Example McDonald's vs. Hardee's

    Refute: Most students never order cafeteria's
               meat/potato dishes

    Support: Tally from cafeteria

Conclusion

    Make appeal for consideration of fast-food franchise

Drafting

Use your outline to guide you, but don't hesitate to diverge from it should something better occur to you. Sometimes our best ideas come in the process of writing, as well as a momentum that directs us to things we hadn't considered earlier. If you get stuck, you can refer back to the outline for ideas and direction.

Revising

Use the analysis questions from Hilson's essay as a guide to evaluating your own essay. In order to see just where you need specific revision, make a chart that corresponds to the basic requirements or features of a position paper. As you apply the analysis questions to each part of your paper, make notes of the problems.

Features of My Position Paper	Problems
Introduction of issue (context, definitions, etc.)	
Thesis statement	
Reasons/support	
Opposition's points	
Organization	
Tone/language	

Peer Response

Add comments from peer readers to the chart. Remember, their response to problems helps you revise.

PROBLEM SOLVING FOR REVISION

Once you (and your peers) have identified a problem, you need to systematically solve it. The following suggestions, paired to the general outline you just used, may help you do that. Add a third column to your chart where you will write your response—specific ideas for revising your draft. For example:

Feature	Problem	How to Solve
Introduction	No sense of why issue really is a problem	Use letter from student newspaper

Introduction of Issue.   Provide more information on how the issue arose and why it affects readers. Consider adding an example or anecdote.

Thesis Statement.   If readers don't recognize your thesis, you will have to rewrite it. It should be explicit, clearly stated.

If readers find the thesis won't hold up because there are legitimate exceptions or very strong counterarguments, rewrite it and modify it; add qualifying words.

Reasons and Support

Generalization Without Adequate Support.   Go back to your notes and brainstorm some more; come up with more examples.

Oversimplification.   Get rid of any either/or statements; qualify statements to show you understand that the issue is complex.

Vague or Weak Reasons. Add explanation, examples, anecdotes.

Weak Evidence.   Review your brainstorming notes; if you can't find better support, consider eliminating that point.

Opposing View

Concessions.   Make some concessions to opposing view; show you recognize legitimacy of readers' views; let readers know you share some of their concerns, values, and the like.

Refutations.   Strengthen.

Acknowledging the Opposition.   Don't ignore counterarguments, especially strong ones—if you can't refute them, concede them.

Organization

Introduction.   If the introduction is dull, try some startling fact, quotation, or anecdote.

Arguments and Major Points.   If the reader has trouble following your arguments, provide a blueprint of them in the introduction.

Support.   If support doesn't follow the main point closely, move it nearer the topic sentence.

Arrangement of Points/Counterpoints.   Reorder for better logic.

Conclusion.   Consider more striking language, an anecdote that sums up the situation or issue, a startling fact, and so on; make it briefer; don't just repeat main points; make an appeal for support.

Editing and Proofreading.   When you have completed revision, check for sentence- and word-level errors. Refer to your personal editing list.

PART TWO

A Writer's Handbook

CHAPTER 9

Working with Sentences

SENTENCE BOUNDARIES

One of the major differences between speaking and writing lies in sentence boundaries. When we speak, we don't always have, or need, boundaries between our sentences. In conversations we have our audience with us. As a result, we are able to run sentences together, blurring the distinction between one thought and the next; we can also utter partial sentences. Our audience can tell us to repeat if necessary, or more likely, understands us without well-formed or correct sentences. Although one might argue that awkward or incomplete sentences can be understood in writing too, the needs and expectations of a reader are different. When we write, we are expected to communicate in complete sentences whenever we write formally, as in school or certain workplace settings. What is appropriate in spoken English—loosely formed and partial sentences—is unacceptable in Standard Written American English.

Fragments

Recognizing sentence boundaries in written English is an important skill. Read the following word groups and decide how you would determine whether or not each constitutes a complete, independent sentence:

A. sitting on the table, a huge red and white cat

B. the youngest student in the class was

C. Jan, who was the youngest student present

D. we have been

It probably didn't take you long to figure out that something important was missing. As readers, we are left hanging, wondering what happened or what about so-and-so. The word groups are incomplete. We have a subject (something or someone) but no predicate (what happened or what about something or someone). We know the "who" but not the "what happened?" Now try these word groups:

E. looked hungrily at the goldfish bowl

F. only twelve years old

G. was the best speaker

H. happy in this house

Again, it probably didn't take you long to realize you had a partial idea—something important was missing. Now we have the "what happened" or "what about" and have no idea who or what we are talking about. If we join the two word groups (A to E, etc.), however, we have complete sentences.

Checking for complete sentences is far easier in an exercise than it is in paragraphs and full essays, especially those we have written. Our brain is wonderful: it can read right through and over incomplete sentences. We know what we wanted to say, so we "fill in the blanks," mentally putting in words that aren't on the paper at all. For this reason, you may have to work sentence by sentence, covering up the rest of your paragraph as you go, in order to isolate and find incomplete sentences. Incomplete sentences are known as *fragments*. When we come across fragments, we need to reread the sentences preceding and following the fragment. Chances are, it will attach to one or the other. We also have the option of completing the fragment, adding information to make a new independent sentence.

Run-on and Comma Splice

Another sentence boundary problem occurs when we fail to use the appropriate punctuation to indicate where one sentence ends and another begins. In Standard American English, a capital letter on the first word of the sentence indicates that we are beginning a new sentence. The end of a sentence is indicated by an appropriate punctuation mark, most often a period or question mark or, less frequently, an exclamation point.

A. The boy in back of me is a pest.

B. Who is that boy in back of you?

C. I can't stand the boy in back of me!

When we fail to put an end mark on sentences, we create *run-on* sentences.

D. The boy in back of me is a pest I can't stand him.

E. I wish he would move he's just too active.

Run-on sentences are just what they sound like: two or more sentences "running together" with no boundary mark or connector between them. A run-on sentence requires work from the reader, namely, to figure out where one idea ends and another starts. Consequently, most readers become irritated and stop reading. To correct run-on sentences, we first have to identify the sentences:

The boy in back of me is a pest I can't stand him.

Where does the first sentence end? How do you know? What end mark would be appropriate at that point (period, question mark, exclamation point)? Other options include using a semicolon, which indicates a close relationship between the two sentences, or adding a coordinator or transition word (see "Ways to Correct").

Sometimes, students understand that punctuation needs to separate sentences but choose the wrong punctuation mark, most often a comma.

F. That guy is driving me crazy, he is such a blab.

G. I saw the dog, I couldn't catch it.

When a comma separates two independent sentences without any connecting or transition word, the resulting error is called a *comma splice*. We have many options to correct the error, as shown in the following box.

Ways to Correct

Replace the comma with a period:

That guy is driving me crazy. He is such a blab.

Replace the comma with a semicolon:

That guy is driving me crazy; he's such a blab.

Add a coordinator (*and, but, or, for, yet*) after the comma:

I saw the dog, but I couldn't catch it.

Add a transition word (*however, additionally*, etc.) before the comma, and add a semicolon before the transition word and a comma after it:

I saw the dog; however, I couldn't catch it.

The only way to become comfortable with sentence boundaries is to continue working with sentences. The more sentences you read, the more familiar you are with how English sentences look and feel. The more sentences you write, the more familiar you become with how to form complete sentences.

PRACTICE: Run-on and Comma Splice

Practice 1   *Run-on Sentences*

Find the spot where one sentence ends and another begins. Add the appropriate end mark (or semicolon). If you use a period, question mark, or exclamation point, be sure to capitalize the first word of the second sentence. If you use a semicolon, do not capitalize.

YO-YO DIETS

1. Yo-yo dieting endangers physical health it is hard on mental health as well.

2. Yo-yo dieting is linked to higher stress worse mental health then occurs.

3. Dr. John Foreyt of Baylor College of Medicine conducted a study of nearly 500 adults he found people who gained or lost no more than 5 pounds in a year to be psychologically sound.

4. Keeping weight stable was important even obese people were better off emotionally.

5. When the scale climbs, it causes distress weight loss is also stressful however.

6. Foreyt says gradual change toward a goal of a healthier diet is desirable a slim body is not necessarily desirable.

7. Exercise and support groups are positive routes to dieting the yo-yo routine is not a positive route, and in fact, dangerous.

8. Despite so many people doing it, the yo-yo routine is bad for physical and mental health the body never adjusts or stabilizes.

9. Yo-yo dieting got its name from the old child's toy up and down on a scale is similar to the uneven, up and down motion of the toy.

10. Many Americans engage in yo-yo dieting even if they don't recognize what they're doing their physical and emotional well-being is being sacrificed. (You have a couple of options as to where you divide the sentences.)

Practice 2   *Comma Splices*

When you locate the comma splice, reread the sentences and think about the relationship between them. Review your options for correction.

TUMMY FAT: WATCH OUT FOR STRESS!

1. An inability to cope with stress might increase tummy fat, this would put women at higher risk for heart attacks.

2. People with a high waist-to-hip ratio of fat have a higher risk of heart attacks, researchers also found a link between uncontrollable stress and building up abdominal fat.

3. Yale University scientists learned women who have no special strategies for coping with stress are more likely to have higher waist-to-hip fat ratios, they also secrete more stress hormones.

4. The scientists, both women, note that they can't say for sure stress is the cause of tummy fat, the high hormone secretions, however, can raise the risk of heart attacks.

5. The tummy has more receptors for the stress hormones than do other parts of the body, given this fact, researchers speculate that poor coping strategies may promote both tummy fat and coronaries.

6. Should women start worrying even more, well, the researchers note that far more research is needed.

7. Because men have been the primary heart attack candidates, women have not been the subject of many studies, the results of any study thus have to be speculative. (Read carefully. Only one of the commas separates two independent sentences.)

8. Research studies are very expensive, scientists often have to write grants for funding to run them.

9. Writing grants takes time and energy, there's no certainty of receiving any money either.

10. Women's groups, however, are pressing for more studies dealing with women's health, they are making some progress but not nearly fast enough.

Practice 3   *Run-on and Comma Splice*

As you read this student essay, check for sentences that are run together without any punctuation or have a comma (without any connecting or transition word) separating them. Make the necessary corrections, including substituting the appropriate end mark on some sentences.

Why Are They Rated Anyway?

I found it ridiculous that on the opening night of White Men Can't Jump almost the entire audience consisted of young teens. The movie has an R rating, doesn't that require that you be seventeen or accompanied by a parent or adult guardian. There were no parents or adults with these kids. A movie is rated to provide a standard as to what one should see and what one should not see. Then, with the restrictions set, isn't is necessary that an adult be concerned as to what their child or children are seeing.

Do parents not care what their children see. Movies that are rated R have adult situations and language, are teens now considered adult enough to attend, without someone over seventeen with them. The theaters allows these adolescents in a movie, containing things such as sex, as long as someone older buys their tickets. Parents need to understand the impact that these movies have on their child, when a young teen sees things such as sex in a movie are they really understanding the real meaning in some movies there are mind games that people play, can an adolescent comprehend that.

The Motion Picture Association of America has very set standards as to who can attend the movies they put out. In 1984, they added a new rating to their list PG-13 means that some material may be objectionable for viewers under thirteen. This should provide for the needs of those ranging between the R movies intended for adults and the PG movies which to them are dumb, boring, and childish.

Children today are growing up fast enough anyway is it necessary for them to attend an R movie alone too? Parents are busy today, they have plenty to do but do they have to drop their kids off at a theater and return later to pick them up? There are never enough hours in a day to tend to everything but once in awhile take time out to go to the movies with your children see what they find so interesting about these R rated movies.

PRACTICE: Fragments

Practice 1 *Fragments*

Read the following sentences slowly. Test each word group: is it complete all by itself, making sense? If it isn't, check the word group before and after it. You might want to attach it to another word group, or you might want to form a completely different sentence from it. In either case, you will probably have to add or subtract words as you correct the fragments.

TEENAGE GIRLS: DWELLING ON EMOTIONS

1. It's hardly a surprise. Teenage girls focus on feelings. Just like women. Dealing with stress by focusing heavily on their feelings.

2. And just like their moms. Their emotion-centered coping style makes them less skilled than males at shrugging off hassles.

3. Masculine strategies, such as going after diversions to gain a new perspective on problems. These seem to make teenage boys less vulnerable to stress.

4. Sheri Johnson, a psychologist at Brown University, studied over 300 teenagers. She found both sexes face stress. A similar amount of stress in their environment.

5. Johnson found females reported a greater amount of stress. A gender difference since the environment was the same.

6. The perceived difference in personal distress. It can be accounted for entirely by girls' greater tendency to dwell on emotions. And maybe magnify their emotions.

7. Boys, however, tend to take time out. Reframing their problems after a breather.

8. Should girls learn new strategies? Would they be less "female"? Researchers don't have all the answers. An interesting idea to consider, though.

Practice 2   *Fragments*

The following student essay has a number of incomplete sentences. In the opening paragraph, the student might have wanted to use one or two fragments for a special effect, but you should decide how you want to handle them. You might need to add or subtract words as you correct the fragments. And you may disagree with this writer's ideas. But for now, just work on the sentence fragments.

Concerts, Concerts

Entertainment. The American way of living. Entertainment comes in a variety of different forms. As a movie, a sports event, a party, and of course, a concert. There are many different types of concerts available to the American public.

Folk music concerts are one type. Music played protesting the black slavery movement. Or also protesting equal rights in the sixties. I often associate folk music as a representative of hard times. A message through song a way of expressing many feelings. People at these concerts express feelings through this type of song. Folk concerts are still around today. Drawing most of their listeners from the 1960s era.

Classical music is another form of music heard at a concert. This type of concert won't be found on the street. Rather in a more formal area. A theater or auditorium. The music played may present a mood somewhat similar to a person belonging to the aristocracy. Most of the music was written in the 1800s. When the aristocracy was well in order. That would probably have something to do with classical music's formality. The music itself is played by a concert orchestra. Or a solo pianist or a quartet of violins. The music provides a rich sound. Enjoyable to the listener's ears. Yet still there is another type of music directing its message towards today's youth.

Rock concerts are very popular. The listeners of rock music are mostly young. The location of rock concerts is almost anywhere. In a field, in a bar, an auditorium, or even in someone's back yard. The rock concert scene is very different than that of folk music or classical. Of course, feelings are brought out in the latter two, but emotions are more apt to be revealed in the loud atmosphere of a rock concert. This type of concert produces more hazards than folk music or classical. Hazards such as drug and alcohol abuse, extremely large crowds, and everyone's friend, general admission.

Rock concerts, classical concerts, and folk music concerts; just a few of the types of concerts available to the American public. They provide a variety in our American entertainment system, and they're well worth it.

Practice 3   *Sentence Boundaries*

Correct the following sentences. You'll find run-ons, comma splices, and fragments.

1. I remember my first day of lifting, I did squats with 125 pounds.

2. You learn to compete with your friends. Not only through sports but also in class.

3. I was addicted and continued lifting, my strength and size increased.

4. I used to get tired and spend a lot of extra time sleeping. Valuable time in which I could have been doing schoolwork.

5. The pride a child has when he surprises his parents with something he made in school, or even a gift for them.

6. A friend of mine told me to come to the phys ed center and start lifting weights it sounded like a good idea so I did.

7. My parents had taken care of me for years, it was time to return the favor.

8. I will not stop either I want to be bigger, more muscular.

9. In high school it was always never, hopefully in college it will be now.

10. If it's not enough that it's against the law, or puts lives in danger, maybe the fact that it will cost a person dearly for driving intoxicated.

BEYOND SENTENCE BOUNDARIES

Sometimes sentences, although technically complete or correct, have other major problems. As readers, we trip over them in some way. Since we want readers to understand our ideas clearly and efficiently on first reading, we need to review sentences for more than their boundaries.

Misplaced Modifiers

Read the following sentences carefully. What's out of place or doesn't make sense?

1. Out of the corner of his eye, the horse jumped the gate.
2. Half asleep from a night on the town, the assignments never got done.
3. Flying high on octane, Lee pushed the Fiat into overdrive.
4. Hanging by a toe, Leslie found her sock.
5. While drinking beer, the TV blew up in the middle of the football game.
6. Trimmed in black lace, Ellie found the perfect gown.
7. At 6'11" tall, the school board was skeptical of Elliot's playing on the grade school team.

Although each word group that starts a sentence provides good information, that information is physically misplaced. The person or thing being described is not the next word in the sentence.

Feeling low, Angela slammed her locker and left.

Who's feeling low? Angela is. In this case, the introductory descriptive information is followed by the person described. In English sentences, we want the description next to the person or thing being described. When we fail to use this arrangement, our readers are distracted—and in some cases, annoyed.

Return to the sentences with misplaced introductory material. There are different ways to repair the sentence:

1. As Jon watched out of the corner of his eye, the horse jumped the gate.

   The horse jumped the gate while John watched out of the corner of his eye.
2. Half asleep from a night on the town, Jon never got his assignments done.
3. Lee pushed the Fiat, flying high on octane, into overdrive.

Make the corrections for sentences 4, 5, 6, and 7. Now try the following sentences, which have the same problem of misplaced description. Remember to ask yourself these questions: Who or what is being described? Is that description next to the person or thing being described?

PRACTICE: Beyond Sentence Boundaries

Practice 1

1. That house is being torn down across the street.

2. The audience can hear the singer in the back of the auditorium.

3. I planted those flowers yesterday in the boxes.

4. The boy chased the dog in his Sunday clothes.

5. Hanging by a thread, Lee found his shirt.

6. Feeling sick, the medication was needed.

7. Remembering the penalty, there was a instant stop to the idea forming in my mind.

8. Returning to the huddle, the crowd yelled at the quarterback.

9. As a member of the army reserve, it would be in my best interest to get my officer's commission.

10. After careful consideration of these criteria, my decision has been made.

11. Because it is viewed as a prime indicator of emotional satisfaction, there is a growing emphasis on sex in a marriage.

12. Because of an inability to see a long-term goal, his recent past has been day-to-day survival.

Parallelism

As readers, we can more easily absorb information when it is presented in similar forms. As you read the following sentences, note which is easier to follow and understand.

A. I like to walk, jog, and riding my bike.
   I like to walk, jog, and bike.
   I liking walking, jogging, and biking.

B. She could be a nurse, teacher, or practice law.
   She could be a nurse, teacher, or lawyer.

You probably concluded quickly that sentences where words were structurally alike were much easier to read: to walk, (to) jog, and (to) bike; walking, jogging, and biking; nurse, teacher, and lawyer.

Practice 2

Make these sentences parallel:

1. He loved playing golf and to go sailing.

2. With the recent Dracula movies, Alex like to see one and then going out for a bite.

3. Sam knew how to drive teachers crazy: he always cracked gum, was chewing pencils, and would light the wastebasket on fire.

4. Shopping and to eat out were Lyn's favorite activities.

5. As a running back, Jeff had great stamina and could outrun anyone.

6. Terry hoped to play left field and wanted to bat first of players.

7. Leo thinks to be a lawyer is better than practicing medicine.

8. Chris tried teaching and to be a singer as careers.

Practice 3

As you read this article from *USA Today*, notice how the author used parallel structure. Underline those words or word groups that use parallel structure.

HOW TO GET SOME SHUT-EYE

Suffering from insomnia? Counting the cracks on the ceiling? Here's what the experts recommend to help you get a good night's sleep:

Go to bed and get up at the same time each day.

Avoid caffeine after 2 P.M.

Exercise in the late afternoon but no later than three hours before bedtime.

Don't do anything too stimulating before bed.

Don't use alcohol as a sedative. It leaves the brain restless later in the night.

Stanford researcher William Dement's studies show that if you miss sleep one night, your body keeps a record of the "sleep debt." If the debt isn't paid back soon, you'll start nodding off in the day. Sleep debt accrues until it's paid back. Most people pay back on the weekends by sleeping or napping.

Some sentences require a bit more study and work. Read the following and look for the comparison, of what to what:

A pair of $200 gym shoes won't last any longer than a boy who buys a $75 pair.

Who or what is being compared? Shoes to shoes? Person to person? We need a parallel: shoe to shoe or boy to boy. Since shoes are the comparison (we can assume the boy will last!), we can make the sentence parallel in this way:

A pair of $200 gym shoes won't last any longer than a pair of $75 gym shoes.

Now try this sentence:

I like my math teacher's lectures better than sitting in English class.

Who or what is being compared? How can you restructure the sentence so that like things are compared? Lecture to lecture or teacher to teacher?

Practice 4

Restructure these sentences so that the parallelism is correct:

1. A good student hits the books daily and is better off than cram sessions at the last minute.

2. Los Angeles' problems seem worse than living in New York City.

3. Going shopping with my sister is more fun than my mother.

4. Cross-country skiing is better exercise than if you were to walk.

5. Anyone who takes up smoking has a good chance of lung cancer than not smoking.

CHAPTER 10

Connecting Ideas

COORDINATION

Writing better sentences may require joining ideas from several sentences. Short sentences that share a relationship can often be joined by a word or punctuation mark that makes the relationship clearer and more focused. As you read the following sentences, (1) isolate the two independent sentences, and (2) circle the word connecting the two sentences. What is the relationship between the two sentences? How does the connecting word (called a coordinator) help a reader grasp the relationship quickly? What punctuation mark is used with the connecting word? Why? How does it help a reader?

A.   Jon dislikes sociology, but he has to take it for his major.

B.   Lynn plans to be a lawyer, so she's majoring in "talk."

C.   Susan lost her cat, and she's really upset.

D.   Mark took the cat to El Cajon, for he was sure it had fleas.

E.   Rich fell over the garbage cans, but he's okay.

F.   Anton will go to Japan, or he will stay in California.

G.   Randi ate two dozen chocolate chip cookies, yet she never gained any weight.

Connector (Coordinator)	Meaning
and	Addition
but	Contrast
yet	Contrast
for	Reason, idea in second sentence explains idea in first sentence
so	Cause and effect
or	Option or alternative

Connecting sentences with one of these connectors is called *coordinating*. It means that we have two sentences, each capable of standing alone, and each conveying equally important ideas. When you began speaking your native language, one of the first sentence combinations you made was with *and* or *but*. And you might have also used these two connectors as your first written sentence combinations as well. The coordinators are endlessly useful. We use *yet* and *for* less often in our speech and writing, but for academic and business writing, you will find them handy alternatives.

Although these coordinators are most commonly used to connect two sentences, we sometimes use *and* and *but* as the first word of the sentence.

> Jonathan is a great guy. And I really mean that.
>
> Krista is a comic. But I can only take so much.

Using the coordinators in this way gives emphasis to the meaning. However, don't overuse this structure, especially in academic or business writing.

One more caution: We use these coordinators not only to connect sentences but also as sentence parts.

> The man is both a doctor and a lawyer.
>
> His weight is okay but not his height.
>
> She'll paint the garage or clean the basement tomorrow.

In the following example, we have one subject and one verb, a single sentence. The word *and* connects sentence parts, not complete sentences. There is *no* comma.

> $\quad$ *S* $\quad$ *V*
>
> The man is both a doctor and a lawyer.

In the next example, we have two sets of subject and verb, two independent sentences. *And* connects two sentences. We need the comma.

   S   *V*   *S*   *V*

The man is a doctor, and he also is a lawyer.

Be sure you have two independent sentences on either side of the coordinator *before* you insert a comma.

PRACTICE: Coordination

Practice 1

Join the two sentences with an appropriate coordinator. Be sure to add the comma before each coordinator. For example:

Leo left the house early. His work wasn't done.
Leo left the house early, but his work wasn't done.

THEIR JUST DESSERTS

1. No amount of cash buys you a seat at the exclusive Barton Bistro.

    Avoiding food fights in the lunchroom might get you in.

2. Good behavior earns a seat at Clara Barton Elementary School's

    most exclusive restaurant. Kids are eager to enter.

3. The restaurant features classical music, a maître d' in tuxedo, real

    silverware, real beef, and ice cream. Kids find it a treat.

4. Principal Leonard Schwartz initiated the elite eatery in the school's

    art room. He believed kids needed rewards for good behavior in

    the lunchroom.

5. A group of 29 second graders found their principal in black tails. He handed them menus and ushered them to their tables. He treated them with the utmost respect.

6. Five waitresses served the children lunch. The children could have beef. They could have pasta casserole.

7. Barton Bistro patrons drink out of cups, not cartons. They use real silverware, not "sporks," a combination fork and spoon made of plastic.

8. The food comes from the regular school cafeteria. There's no special budget.

Practice 2

Examine this student's paragraph for use of coordinators and appropriate punctuation with them. Make any needed corrections.

Week 1

My first week of classes has seemed like an exercise program. Before classes began, I had to buy my books and supplies. Thus I had equipment and I was ready for the first drill. When I started my classes, I needed to find my way around and get used to my teachers. This is what I refer to as my warm-up period. I had to walk up hills so my legs got a workout. I also had to walk for miles between classes. I would run at times for I feared walking in late. And at times, I would end up sitting in front of the teacher or in the worst seat in the class, one behind a pillar. I thus got to stretch out my body or at the very least, I got to stretch my neck a lot. But the final aspect is a continuous

`process. I must make it a routine to get to my classes on`
`time and never give up for like an exercise program I will`
`become useless to myself if I cease the routine.`

Practice 3

Use the following information from the Center for Substance Abuse Prevention to develop a paragraph. You will need to add information from your own observation and experience. Try to use all the coordinators at least once.

THE ALCOHOL THREAT

College students in the United States spend $5.5 billion a year on alcohol.

One study revealed alcohol is one of the major reasons for absenteeism from class.

The same study showed that 25 percent of student deaths are associated with alcohol.

Alcohol was involved in 90 percent of college rapes.

In the 1991 College Alcohol survey, 70 percent of the college administrators responding believed alcohol contributes significantly to campus violence.

Alcohol is a factor in 40 percent of student academic problems.

More than 7 percent of the 1996 graduating class will drop out of school because of drinking.

Out of 12 million college students, more than 250,000 will eventually die of alcohol-related causes.

COORDINATING WITH A SEMICOLON

Semicolons sometimes seem mysterious. They're not. And they're downright useful, especially in academic writing. However, because students sometimes have half-learned rules for this punctuation mark, you're better off going "blank" and starting new here. First, study these sentences and determine how semicolons are used:

The cartoon character Bart Simpson drives some teachers crazy; he is "hell on wheels" in school.

Homer Simpson lost his job at the nuclear energy plant; he fell asleep at the switch.

Why don't we need a coordinator or other connecting word to make the meaning clear? What other punctuation mark could replace the semicolon?

The semicolon separates two independent sentences; on either side of the semicolon, the word group can stand completely alone and and make sense. Because the relationship between the two sentences is so clear, we don't need a connecting word.

PRACTICE: Semicolons

Practice 1

Join these sentences with a semicolon. Remember, you must have two independent sentences, one on either side of the semicolon. You can change the placement of information, as well as add or delete words. You can substitute *he, Thomas, the founder,* and so on. Your goal is two closely related sentences, easily understood by a reader.

BURGERS AND DIPLOMAS

1. Dave Thomas is the founder of a U.S. corporation known to most kids, Wendy's. The corporation has more than $3.6 billion in annual sales.

2. Most people have seen Thomas on television. Thomas does the ads for his restaurant chain.

3. Thomas appears to be a "regular" guy. He's a little overweight, of average height, and white-haired.

4. Thomas, however, is no regular guy. He was a high school drop-out who founded a billion-dollar business.

5. Thomas has received six honorary university degrees. Last week Dave Thomas received his high school diploma.

6. He dropped out of school at age 15 to work full-time in a restaurant. Forty-five years later, he passed the GED exam in Florida, his home state.

7. Thomas urges students to stay in high school. He believes good jobs today demand the knowledge and skills learned in high school and beyond.

Practice 2

Join independent sentences with a semicolon where it seems useful to do so. Remember, the relationship between the idea in the first sentence and that in the second sentence must be perfectly clear to the reader. Use other coordinators as needed. You may substitute *he, Page, judge.* Your goal is a clear, easily read paragraph.

HERE COMES THE JUDGE

Pro football Hall of Famer Alan Page has a new uniform.

Page now wears the robes of a Minnesota Supreme Court justice.

Page, 47, is the first black to serve on the state's highest court.

Page won the seat with 47 percent of the vote in the November 1992 election.

He invited 140 fourth-graders to Monday's swearing-in.

He told them, "Success comes with hard work."

He told them, "It comes with preparation."

"And when you do prepare, then you can achieve your hopes and dreams," said Page.

Page played for the Minnesota Vikings and the Chicago Bears.

Page earned his law degree in 1978 from the University of Minnesota.

He retired from football two years later.

He worked in private practice and as a prosecutor.

OTHER TRANSITIONS BETWEEN SENTENCES

We have one more way to join two independent sentences—a set of transition words. Among the most useful of these transition words are the following:

for example	nevertheless	therefore
in fact	however	thus
as a matter of fact	on the other hand	consequently
for instance		

moreover
additionally
furthermore

> Paul is a perfect student; moreover, he's a great athlete.
>
> Julie lost her scholarship; therefore, she's out of school.
>
> Alan wants to join swing choir; however, he has to work.
>
> Dr. Inkwell gives tough assignments; for example, I have ten chapters to read before tomorrow.

Notice the punctuation used with these transition words. Read each sentence slowly and determine how the punctuation works to help the reader.

What information does each of the transition words provide for the reader?

PRACTICE: Transition Words

Practice 1

With your group or writing partner, develop ten sentences using the transition words listed. Note your reason for using each transition word. How does it help the reader?

Practice 2

Use the following information to construct a paragraph. Use as many transition words as appropriate.

GENTLE GIANTS TAKE TIME TO TUTOR

Jeff Zgonina is gone.

The Purdue defensive lineman is not forgotten.

Zgonina, Big Ten Defensive Player of the Year, graduated in December.

He wanted to leave his college community with something more than football memories.

Last September he organized a tutoring program to help students with special needs.

He called the program Gentle Giants.

"I wanted to leave something behind that I started up," says the 6-2, 270-pound Zgonina.

"Everybody thinks football players just want to play football and not do anything else."

"This is one way to show that we want to help people in the community."

Zgonina and 20 teammates participated in the program, which has been an overwhelming success.

ANOTHER WAY TO USE TRANSITION WORDS

You can also use the transition words this way:

Jon wants to play tennis. However, his left knee is wrecked.

Sara lost the bet. Consequently, she owes Lee $50.

You'll have to read that chapter. Additionally, you have 20 problem sets to solve before tomorrow.

A period marks the end of the first independent sentence. Then, the transition word links that sentence to the one that follows. The period has replaced the semicolon, but the comma following the transition word stays put. As you read, note how you slow down at the comma. The comma acts as an advanced organizer: something important is coming up.

PRACTICE

Add an appropriate transition word to the second sentence, and in some cases, a third or fourth sentence. You want to show the relationship between ideas and help the reader understand them more clearly. Be sure to add a comma after the transition word.

YOUR BRAIN: USE IT OR LOSE IT

1. Certain nerve cells in the brain are short in uneducated people. These cells are longer in people who are educated. People who continue to challenge themselves intellectually have longer brain cells.

2. UCLA researchers examined the brains of 20 people who had died. They learned the dendrites, threadlike portions of nerve cells, were longer in people who remained intellectually active.

3. Researchers analyzed the life histories of the people they studied. They don't know if people with longer dendrites were more likely to attend college, or if going to college made the dendrites grow longer. They believe the latter interpretation is correct.

4. Animal studies provided earlier information on nerve cells. Researchers base their beliefs on these studies. Skeptics can always say, "People aren't rats."

5. Scientists, however, believe in the animal studies. They believe in the link with human studies. They say if you put an animal in an enriched environment, you see an increase in dendritic material and enhanced problem solving. If you move a rat to an impoverished environment, the material decreases.

REVIEW: JOINING INDEPENDENT SENTENCES		
When You Want to:	**Coordinator**	**Transition Word**
Add an Idea	and	additionally moreover furthermore
Show Contrasting Idea	but yet	on the other hand however nevertheless
Show Cause or Effect	for so	therefore as a result consequently thus
Show Alternative	or	
Show Time Relation		first meanwhile then next last

REVIEW: PUNCTUATION JOINING INDEPENDENT SENTENCES

Comma Before Connecting Word: Coordinators

Semicolon Before and Comma After: Transition Words

Semicolon Alone

PRACTICE: Using Various Methods

Practice 1

Try out different coordinators as you connect the following ideas. You may add or delete words as necessary to make a clear, easily read sentence. There are several ways in which to make the connections.

SLIPS OF THE TONGUE

The slip of tongue could have been disastrous.

Professor Daniel Wegner wrote a note about a change of lunch plans to a colleague he didn't like.

He intended to write, "I hope you can dine without me."

He wrote, "I hope you can die without me."

Wegner caught his error before sending the note.

How often has something rude been said when the offender was trying extra hard to be polite?

How often has one been surprised by such a mistake?

The tendency to say or do exactly the opposite of what we intend is a human frailty.

Ever since Freud, psychoanalysts have believed such slips were by-products of the subconscious mind.

Wegner and his colleagues have laboratory experiments that support Freud's hypothesis.

Other psychologists disagree with the theory.

They contend that under conditions of stress or failure, a lot of ideas pop into the mind at the same time.

In this confusion, errors of thinking result.

It doesn't mean there's a lot of unconscious activity.

Wegner and his colleagues believe people are more sensitive to their suppressed ideas than to things consciously being considered.

People can suppress a thought under normal conditions.

They have trouble controlling their thoughts when they are under pressure or have other things on their mind.

They end up blurting out the very thoughts they want to suppress.

Psychologists say there are ways to keep our thoughts in check while dealing with stress or pressure.

One way is to stop trying to suppress unwanted thoughts.

Practice 2

Remember, there are several ways in which to connect the sentences.

GARTH BROOKS: THE PRICE OF STARDOM

Before fame made it impractical, Garth Brooks hung around the stage after his show.

He would sign autographs.

These weren't ordinary autographs.

Women would ask him to sign their undergarments or parts of their bodies.

Garth says he doesn't understand why women find him attractive.

He wonders if they are blind.

He says there are some superhunks.

He is not one of them.

Garth notes he is "pale as a sheet," has three chins, and is losing his hair.

He says if he were a girl, he'd be looking for someone like George Strait.

Garth says the attention he gets is weird.

The attention is also flattering.

From the time he started performing, he attracted women fans.

Garth admits he likes to flirt.

He likes to make love with his music in front of women.

Garth's wife says he has always been a sexual person.

She believes it was his ego making him want to conquer women.

It didn't mean anything to him.

Garth's wife finally threatened to leave him.

The most controversial song on Garth's first album was "Everytime That It Rains," about a one-night stand.

Garth won't say if it were true or not.

He will say that the woman in that song will know who wrote it.

There were two other writers besides Brooks.

Because of his wife, he no longer autographs women's body parts or underwear.

Garth admits temptation is still a problem for him.

Because his music is sexual, it always pushes those buttons.

CHAPTER 11

Subordination

When you coordinated ideas, you created two independent sentences. When you subordinate an idea, however, you create a single sentence with both an independent and a dependent part:

Even though Josie can be really annoying, I like her.

This sentence resulted from two ideas being joined:

Josie can be really annoying.
I like Josie.

The connector (called a subordinator) provides the reader with the relationship between the two ideas. In this case, the writer chose *even though* to express a contrast. The introductory part, "Even though Josie can be really annoying," cannot stand alone; it is dependent upon the second part, "I like her," to complete its meaning. If you cover "I like her" with your hand, you'll quickly conclude that you're left hanging—waiting for the rest of the idea. Working together, however, the two parts provide a reader with good information, efficiently and clearly.

Read through the following sentences and identify (1) the independent part, (2) the dependent (subordinate) part, and (3) the key word in the dependent part—the word or word group showing the relationship between (1) and (2). Note the punctuation: Where does it consistently come? How does it help the reader?

A. Unless my teacher explains problems clearly, I'm lost.
B. When my teacher explains problems clearly, I understand.

C. If my teacher explains problems clearly, I understand.

D. Although my teacher explains problems clearly, I'm lost.

E. Because my teacher explains problems clearly, I'm doing fine.

F. As long as my teacher explains problems clearly, I'm okay.

G. Once my teacher explains problems clearly, I understand.

You can reverse the order of the dependent and independent parts. Notice the position of the key word, the one showing the relationship between the parts, when you reverse order. Also notice the punctuation. What has happened? Can you think of some reasons for this change?

I'm lost unless my teacher explains problems clearly.

I understand once my teacher explains problems clearly.

Whether you place the dependent part first or second is your choice. But you will want some variety in your sentences, so familiarity with both arrangements is important.

PRACTICE: Subordination

With your group or writing partner, discuss the following sentences. Indicate which part is independent and which is dependent. Note the key word linking the two parts. What is its meaning? How does it help us understand the relationship between the two parts?

BART SIMPSON: HERO OF THE 80S

A. Even though Bart Simpson has been one of the most popular cartoon characters of the 1990s, many people find his antics too obnoxious.

B. Because Bart says and does things that many kids would like to do, he's a popular figure with teens and young adults.

C. Some psychologists believe Bart Simpson is popular because he's the underachiever, the kind of kid most teachers ignore.

D. If a few political analysts are right, "The Simpsons" satirizes the 1980s and the Reagan administration.

E. We're all in trouble if Homer Simpson represents the typical nuclear plant employee—totally inept.

F.   Whenever Bart gets a bright idea, trouble follows.

G.   When the police come to the Simpsons' home, the neighbors can only sigh and say, "About time."

H.   Although Marge Simpson often shows compassion and common sense, most viewers are too absorbed with her massive blue hair to notice.

I.   The baby sucks her pacifier more fiercely while any crisis is under way.

J.   Since Bart is the nontypical child, he calls his father "Homer."

COMMON SUBORDINATORS			
Time	**Place**	**Condition**	**Cause**
when	where	although	because
whenever	wherever	even though	since
before		if	
after		once	
during			
while			
as soon as			

Practice 1

Add content to the following subordinators. Think about the meaning of the subordinator before you add material. Remember, you need a subject and verb in both the dependent and independent part.

Example: While _____, _____.

While Jon studied, I watched the ball game.

1. After _____, _____.

2. Even though _____, _____.

3. Since _____, _____.

4. Whenever _____, _____.

5. If _____ , _____ .

6. _____ because _____ .

7. _____ while _____ .

8. _____ before _____ .

9. _____ once _____ .

10. _____ when _____ .

Practice 2

Choose five subordinators and construct a sentence using each one. Remember, you'll have two parts to the sentence: one dependent and one independent. If your sentence starts with the dependent part, be sure to add a comma at the end of the dependent part.

Practice 3

With your group or writing partner, write a brief paragraph or two describing or explaining a favorite television show. Use as many subordinated sentences as appropriate. Underline the subordinator and, if one is needed, the comma.

Practice 4

Combine the following sentences into a paragraph. Review the common subordinators before you begin, and then, as appropriate to your meaning, use some subordinated sentences in your paragraph. You may have to add or delete some words.

FAT CHANCE

The common medical assumption says that women are generally fatter than men.

This assumption may be a slur based upon cultural bias rather than on good science.

An advanced technique for dissecting the human body electronically can measure fat and muscle content slice by slice.

This technique has found no real differences between normal males and females.

Yale University researchers are working on this question.

Women all over America are eager for further results.

MORE SUBORDINATION: EMBEDDING

We can join sentences in many different ways. One of the most useful is called "embedding." What happens in the following pairs of sentences? How does one part "embed" itself into the other? How do the commas around the embedded part help the reader?

A. Stephen King has a large following among teenage readers.

B. Stephen King is famous for his horror fiction.

Stephen King, who is famous for his horror fiction, has a large following among teenage readers.

Stephen King, who has a large following among teenage readers, is famous for his horror fiction.

A. Bart Simpson is irreverent and mouthy.

B. Bart Simpson is a terrible role model for kids.

Bart Simpson, who is a terrible role model for kids, is irreverent and mouthy.

Bart Simpson, who is irreverent and mouthy, is a terrible role model for kids.

We can get even more variety out of embededded sentences. Note how we can simplify and move the embedded part:

Bart Simpson, who is a terrible role model for kids, is irreverent and mouthy.

Bart Simpson, a terrible role model for kids, is irreverent and mouthy.

A terrible role model for kids, Bart Simpson is irreverent and mouthy.

We'll look at these variations in more detail shortly. First, we'll review ways of embedding one sentence into another.

WAYS OF EMBEDDING	
Who, Whom, Whose	Refer to people
That, Which	Refer to objects, ideas, things, places

Stephen King, who lives in Maine, is a prolific writer.

Stephen King, whose best-selling novels have been made into movies, is considered the master of horror.

Stephen King, whom I would like to meet, writes scary stuff.

The book that I liked best was *Cujo*.

Cujo, which I liked best, has left me with a fear of dogs.

Noting Punctuation

Notice what happens when *that* and *which* begin the embedded part. Why are there commas around "which I liked best"? Why can't we set off "that I liked best"? What is its relationship to the rest of the sentence? What rule can you formulate for when we need commas?

I want the beer that is on the table.

The beer that's on the table is the one I want.

Which beer? Any beer?

Sometimes, we don't even bother to put *that* or *that is* into the sentence:

I want the beer on the table.

However, grammatically, *that* is understood to be there. So, we really have two sentences, one embedded into the other. Native speakers of English don't even think about these things; their long experience with the language helps them form many types of sentences unconsciously and easily. It's only when we write, when we have to add punctuation, that we run into some problems.

I want a girl just like the girl that married dear old Dad.

Which girl? Any girl?

Leinenkugel's, which is a small brewery beer, is pretty good.

Do we need to identify which beer we're talking about? What function does "which is a small brewery beer" serve? Do we have to have it to make complete sense? What's the difference between good information and essential information?

Leinenkugel's, which has an Indian maiden on its label, is known throughout Wisconsin.

Leinenkugel's, whose reputation has spread to Chicago through tourists, is considered a specialty beer.

When to Use the Commas

When the idea is added information, good but *not* essential, we use *which* and commas.

When the idea is essential to the sentence, helping us identify the main idea, we use *that* and no commas.

We use commas to set off extra or added information.

PRACTICE: Embedding

Practice 1

With your group or writing partner, embed one sentence into the other. Vary your use of *who, whose, whom, that,* and *which.* Remember to add commas.

A LONG-RUN SHOW: "M*A*S*H"

A. "M*A*S*H" was one of the most popular television shows of the 1970s.

"M*A*S*H" is enjoying reruns in the 1990s.

_____

_____

B. "M*A*S*H" satirized the army and war.
The army was portrayed as bureaucratic and stupid.

_____

_____

C. Hawkeye Pierce was a first-rate surgeon and comic cutup.
Hawkeye covered his anger and pain with jokes.

_____

_____

D. Trapper John McIntyre was Hawkeye's bunk mate.
Trapper was also a surgeon and cutup.

_____

_____

E. Margaret O'Houlihan was in charge of the nurses.
Margaret was called Hot Lips by Hawkeye and Trapper.

_____

_____

F. Radar O'Reilly was one of "M*A*S*H"'s most lovable characters.
Radar was gentle and childlike.

_____

_____

G. Radar kept a teddy bear.
The teddy bear was ragged and tattered.
The teddy bear was his best friend.

_____

_____

H. Hawkeye and Trapper kept trying to defy army regulations.
    The army regulations made no sense to them.

    _____

    _____

I. Henry Blake was the commanding officer.
    Blake's orders made little sense.

    _____

    _____

J. Hawkeye and Trapper kept tormenting Frank Burns.
    They called Frank "Ferret Face."

    _____

    _____

K. Max Klinger was another memorable character.
    Klinger's wardrobe consisted of dresses.

    _____

    _____

L. "M*A*S*H" showed the idiocy of war.
    "M*A*S*H" also showed the excellence of medical care in the field
    hospital.

    _____

    _____

More Ways of Combining and Modifying Sentences

When you were embedding one sentence into another, you might
have noticed that you could delete some words and still convey the
meaning you wanted. For example:

Stephen King, who is a master of horror fiction, lives in Maine.

Stephen King, a master of horror fiction, lives in Maine.

Notice that *Stephen King* and *master* refer to the same person. We often use this writing strategy to provide a bit more information for our reader. However, because this information is "extra," not essential to the meaning of the independent sentence, it is set off by commas. In other words, the same rule operates: Set off nonessential information with commas.

To achieve even more variety in sentences, we sometimes move these "extra info" parts:

A master of horror fiction, Stephen King lives in Maine.

Again note that a comma separates the description from the independent sentence.

Alan, the best point guard on the team, will start.

The best point guard on the team, Alan will start.

Although "the best point guard on the team" is helpful information, it is not needed to complete the main idea of the sentence—Alan will start. For this reason, we need commas. Notice how the commas help us read and absorb ideas more easily.

Practice 2

Examine the following paragraphs for examples of this sentence strategy. Underline it.

HUBBA-HUBBA, BUBBA

We've got a new year, a new president, Bill Clinton—and new words vying for a place in the dictionary. No slouches on research, editors at *Random House Webster's College Dictionary*, the most popular student dictionary, say they are carefully sifting through thousands of possibilities to distinguish between "flashes in the language pan and . . . permanent fixtures in the English firmament." The dictionary staff, a large group of academics, does a massive search of American writing and speech usage to determine the staying power of new words and new meanings given to old words.

Among the front-runners likely for inclusion in the next edition, editors say, is "bubba," a term popularized by the media during Bill Clinton's presidential campaign to characterize the South's good ol' boys. Many promising terms are emerging from the computer world. "Netiquette," the rules of etiquette for using computer bulletin boards, is one such term. Another favorite term is "emoticon," a word formed from "emote" and "icon." This term is used to describe a collection of symbols that can be typed on a keyboard to convey a thought, such as :). When you turn it sideways, you'll see a smiley face—have a good day!

A DOG'S LIFE

Ah, the upscale life of a dog. At Paws Inn, a new storefront-level boarding kennel in Manhattan, the guests can lounge in bed watching TV. On a recent Friday, for example, Chloe and Crystal, two Maltese, were engrossed in an "Oprah" episode about interracial dating. More akin to a spa than a detention center, Paws Inn offers leather couches, enough toys to stock a canine FAO Schwarz, and a VCR. The favorite videos, *101 Dalmatians* and *Benji,* are available 24 hours a day. The cost of this canine pampering, $30 a day, doesn't deter dog lovers.

CLASS-Y DINNER TIME

Kids who have to stay at the table till they clean their plates now have something to do between bites. They can read their place mats. Amy Kallman Epstein of Brooklyn, the creator of Read a Mat, believes that her invention fits the parents of the 90s. Read a Mat, an educational place mat, perfectly fits the mindset of the modern parent, a mindset that abhors downtime for children. The 61 patterns range from the alphabet, shapes and numbers to the solar system, rain forests, foreign languages, great American women and maps of the world. Epstein's company, Straight Edge, sells more than $2 million in mats annually at stationery shops and toy stores in all 50 states.

ONE MORE STRATEGY: USING "-ING" AND "-ED"

Here is one more way of adding information without adding another sentence:

Crashing into the mailbox, Ellen mailed her letters the hard way.
Signaling to the referee, the quarterback stopped the clock.
Thinking about the exam, Josh got a massive headache.
Worried about the results, the math teacher junked the test.
Convinced that half the class failed, the teacher wept.

How does the *-ing* add to our understanding of the action? How does *-ed* add to our understanding? What is the relationship between the information in the *-ing* or *-ed* part and the independent sentence?

Again note that the punctuation sets off extra information—good information but not essential to the meaning of the independent sentence.

PRACTICE: Using "-ing" and "-ed"

Practice 1

Examine the following for examples of this sentence strategy. Circle introductory word groups that modify or describe through use of *-ing* or *-ed*.

ELVIS, SPECIAL DELIVERY

Leaving his stamp on the world of rock 'n' roll, Elvis Presley now has left his stamp on the doors of the U.S. Postal Service. The first official Elvis Presley stamp was sold to his daughter, Lisa Marie, on January 7, 1993. Featuring live cut-in spots from the ceremony, the cable television network celebrated Presley's 58th birthday. Thousands of fans came to Graceland to participate in the King's birthday and the new stamp honoring him. Milling about the grounds, approximately 15,000 people waited in pouring rain to buy the first Elvis stamps. Timed to coincide with Presley's birthday, a five-day *Elvis: Special Delivery* tribute featured back-to-back Elvis movies on TNT.

Practice 2

Using *-ing* or *-ed,* create introductory word groups that modify or describe. If you're not sure about the spelling of an *-ing* or *-ed* verb form, check the dictionary. For example:

_____, Lee left the party.

Losing his date, Lee left the party.

Or:

Torn by indecision, Lee left the party.

1. _____, Sally took the exam.

2. _____, Paul passed the ball to Ken.

3. _____, Kerry thought about the movie.

4. _____, Ellen and Jan went shopping.

5. _____, Sam drove out of the driveway.

6. _____, the mail carrier ran.

7. _____, the barber made some mistakes.

8. _____, the halfback started to run.

9. _____, Abner gave up golf forever.

10. _____, LuAnn charged out of the room.

REVIEWING WAYS TO JOIN IDEAS			
When You Want to:	**Coordinate**	**Subordinate**	**Transition Word**
Add an Idea	and		also additionally furthermore moreover
Show Contrast	but yet	although even though	however nevertheless
Show Cause or Effect	for so	because since	therefore thus consequently as a result
Show Condition		if unless once	
Show Time Relation		before during when after	first meanwhile then last next
Show Alternative	or		
Use Punctuation Only	;		
Embed One Sentence into Another:	who whose whom that which		

PRACTICE: Ways to Join Ideas

Using the following information on sharks, write a paragraph in which you practice the various sentence strategies in this chapter.

KING OF THE SEAS

It took millions of years of evolutionary honing.

The shark became king of the seas.

The shark is the predator at the head of the aquatic food chain.

It's taken only about ten years for the shark to be overmatched.

Man has overmatched the shark.

Man is the most deadly killer on earth.

Each year tens of millions of sharks are killed.

The sharks are killed for food.

Sharks are also killed accidentally.

Sharks are caught in nets intended for shrimp, swordfish, or tuna.

Sharks caught in nets are often clubbed to death aboard ship.

Sharks are then tossed back into the water.

Many sharks are dying.

Some researchers are afraid the species will die out.

Environmentalists and fisheries scientists have been pressing a shark-saving plan on the U.S. Department of Commerce.

They began pressing in 1989.

The Bush administration never acted on the issue.

Enthusiasts may go to court.

Enthusiasts may look to the Clinton-Gore administration.

Selling the shark's cause is not easy.

Sharks are generally portrayed as mindless killing machines.

Sharks are considered more like the Saddam Husseins of the natural world.

Sharks are not the kind of animals that inspire films like *Born Free*.

Sharks are like lions and tigers.

Sharks are important predators and scavengers.

They prune weak and dying animals from their habitat.

Few children fall asleep clutching a stuffed, saber-toothed fish.

Must we kill what we haven't learned to love?

CHAPTER 12

Revising Sentences

People sometimes use the words *revising* and *editing* interchangeably, as though they meant the same thing. They don't. When we revise a sentence, we are reworking it. We are trying to make it better: clearer, more effective, more vivid or interesting. When we edit a sentence, we are correcting it, making it correspond to Standard Written English. In editing, we are checking that grammar, punctuation, and spelling are correct. However, it's important to note that a correct sentence doesn't necessarily mean a good sentence—one that is easy to read and clearly reflects the intended meaning of the writer. For this reason, we'll concentrate first on revising sentences and second on editing them.

We revise sentences through expanding them, deleting words or phrases from them, or combining them. We also revise by changing single words.

EXPANDING

We can expand sentences by adding descriptive words or phrases. Here are some questions that help us expand:

What detail would help describe more clearly?

Who's this sentence about?

What's this sentence about?

Why?

Where?

When?

Some adults don't like the cartoon character Bart Simpson.

teachers	a mouthy, aggressive fourth grader
parents	disrespectful
	defies authority
	mocks learning

Some parents dislike the cartoon character Bart Simpson, a mouthy, aggressive fourth grader who defies authority.

The revised sentence is more precise and gives the reader some reasons why adults wouldn't like this character.

Note the differences in the following pairs of examples:

A. My math teacher is hard to follow.

B. Dr. Inkwell, my math teacher, speaks in short, rapid sentences, swallowing words as he goes.

A. He gives too much work.

B. A typical daily assignment from Dr. Inkwell consists of three chapters of problems. Each chapter takes most students at least two hours to complete.

A. I was late for math class once and felt upset.

B. The door was tightly shut when I reached math class. Through it, I could hear Dr. Inkwell's booming bass voice, yelling about lazy students. Trembling, I opened the door and tiptoed to the first empty seat, trying to avoid his steely eyes.

What role is the comma playing in these expanded sentences?

PRACTICE: Expanding Sentences

Practice 1

Giving exact names when possible, substitute general words with concrete sensory (sight, sound, taste, touch) words, and replace verbs with more active ones.

1. My cousin is talented.

_____

2. The basketball team is the worst.

_____

3. Her hair is unusual.

_____

4. My boss is too picky.

_____

A Word About Commas

Most punctuation helps us read and understand ideas more clearly and more efficiently. You may have been exposed to punctuation as rows of rules. Here, we'll look at punctuation as part of constructing and revising sentences. Learning how to use commas, for example, helps you express yourself more clearly and at the same time helps your readers understand you. When we speak, we use our voice—intonation, pitch, pauses, and so on—as punctuation. In writing, we have to learn how to give that same life through good punctuation.

When we expand sentences, we often have to set off those additional words and phrases with commas. In fact, most commas are used for this purpose. Notice the following:

Jeff, tired but happy, left the playing field.

Angry at the pay cut, the workers walked out.

Jess sat at her desk, wondering what to start first.

Why are the commas there? Could you eliminate the information enclosed with commas and still have a sensible, stand-alone sentence? What rule can you form about the use of these commas?

Jeff, my best friend, is a great musician.

Jeff, a great musician, is my best friend.

Jeff, whose mother is a rock star, is my friend.

Nashville, the home of country western music, is a great place to visit.

Minneapolis, site of the 1992 Super Bowl, surprised many fans.

Does the comma rule hold for these sentences too? Why? What does the material enclosed by commas do for the reader?

Practice 2

With your group or writing partner, expand the numbered sentences by modifying key words. You will probably need to add commas to set off descriptive words or phrases. For example:

Dame Edna Everidge is in reality a male.

Dame Edna Everidge, a lavender-haired, sequined entertainer, is in reality a male.

Dame Edna Everidge is in reality a male, Australian Barry Humphries.

1. The photographers swarmed around Madonna.

   _____

2. The crowd loved M. C. Hammer.

   _____

3. Roseanne Barr shocked baseball fans.

   _____

4. Kevin Costner lived with the Lakota Sioux.

   _____

5. Tom Cruise plays squeaky-clean characters.

   _____

6. Arsenio Hall entertains late-night television watchers.

   _____

7. Dan Marino does ads for Isotoner.

   _____

8. George Bush lost the 1992 presidential election.

   _____

9. Bill Clinton won the 1992 presidential election.

_____

10. Spike Lee made the film *Malcolm X*.

_____

CHANGING A SINGLE WORD

Sometimes, changing a single word changes the sentence into a far more lively or precise one. When we talk, we often make such changes without even thinking about it. If you tell someone that the concert was "awesome," you don't stop there. You go on to describe and explain, so the general "awesome" is broken down into flesh and blood terms. When we write, we have to be careful to break down a general term, sometimes by expanding but just as often through substituting one word for another. A good vocabulary is a writer's tool. Fortunately, we have reference books to help us enlarge that vocabulary. If you are not familiar with books such as *Roget's Thesaurus*, check them out in the bookstore or library.

The boy looked at the car.→
The fifteen-year-old couldn't keep his eyes off the Mazda RX-7.
The teenager stared at the vintage Mustang.

The old man walked into the store. →
The old man stumbled into the store.
The old man shuffled into the 7-Eleven.

PRACTICE: Changing Words

With your group, make as many substitutions as possible.

1. The student left class.

_____

2. The girl ate the food.

_____

3. The team left the field.

_____

4. The teacher looked at the class.

_____

WORKING WITHIN PARAGRAPHS

When we isolate sentences, as in these exercises, we end up working differently than when we work with paragraphs and complete essays. Within paragraphs, and ultimately full essays, we have to deal with what we just said, as well as what we go on to say. Therefore, our changes have to match a great number of thoughts, not just a single one in a single sentence. Moreover, it's always harder to change our own sentences. We know in our heads what we want to say, and we tend to think that we have—the first time! However, that's seldom the case, and reworking sentences is a necessity.

Notice the vocabulary in this excerpt from a _Newsweek_ article about movie maker Spike Lee:

> About a year ago, as Spike Lee tells it, he was setting up a rally scene for _Malcolm X_ on a Harlem Street when an empty car suddenly came hurtling toward him and his crew. Although the car crashed before injuring anyone, its interior chilled the blood. "Someone," says Lee, "had tied a brick to the accelerator and gunned it in our direction."

Three words stand out: _hurtling, chilled, gunned._ They provide the reader with a very precise sense of action and feeling. When we read a paragraph, we aren't always aware of the impact of individual words; we simply absorb and benefit from them. As writers, however, we have to be aware.

PRACTICE: Paragraphs

Practice 1

The following "Profile" from _Sports Illustrated_ offers some practice with a paragraph. First, underline the words and phrases that give us a specific picture or idea of what Tim Green is like. Then, consider how the paragraph would read without them. Would the reader have the same sense of Tim Green?

RENAISSANCE MAN

Since his days as an All-America defensive end and English major at Syracuse in the mid-1980s, Tim Green of the Falcons has successfully balanced two passions—football and writing. A first round draft pick by Atlanta in 1986, Green spent his first four years as a pro fighting through injuries and position changes. But in 1990 he was moved back to end, and he has become the most dependable performer on the Falcon defensive front, despite being small (6'2", 245 pounds) for his position.

After attending an emotional retirement dinner for Atlanta defensive end Rick Bryan, who had suffered recurring neck injuries, Green wrote:

Back in the locker room the next day, I checked my protective neck padding and I pumped some extra air into the padding inside my helmet. Like a gypsy gazing into a crystal ball, I looked at my own distorted reflection in the glossy black surface of my Falcons helmet. The smile let me know I was glad to be there. But there was nothing I could see that told me how long I would last. I'm 28, remember. A 28-year-old defensive lineman. I'm old.

As you worked through the paragraph about Green, you no doubt found a physical picture (a defensive end, height, weight) and perhaps a more interesting picture of the man himself—one who thinks about his future. Green's description of himself holding his helmet, "Like a gypsy gazing into a crystal ball," gives us both a physical picture and a comparison that adds meaning to his action. He then notes his "distorted" reflection in the helmet's "glossy black surface." The word *distorted* is important because it helps us envision Green. *Glossy* also provides instant visualization for us as readers. As writers, we want to do just that: provide our readers with visualization. We also want to appeal to the other senses (hearing, touch, taste). In brief, we want our readers to enter into the world we are sharing with them.

Using the following information from "Renaissance Man," write a paragraph about Tim Green that allows the reader to know Green better. Add your own words to liven things up, but keep the portrait of Green as true as possible to these facts.

Green has written a novel. Its title is *Ruffians.* The novel tells what pro football is really like. It's not published yet.

Green comments on pro football for National Public Radio. He writes a weekly column for the *Syracuse Herald-Journal* during the football season. Green uses a laptap computer during flights to road games.

Green writes well and with feeling. He shows a side of football fans rarely see. There is stress and anxiety. There is love and hate. There is human drama. It's not all anguish.

Green has finished two years of law school at Syracuse University. He'd like to be a trial lawyer. He says he loves reading and writing.

Practice 2

David Gelman, a writer for *Newsweek,* wrote about professional football injuries. In the following article, Gelman uses very specific words to describe what happens. Underline those which provide us with a vivid picture, especially of actions.

THE MOST DANGEROUS GAME

David Gelman

It was a good thing for Kansas City Chiefs quarterback Dave Kreig that he moved out of the pocket at the last moment—and as it turned out, a terrible thing for Jet defensive end Dennis Byrd. As Byrd and teammate Scoot Mersereau thundered toward Kreig like two runaway freight trains on a collision course, the quarterback stepped forward ever so slightly—just enough so that Byrd rammed headfirst into Mersereau's formidable sternum. Byrd doesn't remember what happened next, but when he came to moments later, he told worried doctors he could move his arms a little and his legs not at all.

Football players put their bodies on the line, and injuries of all kinds come with the turf they fight for. This season alone several hundred players have been shoved, shouldered or butted out of action.

Practice 3

Choose someone whom you follow, either admire or dislike, from the world of sports or music. Write a brief paragraph about that person. Try to capture this person through striking words and phrases. In your first draft, just get the ideas down. Then go back and revise the sentences for clarity, vividness, and the like. Remember:

> Who or what is this sentence about?
>
> What details would help the reader see or understand this person more clearly?
>
> How can sensory details, those appealing to sight, sound, and touch in particular, help convey the image you want?

Brainstorm words on the following lines. Then work with your group or writing partner to refine the list.

_____

_____

_____

_____

DELETING WORDS AND PHRASES

Besides expanding sentences, we sometimes have to do the opposite—cut them down. Taking out the "deadwood" is another important step in revising sentences. Deadwood is any word or phrase that can be removed without any loss in meaning. For example:

> In today's society the average teenager will find that there are few jobs available unless some advanced schooling has been taken.

What's the main idea in this sentence? What's essential?

> Today's teenagers will need advanced schooling for most jobs.

Now try this one:

> In my opinion, there are many reasons why I believe we should attend this upcoming tournament in the next few weeks.

Cross out nonessential words or repetitions. Then rewrite the sentence:

_____

_____

And this:

> It is my belief that it is a matter of great importance for a student to plan a schedule for one semester in order to get prepared for all the work and exams.

_____

_____

Another common piece of deadwood occurs in sentences starting with "It is" or "There is." For example:

> There were four problems that caused the flight delay.
> Four problems caused the flight delay.
>
> It was the chili dog that caused me to get sick.
> The chili dog caused my sickness.
> This chili dog made me sick.

PRACTICE: Deleting

Practice 1

Cut the deadwood out of these sentences:

1. It was early in the morning when the sun was just coming up when I saw the neighbor's dog.

_____

2. There were a couple of kids playing in the yard.

_____

3. It is my opinion that women still don't have the kind of equity in pay that men have.

_____

4. There are too many barriers that keep women who are qualified out of the very top corporate jobs.

_____

5. I am of the belief that the school term is excessively long and lasts too late in the year.

_____

6. He responded that I should spend it on something special that I would never usually spend money on.

_____

7. Seeing that there were no other seats on the bus Ella was forced to sit next to the young man who seemed odd.

_____

8. In today's society, I myself find too many choices of things I might do.

_____

More Deadwood

Certain phrases are always deadwood. Recognizing them gives you an immediate start on deletion:

the reason being that	because
due to the fact that	because
for the reason that	because
in spite of the fact that	despite

Jeff lost the scholarship, the reason being that he broke his leg.
Jeff lost the scholarship because he broke his leg.

Jean lost the scholarship in spite of the fact that she had good grades.

Jean lost the scholarship despite her good grades.

Occasionally Deadwood: Passive Sentences

Passive and *active* can describe sentences as well as people.

Active   The first baseman threw the ball to the catcher.

Passive   The ball was thrown by the first baseman to the catcher.

If you're thinking that there is action in the passive sentence, you're right. However, the "doer" of that action is set off in a phrase rather than directly acting. The result is a longer, less clear sentence.

Passive sentences can be useful when we don't know who the doer is, or for some reason, do not wish to indicate who the doer is.

The law was supported by several important, unnamed jurists.

The car was smashed sometime between midnight and dawn.

Passive sentences, usually, are longer and far less clear than active ones. For that reason, most of our sentences should be active ones.

Practice 2

Turn these passive sentences into active ones. You may add or subtract words.

1. Her hair was braided by her mother.

   _____

2. The books were handed over to the new students by the principal.

   _____

3. The vandalism was done by three kids who had been suspended.

   _____

4. The football was caught by the wide receiver at the last moment.

_____

5. The exam was graded by the substitute teacher.

_____

6. That awful decision was made by the Mayor's Commission.

_____

7. John was run over by the Frito-Lay Potato Chip truck yesterday.

_____

8. The results were announced by the Pentagon's spokesman.

_____

9. I had been seen by my folks at the movies.

_____

10. The artwork was taken down by the principal.

_____

Many sentences require adding words or phrases to make them clearer and more effective. However, many other sentences require fewer words to achieve the same effect. We have to eliminate words that don't contribute to the sentence's meaning or that repeat what we've already said. At this point, you may be wondering why we add words only to face deleting some later. That's a good question, and the best way to understand the use of these two processes is to consider revision as experimentation with words. We want our sentences to say what we mean—and achieving that purpose takes experimenting with words and phrases. By experimenting, trying out different words or phrases, you'll learn when to add and when to delete. Ask yourself if you really need all those words. Ask yourself if there is a better word to express your meaning. Revising sentences requires time and concentration, but the end result is worth it—your intended meaning comes through.

CHAPTER 13

Editing Sentences

When we revise sentences, we are concerned with making them clearer, more easily understood by our readers; we also want to improve their "punch." Readers appreciate active, vivid sentences and a sharp focus on the idea being presented. When we edit, however, we turn our attention to making our sentences correct; we make them conform to Standard Written American English. Despite the fact that every language and dialect is equally useful and important as a communication system, most languages have a standard form that is taught in school and used in the workplace. In those settings, teachers and employers expect the standard form, and when they don't find it, they get annoyed and even stop reading. Thus, in order for our written thoughts to be taken seriously, we have to use Standard Written American English. Editing is the process that allows us to do so. Although we may make some corrections as we draft or revise, editing should be considered the final process in readying our text for a reader. Editing too early in the writing process could be a waste of time, mainly because the edited sentences could be deleted in the revising process.

GENERAL EDITING STRATEGIES

You need to develop your personal approach to editing. However, knowing a few general strategies can help you be systematic about the process. Some students use the following:

1. Reading the essay aloud, slowly and deliberately. There's considerable difference between reading silently and aloud, and

many students catch their errors when they switch to an oral reading.

2. Using a ruler or a piece of paper to force a slow and careful reading of each sentence. We can skim right over sentences we have written, and the tendency to do so lessens when only one or two sentences are visible.

3. Reading "backward" from the end to the start of the piece. This action forces us to concentrate on a single sentence.

4. Writing a note on the top of each page of the draft: "Check for _____." It's easy to overlook certain errors, so the note serves as a reminder.

5. Using an error log. Data from the log can be applied to the next writing task. We can anticipate places where we are likely to make errors, and then check the piece for those errors. What most students find is a pattern: they tend to make certain kinds of errors. It's usually comforting to see the log: students know they are making fewer errors than they thought; they can zero in on errors giving them the most trouble; and they can refer to something concrete as a guide to editing.

SAMPLE LOGS

Error	Correction	Cause of Error
There is plenty of boys	There are	Starting with there
The boys, they knew	The boys knew	Repeating oral pattern

Type of Error	Examples	Probable Cause	How to Correct
Apostrophe	Idea's value	Not think of ownership unless person	Check for ownership

You'll find that the time and attention given to maintaining logs pays off. Writing becomes easier when we have definite strategies to help us revise and edit, as well as specific areas where we know we tend to make mistakes.

SUBJECTS AND VERBS

Before looking at some of the problems that occur with subjects and verbs, we need to review briefly just what we mean by the terms *subject* and *verb*.

Subject

When we talk about the subject of a sentence, we are taking note of *who* or *what* that sentence is about:

Who	Jon (a specific person)
Who	neighbor, boxer, athlete (person)
What	cat, pencil (concrete things)
What	idea, value (abstract things)

Jon left the car running. (Who left it running?)

That athlete is a jerk. (Who's the jerk?)

My cat is a nuisance. (What's the nuisance?)

His idea was the best. (What was the best?)

Their values are really different. (What's different?)

Verb

When we talk about the verb of a sentence, we are taking note of what the subject does, is, or has. We are saying something about the subject: "What about _____?"

Does	Jon runs marathons. (What does Jon do?)
	That athlete competes nationally. (What does that athlete do?)
Is	My cat is classy. (What is my cat? What about that cat?)
	Their ideas are welcome. (What about their ideas?)
Has	Their plans have merit. (What do the plans have? What about the plans?)

Examine these sentences:

The kid in the last desk seems tired.

Who or what are we talking about? What is the key word?
What about this kid? What information do we get?

That information is practically useless.

Who or what are we talking about?
What about it?

Playing basketball can be fun.

What are we talking about? And what about it?

Mel runs the best marathon in the city.

Who? What does he do?

Verbs that show physical or mental action are usually easy to pick out: *run, talk, hit, think, believe,* and so on. Verbs that act as connectors (that is, have no action) sometimes are a bit more difficult to spot: *is, are, were, seem.* However, if you keep in mind that we need information on both "who or what" and "what happened," you'll keep the sentence sense.

Subject-Verb Agreement

In Standard Written English, the subject and verb must agree in number—singular to singular and plural to plural.

$$s \quad v$$
The boy sings too loudly.

$$s \quad v$$
The boys sing too loudly.

$$s \quad v$$
The idea is really good.

s   v

The ideas are really good.

One of the obvious problems for many speakers is the way in which English uses -*s*. We use it on nouns to indicate a plural and on verbs to indicate singular! Students who are learning English as a second language usually have to make subject-verb agreement an editing check for themselves.

Some American dialects, notably Black English, don't require subject·verb agreement. Because our home languages are automatic, speakers of other dialects often need to check on this feature of Standard Written English. Making a shift from automatic to deliberate and conscious takes concentration, so an editing check is usually needed.

Because we write more complex sentences as we mature, anyone can lose agreement between subjects and verbs. By the time we get to the end of the sentence, we may have lost track of the subject. And that's okay. In the editing process, we have a chance to double-check our text and correct any errors in subject-verb agreement.

Strategies for Subject-Verb Agreement

1. As a general rule, ignore words separating the subject and verb. Usually, they don't count in terms of subject-verb agreement.

s   v

The man [in the back seat] is my dad.

One [of the roses] looks dead.

The boy [who bit me] left.

2. Ignore word groups beginning with the following:

about	before	in	through
above	below	into	to
across	beside	near	under
after	between	of	upon
among	by	off	with
around	down	on	within
at	from	over	

These words are called *prepositions*. They are very handy for providing us with description and specific information about someone or something. Note how they work:

The box near the sink is pretty heavy. (Which box?)

Jon is playing under the table. (Where?)

The house around the corner is being torn down. (Which house?)

Some member of Congress is under attack. (Of what?)

Dr. Paul's lectures on astrophysics are beyond me. (On what?)

The key word in each of these sentences (the subject), however, comes before the preposition:

box is

Jon is playing

house is

member is

lectures are

Asking "Who or what is this really about?" or "Who or what is doing something?" will keep you on track with finding the subject. Being aware of the preposition will help too. Don't try to memorize them though. You can always refer to the list when you edit.

The other word groups that separate subjects and verbs are these:

who	The boy *who lost his coat* is crying.
which	My coat, *which is too long*, is ugly.
that	The beer *that sits too long* goes flat.

One more special problem involves *-ing* words:

The coat *lying on that chair* is mine.

The box *sitting next to the desk* is yours.

The man *fixing the TV* will charge me $100.

Again, asking "Who or what is this all about?" helps isolate the key word, the subject of the sentence.

3. Remember the only time we have to add *-s* or *-es* to make a verb agree with its subject occurs in the present—not the past or the future. If the subject is singular (one), add *-s* or *-es* to the verb:

The test stinks!

This machine crunches numbers for me.

Allen runs too much.

If the subject is plural (more than one), leave the verb alone:

Tests stink!

These machines crunch numbers for me.

Allen and Paul run too much.

4. We have a parallel to the *-s* rule in some heavily used verbs, such as *to be* and *to have:*

Singular   is   was   has   (all end in *-s*)

Plural   are   were   have

The form for *you* is always plural, no matter what.

You (one person) are right.

You (more than one person) are not telling the truth.

You (one person) have the personality for it.

You (more than one person) have a lot of nerve.

The form for *I* is unique.

I am ready for the test.

I have the right page.

PRACTICE: Subject and Verb

Practice 1

Supply the correct form of the verb:

1. The baby in the crib (scream) _____ every night.

2. Those kids from La Crosse (run) _____ the marathon every year.

3. The guys in the apartment next door (play) _____ the stereo at full blast all night.

4. Those girls near the elevator (seem) _____ approachable.

5. Dr. Lyon's lectures on math continually (bore) _____ me.

6. The house between mine and the corner (shed) _____ paint.

7. The pages within that book (sell) _____ because of photos.

8. Some colleges in the Midwest (draw) _____ students from every part of the United States.

9. Singing in the choir every day (take) _____ time.

10. Working at McDonald's on weekends (give) _____ some financial freedom.

Reversing Order

The usual pattern for subjects and verbs in English sentences is the subject before the verb:

       S   *V*
My neighbor chases his dog every night.

         S   *V*
That idea is pretty weird.

       S   *V*
Sailing is a great sport.

However, we sometimes reverse that order:

                      V   *S*
Sitting on the window were ten bottles.

           V   *S*
There were ten bottles on the window.

         V   *V*
Here are the books.

When we start a sentence with *there* or *here*, the subject will follow the verb. When you check for subject and verb agreement, then, you will be searching in reverse order. Keep in mind that *there* and *here* are introductory words, not subjects.

Compound Subjects

When we have a compound subject, we have to pay attention to the connecting word:

       S   *S* *V*
The old man and his son were hurt in the accident.

    S   *S*   *V*
Rain and sleet made the roads icy.

    S   *S*   *S* *V*
Dogs, cats, and ponies are the featured animals.

And indicates a plural subject. Therefore, we need a plural verb.
Or indicates a singular subject. We are talking about one or the other, not both. Therefore, we need a singular verb.

The teacher *or* the lawyer writes the script.

Snow *or* sleet makes travel impossible.

A party *or* a basketball game consumes Jim's time.

and = both	Use a plural verb
or = one	Use a singular verb

Repeating the Subject

When we speak, we sometimes repeat words, including our subject. In the context of conversation, some repeating makes sense and may help the listener. Moreover, in some languages and American dialects, repetition of the subject of a sentence is the normal pattern and expected. However, in Standard Written English, repeating the subject is considered an error.

Jon he left at noon.

That *girl* next door *she* has a hot car.

My *teacher,* who never shuts up, *he's* a real bore.

That *movie,* you know, the one with Madonna, *it's* wild.

If your oral language uses the repeating subject pattern, you'll need an edit check for this feature.

Practice 2

Circle the correct verb.

1. There (is/are) at least 15 students signed up.
2. Here (is/are) the test you asked for.
3. Lying on the davenport (is/are) 20 beer bottles.
4. Across the street (was/were) the fire station and police headquarters.
5. Classes and work (take/takes) all the time I have.
6. The teacher or his assistant (mark/marks) the exams.
7. Jon or Ellen (take/takes) the boxes to the dump.
8. Physics and mathematics (is/are) two areas I avoid.

Checking Verb Tenses

When we write, we have to be consistent about time. Usually, we stick to *present or past* throughout a single piece of writing. We have to have a very good reason to switch from one to another, or we risk losing our reader. *Present* refers to what is happening right now or what usually happens, habitually. *Past* refers to what has already happened.

Too much beer causes trouble.

Too much beer caused trouble.

ENGLISH VERB TENSES		
Tense	**Example**	**When to Use**
Present	Alice likes Paul. He eats slowly.	Present time Habitual action
Past	Alice liked Paul.	Action completed/over.
Future	Alice will like Paul.	Action after present
Present Perfect	Alice has liked Paul.	Action began in past but continues
Past Perfect	Alice had liked Paul, but she left him.	Action completed before second action in past
Future Perfect	Alice will have dated Alec for two months.	Action from present to future/continuing

Forming Past Tense.   The past tense in English indicates that the action or condition is over. The most common way of indicating past tense is the addition of *-ed* or *-d* to the verb:

She talked for an hour.

They required a written application.

However, we do have English verbs that do not follow this pattern. These verbs, called *irregular*, change their spelling.

> I knew the answer.
>
> Ellen rang the doorbell.
>
> I spoke to her yesterday.

If you are not sure whether a verb adds *-ed* or changes form altogether, check the dictionary. Look up the present-tense form of the verb; the dictionary will list forms (present, past, and past participle) of each irregular verb.

The *past participle* is a verb form heavily used in English. It expresses actions or conditions that began in the past but are still in progress. The past participle is used after the helping verb:

Main verb:	I have a book in my locker.
Helping verb + past participle:	I have spoken to him about it.
Main verb:	I had the answer right.
Helping verb + participle:	I had learned the entire lesson.

The past participle of most English verbs is formed by adding *-ed* to the present form, just as we do to get the past verb form:

Past:	I walked the entire course.
Past participle:	I have walked the entire course.

However, many of our irregular verbs have different forms for past and past participle:

Past:	I saw the teacher yesterday.
	Jon tore up the test.
Past participle:	I have seen the teacher.
	Jon has torn up the test.

Note: Check your dictionary for the correct spelling of the past and past participle forms. In written work, you will be expected to use the Standard Written English form.

Problems with "-ed" Endings.   Sometimes we drop off the *-ed* endings when we speak, especially in casual conversations. Our listeners don't mind because the sounds blend together:

> I use to visit the library every week. (used)
>
> I was suppose to do the laundry. (supposed)

You might have noticed that the word following the verb started with a consonant. When this combination occurs, we find it hard to distinguish *use* from *used.* Most of us don't even notice the missing *-ed* ending, nor do we have any trouble understanding that the verb refers to past.

In Standard Written English, however, we have no such leeway. We must write the standard form of the past tense and past participle. When you edit, you'll need to check your verbs for *-ed* and *-d* endings.

PRONOUNS

We use pronouns to vary our writing. Without them, we would be forced to repeat the same word again and again through a piece of writing.

> Jon isn't here. Jon is working.
>
> College is different than I expected; college is harder.
>
> I liked the pizza. The pizza didn't have too much sauce.
>
> Jon isn't here. He's working.
>
> College is different than I expected; it's harder.
>
> I liked the pizza. It didn't have too much sauce.

Pronouns, then, are very useful. When we use them, however, we have to make sure they agree with the word they replace and represent—singular to singular and plural to plural.

> If students miss class, they'll risk failing.
>
> Valentine's Day has charm all of its own.

Singular	Plural	How Used
I	we	Subjects—actor
you	you	
he, she, it	they	
me	us	Objects—receiver
you	you	
him, her, it	them	
mine	ours	Possessives—owner
yours	yours	
his, hers, its	theirs	

Standard Written English has distinct slots for pronouns:

Subject   I took the bait.

Object   Milo gave me the bait.

Possessive That bait is mine.

For most people, the problem with getting the right pronoun in the right sentence slot occurs when there is a compound subject:

Kyle and him are coming over tonight.

He runs faster than me.

A subject pronoun, *he*, is needed in the first sentence, and because speech patterns may suggest that *him* and *me* are correct, we need to double-check.

With subject pronouns, mentally erase the other subject:

him are coming

Most native speakers of English would catch the problem at this point. However, speakers with different home languages may need to consult the list of subject pronouns.

The second sentence, "He runs faster than me," is more bothersome. It sounds right to most of us. If we completed the sentence with what is implied, though, we find the problem:

He runs faster than *I do*.

He runs faster than *me do*.

So again some mental deleting and adding will help solve the problem.

PRACTICE: Pronouns

Practice 1

Place an appropriate pronoun in these sentences:

1. Jan and _____ are coming to the party tonight.

2. Please give the pizza to Paul and _____.

3. I know I can do better than _____.

4. _____ and I plan to do that work today.

5. If that book is yours, this is _____.

6. Alex gave Leo and _____ the tickets.

7. The car lost _____ wheel cover.

8. Ellen always runs better than _____ in the 400 relay.

9. Jeff and _____ planned the party last night.

10. You know you can figure that out faster than _____.

Avoiding Sexist Language

Besides needing agreement in number (singular or plural) with the word they stand for, pronouns must also agree in gender (male, female, neutral). This requirement brings up a special problem: sexist language. Prior to the feminist movement, writers used the male pronoun when referring to someone who could be male or female. Today this practice is considered sexist, implying that women either aren't important or don't exist. Sexism can work in reverse as well. For example, using a female pronoun when referring to a nurse implies that there are no male nurses. Some writers try to use plural forms whenever possible, thus avoiding the he/she distinction. In any case, check your pronouns as part of your editing process. Trace each pronoun back to the word it stands for.

Male:	he, him, his
Female:	she, her, hers
Neutral:	it, its
Male-female:	he or she, his or hers
	they, them, their, theirs

Practice 2

Use an appropriate pronoun (or two) in these sentences:

1. The police officer looked at _____ records.

2. A football coach has to watch out for _____ team.

3. The committee asked _____ members to do some studying.

4. The flight attendant lost _____ keys in flight.

5. The class gave _____ response in writing.

6. The school board based _____ decision on the facts.

7. Jo and Ellen said the problem is _____.

8. The basketball team lost _____ first-place ranking.

A Special Set of Pronouns: Indefinites

You're probably unaware of how often you use a special set of pronouns:

everyone	anything	neither
everybody	anyone	every
everything	anybody	nobody
something	each	none
somebody	either	nothing

When you use these pronouns as the subject of a sentence, use a *singular* verb. One of the problems in remembering this rule lies in how we often use them to mean many people; some of these pronouns are *psychologically plural*. Grammatically, however, they are all singular.

Everyone in the room was happy with the outcome.

Everybody contributes to the project.

Anybody is welcome to join.

Neither runs very fast.

Each of the toys has some merit.

Practice 3

Complete the sentence. Remember these pronouns take a singular verb. Stay in the present tense.

1. Anyone _____ welcome to attend the meeting.

2. Someone _____ responsible for the error.

3. Everybody _____ coming to the party tonight.

4. Every kid in school _____ in the school cafeteria.

5. Nothing _____ right when Sara's in charge.

6. None of the students _____ in the room then.

7. Neither _____ good etiquette at the supper table.

8. Something _____ happening tonight.

Note: When we separate the subject pronoun from its verb, as in the last example, it's easy to get confused. Remember that the words coming between the subject and its verb have no effect on the correct form of verb, singular or plural.

Each (singular) of the toys has (singular) some merit.
Neither (singular) of the boys seems (singular) well suited for the job.

The following pronouns may be either singular or plural; it all depends on the meaning of your sentence:

some   none   any   most

None of the boxes are the right size.
Some of the pages are missing.
Some of the ink is smeared.

A final special rule: When you join two or more subjects with *or* or *nor,* you will use the subject closest to the verb as the determining factor for singular or plural.

Neither my sister nor her friends like the outfits.
Neither her friends nor my sister likes the outfits.

Either that box or those crates are okay.
Either those crates or that box is okay.

Matching Pronoun with Pronoun

Just as we have to be concerned with pronouns agreeing with their verbs, we also have to check that indefinite pronouns are correctly matched with other pronouns. We use indefinite pronouns when we don't know names or simply want to be more general in our discussion. As noted earlier, the indefinite pronouns are singular; therefore, they require a singular pronoun:

Everyone in the cafeteria was throwing his or her books.
Anyone caught throwing food will have his or her activities taken away for the week.

Matching Pronouns with Collective Nouns

A collective noun—words like *team, family, group, committee, class, army*—requires a singular pronoun whenever the noun refers to a single unit, a group.

The team has lost its tickets.

My family takes its vacations in warm places.

If, however, you are referring to individual members of that unit, you would use a plural pronoun.

Practice 4

Match the subject pronoun with an appropriate form of the verb.

1. Either the blue dress or red suit (is/are) _____ workable.

2. None of those books (is/are) _____ very good.

3. Each of the tests (shows/show) _____ promise.

4. Everyone in the room (has/have) _____ contributed something.

5. Nobody ever (tells/tell) _____ me anything.

6. Either the books or the stereo (has/have) _____ to go first.

7. Neither the rain nor snow (stops/stop) _____ the mail.

8. Neither my brother nor my sisters (is/are) _____ here.

9. The team (has/have) _____ lost the game.

10. My class (takes/take) _____ all day for the trip.

Pronoun Antecedent

Pronouns have to agree in number (singular/plural) with the word they stand for:

The boys lost their books on that trip.

The neighbor boy lost his books on that trip.

The cat found its box in the basement.

In short and uncomplicated sentences, we can usually make the connection easily. Many of our sentences, however, are fairly complex. Then, keeping track of pronouns becomes an editing task.

If *students* insist on missing the 8:00 A.M. class, and then ask for makeup work, *they* will have to see the dean.

Because of *its* prestige and power, the American Heart *Association* is able to raise millions of dollars for *its* research.

Keep gender problems and collective nouns in mind as you work with pronouns.

Practice 5

Circle the noun that the pronoun must agree with. Then fill in the blank with the appropriate pronoun.

1. For Christians, the Christmas season has (its/their)

   _____ own rites associated with religion.

2. The record industry did not want government interference;

   (it/they) _____ preferred to monitor the issues.

3. Several members of that fraternity volunteer (his/their)

   _____ time for community service work.

4. The ski club will hold (its/their) _____ dance next week.

5. Every year violent crimes against women rise; however, (it/they)

_____ may only be a reflection of the increase in reported crimes.

6. Unlike many colleges, my school still requires English as part of

(its/their) _____ graduation requirement.

7. Watching the duck swim to shore, I began to wonder if something

were wrong with (its/their) _____ feet.

8. The performers on *Saturday Night Live* had a great time with polit-

ical candidates, exaggerating (his or her/their) _____
personal mannerisms.

Practice 6

Rewrite these sentences, correcting pronoun errors:

1. Even if one does not lose their license, the violation will cost
   money.

   _____

   _____

2. The youngest child can take advantage of learning from their older
   brothers and sisters.

   _____

   _____

3. When the oldest child gets a D, they want to hide it from parents.

   _____

   _____

4. Not only does it help the relationship but this sharing has also been good for us.

_____

_____

5. He likes to do this mainly because of the recognition they receive in the process.

_____

_____

6. Most colleges will not look at an athlete, no matter how good they are, unless they have halfway decent grades.

_____

_____

CHAPTER 14

Mechanics: Punctuation, Capitalization, Spelling

APOSTROPHES

Quite a few generations of students have hoped that the apostrophe would drop out of use, but it's still with us. We use it for two reasons: to show possession and to make contractions.

Showing Possession

Possession means ownership: Someone or something "owns" someone or something else. We can understand this relationship easily enough when "someone or something" is concrete, a person owning an object, for example:

Jon's hat is ten sizes too large.

The girl's dress is torn.

The process is a bit more difficult when something is not concrete, when we can't see it:

Paul's ideas are good ones.

That child's attitude needs adjustment.

The coach's stupidity lost the game.

We have to visualize this relationship as "owns" or "of":

> The stupidity of the coach

And we have a bit more trouble when both the "owner" and "what's owned" are less immediately visible and concrete:

> The idea's value was questionable.
> The organization's ideals got lost.
> Our society's attitudes have changed.

Once we have decided who or what is doing the possessing, we simply add -'s to that word. We could think of the -'s as replacing *of the* and saving us time and space.

PRACTICE: Apostrophes

Practice 1

Use an apostrophe to show ownership:

1. the rights of the student _____

2. the liberation of the people _____

3. the conclusion of the committee _____

4. the talent of the team _____

5. the usefulness of the idea _____

6. the decision of the teacher _____

7. the merit of his work _____

8. the antics of the star _____

9. the flaws of the contract _____

10. the cell of the plant _____

So far, we have been working with singular words. But what if the word is plural and already has an -*s*? If it does have the -*s* as its last letter, simply add the apostrophe:

The boys' coats were thrown on the floor.

The horses' harnesses were torn.

He listened to the workers' complaints.

The uniforms' logos had to be changed.

Practice 2

Rewrite with the apostrophe:

1. the problems of the workers _____

2. the voices of the teachers _____

3. the skins of the rattlesnakes _____

4. the software of the computers _____

5. the books of the students _____

6. the appetites of the wrestlers _____

7. the beliefs of the Muslims _____

8. the noise of the agitators _____

9. the fare wars of the airlines _____

10. the interdependence of the companies _____

So far, so good. But some words form their plurals without adding an -*s*:

man   men
child   children
woman   women

And some keep the same form, singular or plural:

sheep

deer

There aren't many of these oddities in English, and in any case, we follow the same rule:

To Show Possession:

If the word showing ownership does not end in -s, add 's.
If the word showing ownership already ends in -s, add the apostrophe only.

The man's hat was stolen.
The men's club meets tonight.

The child's toy is too expensive.
The children's stories are wonderful.

The sheep's coat is ready to cut.
The sheep's coats are ready to cut.

Los Angeles' smog is world famous.
Ray Charles' Pepsi commercials brought a ton of money.

Practice 3

Show ownership with the following words. You'll have to add whatever it is that they "own."

1. Jimmy Conners _____

2. Rolling Stones _____

3. women _____

4. freshman _____

5. Los Cerritos _____

6. lemons _____

7. rug _____

8. CD _____

9. children _____

10. freshmen _____

A note about a different kind of possessive:

The book is *yours.*
His ideas are old-fashioned.
Their car is unreliable.

The pronouns showing possession have *no* apostrophe. The word itself indicates ownership.

Contractions

Another common use of the apostrophe occurs in contractions. When we use a contraction, we are using a shortcut. We omit a letter or two and push two words together where we have omitted letters:

she is   she's
I will not   I won't
you have   you've
do not   don't

In most college and business writing, however, we usually write out the complete words—no contractions. In personal letters and other informal writing, we can use them.

COLON

The colon (:) can give versatility to your writing. Examine the following sentences, and note the relationship between the sentence before the colon and the word group that follows it.

My brother has some weird exercises: hanging from trees, wrapping his body around poles, and swinging from lights.

I got the shock of my life: my roommate was reading my mail.

In the 1980s, people had one goal: making money.

World problems are serious: starvation in Somalia, civil war in the former Yugoslavia, and confrontation between the Arab and Western worlds.

Don't forget to check this list: soup, pizza, candy, soda pop, and beer.

What does the colon do? You might have noticed that it takes the place of saying, "I'll tell you what. . . ." For example, "the shock of my life" *is* the roommate snooping in mail; "the goal" *is* making money; and world problems *are* the situations described after the colon. Colons make our writing efficient and easy to follow. We can provide lists, descriptions, and explanations clearly and economically.

Note the following:

Before the colon, we have a complete sentence.

Do not use a colon right after the verb.

After the colon, we can have any structure—a complete sentence, a single word, or word groups.

PRACTICE: Colons

With your group, set up some lists:

1. Jobs you'd like
2. Jobs you'd hate
3. Favorite foods
4. People you admire
5. Places you want to travel
6. Television shows you hate the most
7. Classes you want to avoid
8. Movies everyone should see

Create sentences that use a colon. Be sure to use a complete sentence before the colon.

COMMAS

Separating Items in a Series

In academic or business writing, use a comma to separate three or more words or word groups in a sentence:

Gum, popcorn, and candy bars are high-priced at the movies.

Jon was running, hopping, and skipping.

May, June, July, and August are best for travel.

Note: If you have three items, two commas; if you have four items, three commas; and so on. In brief, use one less comma than the number of items you are separating.

Separating Places and Dates

Within a sentence, separate the city from the state and the state from the rest of the sentence:

I've been visiting San Diego, California, for ten years now.

Also separate the parts of a street address:

Send it to 1500 West Park Place, Chicago, IL 60618.

Note: Do not separate the state from its zip code.

Separate the following parts of a date:

He will return on January 15, 1994, if everything goes as planned.

Note: Do not separate the month from the day.

Using Commas with Modifiers

In the sections on coordination and subordination, we reviewed the use of commas with modifiers. Briefly, here are the rules once more:

Use a comma to separate introductory material from the main sentence:

Listening to Paul, I got a headache.
According to the manual, the plug goes here.

Use a comma to separate words or word groups that provide an extra bit of information. This information may be good, but it is not essential. If we pull it out, the main sentence can stand alone and expresses the same meaning.

My brother, who's a bit of a pest, is only six.
Jon Landen, the best swimmer on the team, dropped out.
I gave the book to Ellen, my best friend.

Contrast the preceding sentences with this one:

The girl who ate the ants got sick.

Who got sick? Any girl? We need "who ate the ants" to provide the identification, to know just which girl we are discussing. Therefore, no commas are needed.

QUOTATION MARKS

Direct Quotations

We use quotation marks to set off someone's exact words:

The coach of the Dallas Cowboys said, "We win because we love each other."
"We win because we love each other," said the coach of the Dallas Cowboys.

Note: The comma sets off the speaker from what is said.

We use quotation marks only when we quote directly, the exact words, of the speaker. Here is an indirect quote:

The coach of the Dallas Cowboys said that they win because they love each other.

No quotation marks are used because it is an indirect quotation.

Punctuation with Quotation Marks

Place periods and commas within the closing quotation mark:

The coach said, "You guys are the greatest."
The players said, "We know we are."
"You're supposed to be more modest," said the coach.

Place colons and semicolons outside of the closing quotation marks:

My math teacher said, "This assignment will take only an hour"; however, he later added, "for most of you."

Place question marks, exclamation points, and dashes inside of the closing quotation mark when they are part of the quoted material:

My math teacher asked, "Will each of you take one problem?"
My English teacher said, "This is the greatest class!"

However, if these marks are part of a larger sentence and not part of the directly quoted material, the marks go outside:

What does the math teacher mean by "one problem"?

Titles

Use quotation marks to set off the following titles:

Short stories	I read "The Frozen Tundra" yesterday.
Poems	He likes Robert Frost's "The Road Not Taken."
Magazine articles	"Too Old, Too Fast?" in *Newsweek* suggests high school kids shouldn't work.
Chapters of books	You should read "The Love Connection" in *Growing Up Male.*
Songs	"You've Got That Loving Feeling" was used in the sound track of the film *Top Gun.*

> **Note:** In academic and business writing, titles of books, magazines, films, and videos are underlined or printed in italic type. One way to remember the rule: the shorter works use quotation marks.

CAPITALIZATION

In standard written English, we are expected to capitalize the following words:

1. The first word of every sentence, including sentences that are direct quotations within a larger sentence:

   The boy screamed, "That is the wrong car!"

2. The names of specific people, places, or groups:

   Patty Lehman visits Miami, Florida, every year.
   Some people are crazy about the Miami Dolphins football team.
   The U.S. Air Force is cutting its recruits.
   The Lakota Sioux were central to the film *Dances with Wolves.*

3. The names of specific events:

   He is a veteran of the Vietnam War, and his dad is a vet of World War II.

4. The names of specific businesses and brand names:

   Cray Research builds computers for the world.
   I had a Pepsi for lunch.
   Hand over the Milky Way bar.
   Is that a Sony?

5. The names of specific languages, religions, and organizations:

   I wish I knew what these French phrases mean.
   He says he is Hindu, but I think he's Catholic.
   The Democratic party has its headquarters downtown.

6. The names of specific courses:

    Jan is taking Math 203 this semester.
    I'm struggling with Chemistry 100.
    Take Psych 100, Introduction to Psychology.

7. The titles of books, articles, poems, songs, and artworks:

    Rising Sun explores the clash between Japanese and American ways of doing business.
    The *Mona Lisa* is one of Leonardo da Vinci's most famous paintings.
    I have to read "Ode on a Grecian Urn" for tomorrow.

PRACTICE: Capitalization

Correct the capitalization in the following sentences:

1. The reverend jesse jackson is a baptist minister who doesn't limit his congregation to a single church.

2. Reverend jackson has been involved in the civil rights movement for several decades.

3. We've been studying martin luther king, jr., and his leadership of african-americans in political science 100.

4. I've been reading malcolm x for my book report in poly sci.

5. The poetry of gwendolyn brooks, such as "we cool," is relevant today.

SPELLING

Why It Matters

English spelling can be frustrating, mainly because we represent sounds by many different combinations of letters. We don't have many useful spelling rules either. Regardless, we are expected to use standard spelling in school and the workplace. For most people, this expectation entails careful editing. Spelling errors, perhaps more than any other aspect of writing, distract and annoy readers. Further, some readers will judge the writer to be unintelligent and uneducated if spelling errors are present—no matter how good or well-developed the ideas in that piece. For this reason, checking for spelling errors is crucial.

Strategies

1. Know your typical errors. Keep a spelling log.

Word	Misspelling	Cause or Type of Problem
definite	definate	Sounding like a
athlete	athelete	Adding a sound
site	sight	Confused sound-alike

2. Understand your own spelling error patterns. Analyze your log for recurring patterns—there'll be some.

   The following are common causes of error:

   Addition   Adding a letter because of pronouncing an additional sound (like athelete).

   Substitution   Substituting a letter for one that sounds similar (like definate).

   Deletion   Dropping a letter because it's not pronounced (like goverment instead of government).

   Confusion   Mixing up two or more sound-alike words (like there/they're/their).

   Demons   Never quite getting the number of double letters right (like necesary instead of necessary).

   Reversals   Interchanging letters (like recieve for receive).

3. Use your personal spelling demon list for editing. Careful reading and the use of a computer spell-check program will help you most. One caution, however: The spell checker cannot distinguish the

sound-alike words or errors that result in another acceptable English word.

4. Use a dictionary. If you have trouble with the first letters of the word, ask someone for help.

5. Develop your own methods for remembering problem words.

6. Keep spelling in its correct place: at the end of the drafting and revising processes.

PRACTICE: Sentence Boundaries and Other Punctuation

Read the paragraphs slowly. Try the editing strategies discussed earlier. You may add or delete words.

A

I came home from an average day at school. Except for my mom was crying and packing her suit case. Great my parents had an argument and now theyre getting a divorce. Well at least thats what I thought. What was really wrong was that my grandfather who of course was an alcoholic almost all of his adult life. Was in the hospital after falling off my aunts porch, because he was too drunk to walk up the stairs. He was in a coma and the chance of him coming out of it was very slim so what was my mom upset about. Time passed with our family in ruins but every day we prayed for him to come out of the coma. A month later he finally woke up, and came out

with only partial brain damage. He understands everything you say but he can't reply since he doesn't remember how to talk. But boy he has got a great life now
he's got people to care for him all day long, he doesn't
have to work, he can eat all he wants and each day he
can get fatter and fatter until he dies. But there is
nothing we can do about it. Because alcohol has already
ruined his life.

B

Concerts come in all different types sizes and forms.
First for example there is the hard rock concert for the
people who like to get rowdy, and party. Another example
of a concert would be a jazz concert for the person, who
likes to relax and enjoy some mellow music, while eating
lunch. I think that this type of concert is the most
popular for people who think about and spend time with
their boyfriend. This type of concert would be a Lionel
Richie concert for example, because he expresses the
true feeling of love. In all the songs he sings. One
thing that some people do is that they would cut on people for example of a 50 year old man, would attend a

hard rock concert people would probably think that he

should be attending a jazz concert.

PRACTICE: Mechanics (Punctuation, Capitalization, Spelling)

Edit these paragraphs with special attention to mechanical errors:

A

I was born on february 26th. That gives me some interesting qualities. For example I'm creative and artistic. I've always known that my bad grades in my Music Drawing, and Painting classes were all the teachers fault. They just didnt see what an incredable talent they had in there classes. Linda Goodman had more things to say about me in her book Sun Signs. She could even describe the way I looked. My eyes were simply beautiful my feet a bit small and my hair was light.

B

My astrological sign is gemini as I was born on may 30. Geminis symbol is the twins and mercury is the ruling planet of this sign. In Liz Greenes Star Signs for Lovers people born under this sign are generally talkative charming witty, and extreamly unpredictible. In addition they have the attention spans of house plants. I was very surprize reading this. Although I feel my attention span is a bit longer than that of a Geranium I found Greenes analysis chillingly accurate.

PART THREE

Evaluating Writing

Many students in English or composition classes wonder just how their teachers come up with a grade, especially on an essay. The process appears to be quite subjective, especially compared to courses like math, where there is one answer, either right or wrong. The grade is calculated from numerical data—so many right, so many wrong. Composition grades, by contrast, emerge from many factors that may not be easily identified by inexperienced writers. As a result, students may get the idea that composition grades are mysterious or even unfair. In most cases, they are neither. Most teachers evaluate the essays on a set of criteria:

Content

    Controlling idea clear

    Relevant and adequate support

    Appropriate organization and transitions

Style

    Writer's voice and individuality

    Wording and phrasing

Form

    Sentence structure

    Grammar

    Punctuation

    Spelling

Additionally, teachers consider the depth of thinking about the topic. Students who present a thoughtful essay will score higher than those who are superficial. Students who show control of the essay—not mastery, but control—will score higher than those who wander off topic or have a fuzzy focus. Students who have not yet gained control of sentences or punctuation will score lower than those who have.

Teachers aren't expecting perfection, and most give students a wide berth in which to assimilate and apply new skills. Learning to write takes time and sustained practice. Nonetheless, writing must be evaluated and grades assigned.

If you have not been shown the evaluation process, you no doubt have mixed feelings about it: you understand it must be done, but you don't like it. Many teachers have mixed feelings as well. Nonetheless, evaluating and assigning grades is a responsibility they take seriously. To get a sense of just how teachers and other readers evaluate writing, you will try out the process yourself. The better you understand the criteria used in evaluation, the more easily you can use them as you revise and edit your own work.

EVALUATING STUDENT RESPONSES

Before you read the responses, you need to understand the writing task these students were given. They read a short story entitled "To Kill a King." Then, they were given a single question asking them to respond to the theme of the short story: Explain the boy's action, the "murder." The students wrote their responses within a 50-minute class period.

The main character in "To Kill a King" is a young farm boy who loves wildlife, especially birds. The boy is drawn to a majestic hawk, which becomes the focus of his life and actions. Here are excerpts from the story; they will provide you with enough information to evaluate the students' responses:

TO KILL A KING

Sue Gross

The introductory paragraphs tell of the boy's love of birds of all kinds and of his close relationship with and sensitivity to nature.

But the hawk was different. It was big, aloof, and lonely. The boy thought of how it was always alone when he saw it, far away, remote as the little stars he saw at night. He wondered if the hawk had a mate; if the hawk had a nest to come to at evening, when his side wings ached with weariness and his eyes burned from soaring all day in the sun. He would never know. He could never follow the hawk as he did the redstarts [a bird], could never be intimate with him as with the friendly cardinals. The hawk was a thing apart, unapproachable.

The boy began scanning the sky as he came near the place where he would see the hawk. He stood alert on his hilltop, waiting—watching.

It came floating down out of the east, superb and lazy and lordly. Its movements were all the grace the boy knew, all the art he ever saw. He gazed up at it, letting it be the only thing in all the vast blue sky. Then he raised his glasses, shutting the bird with him in their small circle, getting close to it in the only way he could. His neck began to ache, but while the hawk was there, he was powerless, compelled to watch it. It turned at last and pounded silently away over the far woods. The boy lowered his head, wincing with pain. He stood numbly, rubbing the crick out of his neck with his hand, remembering the hawk: the wide wings, the fanned red tail, the magnificence. He went down the wooded hill. The sparrows bounced along beside him, chattering; he did not hear them. A pewee called and called from a tree somewhere in the forest; he did not care to find it.

The next day the boy takes his rifle and, asked where he's going, says he's going hunting for squirrels, his face burning because of the lie. He climbs to the hilltop and awaits the hawk.

Wheeling, high over the trees, it spread its broad rounded wings and flashed its rust-red tail as it veered away to climb at the sun, and soared down again in long, easy spirals. Through the glasses, the boy followed the hawk's easy flight. He drank in the cruel grace, the mastery, the majesty of the bird, as he had done for days past, and it made him dizzy. He watched the hawk and thought of the gun leaning against the tree trunk! If he could bring that great brute down . . . If he could kill the hawk and tell his friends . . . He knew it wasn't a harmful bird, but it was a king, and to kill a king! He could not take his eyes off the hawk, or his mind from the gun.

He had admired the bird; now he longed to conquer it. He let the glasses drop down on his chest, and moved toward the gun. He held the gun in his hand, still looking at the bird veering over his head. He took a bullet in his fingers, loaded the gun without looking. Then once more he gave himself up to the hawk. It hung in the sky like a golden crumb in an upturned bowl. The boy raised his rifle and aimed carefully, keeping the little black dot of the sight on the hawk's streaked breast as it circled over the forest. Then his brain went white and he fired. The bird fell out of the sky like a plumb cut from the line. Marking where it crashed into the brush, the boy ejected the empty shell and walked down the steep hillside with the smoking gun over his arm.

Twigs lashed his hot face, and long, thorny vines tangled around his feet and tore at his ankles. Cobwebs stretched and broke across his mouth. He stumbled over a root, and then he heard the noise in the underbrush ahead of him. He saw the hawk thrashing in the leaves, dragging one wing on the ground and beating the other in an hysterical effort to rise. He saw the bloody hole where his bullet had torn through the hawk's shoulder. The bird's eyes were dim, its beak opened wide in terror as it clawed deep gashes in the dirt. It would rage that way all night, the boy knew, dragging itself in a pitiful circle, bashing itself to exhausted death.

The boy took another bullet from his pocket, thrust it into place, and slammed down the breech. He cocked the rifle, lowered the muzzle to the hawk's head, squeezed the trigger. The bird jerked and lay still. The boy snapped out the shell, and stood staring at the hawk's crumpled body; the torn wing, the smashed head, the dark blood soaking down through the rotten leaves. His heart hurt suddenly; tears scorched his eyelids. With the butt of his gun, he scraped a little mound of earth and leaves over the body. Then he turned away. With tears running on his dirty face, he walked through the stubbly fields. The rifle weighed a ton in his hands.

The boy's father sees him walking to the farm, quickly understands exactly what has happened, and tells his wife to forget about squirrels and dumplings for supper; in fact, he tells her to throw out the dumplings. The wife protests, and they argue about it. The father finally commands, "There'll be no talk o' squirrels or huntin' tonight," and she responds, "All this fuss over a squirrel or two." The father then says, "It ain't squirrels, Mother . . . You never been a boy . . . or done a murder."

The Writing Task

Explain the boy's action, the "murder," in "To Kill a King."

Students were expected to use information from the story to explain why the boy did what he did. If he loved birds, especially the hawk, why did he kill it?

Questions for Evaluating Student Responses

Teachers may not write out questions like these, but they are nonetheless using them "mentally." The questions are a guide to the effectiveness of the response. Keep in mind that such questions evaluate the written response; they are not questions about the short story.

1. What main point does the student writer make? Does the writer explain the boy's action?

2. How does the writer support his or her main point?

3. Does the writer provide enough support? Or does the writer leave the reader with unanswered questions? Does the writer provide good examples or details to support his or her point?

4. Is the support relevant? Or does the writer go off track somewhere, presenting information that is not needed or wrong for the writing task? Does the writer answer the question asked?

5. Does the writer's voice come through? Does the reader get a sense of a human being talking to another human being?

6. Is the response organized well? Can the reader move from idea to idea easily?

7. Is the response difficult to follow because of incomplete or illogical sentences? Is the response difficult to follow because of awkward sentences?

8. Are there errors in Standard Written American English: usage, punctuation, spelling?

9. What would the writer have to do to make his or her response clearer or more convincing?

10. Overall, what are the strengths of the response? The weaknesses?

Rating the Response

Some teachers and students use an evaluation scale to sort out the strengths and weaknesses of a piece of writing. Use the following one to evaluate each of the five responses to "To Kill A King." On this particular scale, the development of the essay is more important than anything else. The multiplication of the score turns the 45-point scale into a 100-point scale.

Scale: 1 = poor   2 = fair   3 = adequate   4 = good   5 = excellent

Content (60%)

Clear controlling idea	1	2	3	4	5
Relevant and adequate support	1	2	3	4	5
Organization and transitions	1	2	3	4	5

_____ $\times 4 =$ _____

Style (20%)

Writer's voice/individuality	1	2	3	4	5
Wording and phrasing	1	2	3	4	5

_____ × 2 = _____

Form (20%)

Sentence structure	1	2	3	4	5
Grammar	1	2	3	4	5
Punctuation	1	2	3	4	5
Spelling	1	2	3	4	5

_____ × 1 = _____

Total grade = _____%

TRYING OUT THE EVALUATION PROCESS

Most teachers first read through the piece quickly, to get an overall sense of the essay. They then do a second reading, slowly and thoughtfully, applying the evaluation criteria as they read. You can try out the process yourself on the following brief response. Then read the explanation that follows.

The boy's action for killing the bird was that he wanted to conquer it because he could only admir it from far away and he wanted to tell his friends about killing a king. After the boy killed the hawk, he started crying because he didn't really conquer the bird, he had killed it and the bird was very beautiful. The father's reaction is to leave the boy alone, he leaves the boy alone and doesn't want his wife talking about hunting because he was once a boy and had probably murdered some kind of animal.

Explanation

The student certainly has the right idea initially, but it is not expressed very clearly. The essay is not well developed either. We don't get a good sense of the boy's relationship with the hawk. The part about the father's reaction has nothing to do with the boy's motivation for killing the hawk, so it is irrelevant. The organization isn't bad, but it makes little difference since the writer failed to develop the point.

If we award the student ratings of 2, 1, 3 under "Content," the subtotal is $6 \times 4 = 24\%$ on that part.

The student's voice comes through okay, but wording and phrasing are unclear and at times quite awkward.

If we award the student ratings of 3 and 1 under "Style," the subtotal is $4 \times 2 = 8\%$ on that part.

Most of us have a combination of strengths and weaknesses in the technical aspect of writing—mainly because it takes a long time to learn how to write. This student is no exception. Quite a few of the sentences are unclear, and a couple are strung together with commas, creating errors. Sentence boundaries require a connecting word with the comma or replacement of the comma with a period or semicolon. The grammar is generally okay, though. There are a couple of punctuation errors. With one exception (the silent *e* on *admire*), the spelling is fine.

If we award ratings of 2, 3, 2, 4 under "Form," the subtotal is $11 \times 1 = 11\%$.

The total for the entire piece is 43% out of 100%. This student would have some significant revising and editing to do before the piece would be acceptable.
What positive remarks would you have for this writer?
What would you suggest for revision? Be specific.

SAMPLE RESPONSES TO "TO KILL A KING"

Even on the preceding short piece, you probably got a good sense of what evaluation is all about. Most teachers I know, including myself, are often unhappy with having to assign a grade. Sometimes it is very evident that a student has shown significant improvement, but nonetheless has not yet achieved a C. At other times, it is evident the student has produced a technically correct paper, but the essay is "empty." It has little sense of the author or of engagement with the topic. It could have been written by a robot. These situations cause real dilemmas in evaluation and the assigning of a grade. The criteria for evaluation become very important; they help teachers determine if an essay meets the standards of acceptability for academic writing.

SAMPLE 1

If you ever watch birds up close, you'll know that the beauty and grace they have is a treasure to watch. The boy was one of the constant, vivid bird watchers. It seemed he was friends with all birds of every sort, except the hawk. The hawk was a loner, and sang no songs or did any dances for the boy. It preferred to be alone in it's own domain, and was content to stay there.

The boy, on the other hand, felt possessed by it and continued to watch it for days. It didn't fit in with the other birds, and yet it was a bird. When he killed it, he killed it to prove that he was better than the hawk. But afterwards, he saw that it was just a bird like any other bird, and that the act was worthless and had no meaning. I think the father knew this when he saw his son comeing up the drive. He was a boy once and went thru the same thing. He understood the need to be alone, and not to bring up anything that might bring back the memory of the murder.

SAMPLE 2

To explain the boy's action in "To Kill A King" we are going to have to go back and look at how he viewed the hawk he shot. In the boy's eyes, the hawk was an admired bird of beauty, and through days of watching it, became attached to it. The boy regarded the hawk as the king of birds, and to shoot such a king would make the boy feel just as great. After he shot the bird, a great remorse came over him. He had lost an admired friend. When the boy came home, the father could read write through him. The father was quite sympathetic to the boys

feelings, for the father had also gone through such a
period as a boy. The father figured the boy would want to
be left alone, so the father left the boy to do chores
by himself.

SAMPLE 3

The boy had an incrediable feeling for birds. He loved
them. But what he really wanted was "the king," a hawk.

The hawk was a lonely, big, lordly beast. The boy was
powerless when watching the hawks flight. The reason for
the boy's urge in killing the hawk was to tell his
friends. If he brought the hawk down, he brought down a
king. So after viewing the flight of the hawk, he finally
shot it down. His heart was in pain. When he reached the
hawk, he decided to bury it where it laid rest. On his
arrival home, the father saw he didn't have any squirrels. Matter of fact, the father knew what the boy was
after when he departed. He knew the boy wanted the ulti-
mate: to kill a king. There feeling was rather mutual.
His father knew that killing the hawk was going to make
the boy feel power: but what it actually showed was pain
in the boy.

SAMPLE 4

The boy liked to go out to the hilltop every morning
to watch the hawk hunt the field. His father knew he
liked to do that, so he always let the boy go, after
the chours were done. One day the boy brought his .22
rifle along and his dad asked why he was bringing it.
He was haveing thoughts of shooting the hawk, but he
told his dad he might snag a few squirls for supper.
That day when the hawk flew over the boy had already
through whether he should shoot the hawk or not many
times. The hawk kept coming closer and closer until the
boy shot. When the hawk was flopping around on the
ground the boy felt bad about shooting it, and wished
he hadn't have done what he did. Had the hawk stayed

far enough away, the boy wouldn't have shot it, but
with all the excitment, wonder and unsureness the boy
shot it without thinking. Now he was suffering over it,
and would think of that hawk every time he went to the
hill. On the way home the boy slowly dragged his feet
along the dirt. From a distance the father could see
the boy had no squirls so he told his wife not to mention any to the boy because he knew the boy had killed
the hawk, or done something. The father told the boy to
do the milking himself tonight because he wanted the
boy to forget the hawk. The father figuered if the boy
could fill the rest of the day with work or something
it would help the boy forget. This was a learning expe-
riance for the boy, and the father wanted to help him
any way he could.

An evaluation of writing, whether by a teacher or peers, provides
the writer with specific information for revising and editing. The more
specific the information, the easier it is to take a hard look at our own
writing.

PRACTICE ESSAY

With your group or writing partner, evaluate the following student essays. The writing task asked students to respond to a question
parents or caregivers face: whether or not to tell children the truth
about serious family problems (e.g., impending divorce, life-threatening illness, financial trouble).

You will find two views in the essays. Keep in mind that you no
doubt have an opinion, and because of it, you have to guard against
being biased as you evaluate. You are evaluating the essay, not the
view expressed.

Review the evaluation questions. These are your criteria for judging how well the student presented and developed his or her main
point. Read the essay through once. Then return to read slowly and
carefully as you evaluate.

STUDENT ESSAY 1

How to Tell Kids a Crisis Problem

A child ranks toys, bikes, playtime, and TV time at the top of his or her list of importance. An adult on the other hand ranks job security, income and safety at the top of his or her list of importance. It is obvious that adults and children seen things differently.

Certain things like financial troubles, marital problems, life-threatening illness, and other serious matters should not be discussed with children until certain times.

I believe it is important that children learn about these things, but it is a bad time to discuss them while in the middle of a crisis. The first thing a child will do is to ask questions when told about something new. For adults trying to deal with a stressful problem, like a death in the family or money problems, a child asking questions is just added frustration. In time of a crisis, adults need their full attention on the problem at hand. If they have to take time out to explain to a child what is going on, they get even more stressed out and edgy, and the chances increase that the adult will yell at or strike the child.

I believe the best way to deal with the situation is to not tell the child what is going on during the crisis. I do believe that the child should learn about these situations, but during the crisis. A parent can take time out before or after a crisis to explain things. This will give the child a better chance to understand the problem. It would also ease any frustration of the parent if the child does not understand.

Although children are bright, some things they will not understand until they experience them. One such example is money. To a child, money is an item that comes out of mothers purse when food, toys, or candy is needed. A child does not understand how hard adults work to earn money. They can be told about crises that deal with money, but to fully understand they must experience the work required to earn the money.

Children do view things differently than adults. They should not be told about crisis problems until the adult has the time and the patience to sit down and really explain things to them.

Student Essay 2

Include the Child

Over the past few years parents have been faced with many hard problems, such as financial trouble, marriage problems, life-threatening illness, and differences with inlaws/siblings. The most popular thing for parents to do in these situations is to keep the children in the dark about what the problem is. What parents don't realize is that they may be doing more harm than good.

From the outside a child look weak but on the inside they are strong. When there are problem within the family structure, a child notices it and wants to help. If the parent allows that child to help, he/she may be able to give the parent(s) that push to keep trying, which in turn could possibly solve the problem.

Another problem if parents covering up the truth, is that children feel as though they are the cause of the problem. Children who recive this type of message tend to look elseware for the love and effection they need. Some children choose drugs and alcohol, and other seek love from the wrong people. These coping strategies are harmful to the childs health and may cause major problems, such as addiction or death.

Some people who feel that covering the child ears maybe the answer, are not giving that child a fare chance. Even if protecting the child seem like the thing to do, pleae at least talk with the child and let him/her know that they are not the problem.

When I see a child who is sent away or to his/her room because of family troubles I can only hope that he/she doesn't blame his/her self and cause problems of their own.

PART FOUR

Student Essays for Revision and Editing Practice

SHORT TAKES

SHORT ESSAY A

Did You Ever Notice a Freshman?

Let's face it freshmen stand out, they do everything wrong, nothing ever goes well for them. They run into all kinds of problems, bad situations, humilaties, put downs, and fowl language from upper class.

But did the socalled "Big Shots" on campus every figure out if they offer help and support in a nice way. They wouldn't do those fun little mistakes like, carrying their tray backward in the cafeteria, walking around the halls aimlessly or for the 3rd, 4th, and 5th time. They just watch and laugh and holler obsinaties.

All a freshman wants is to fit in, to do well and have some fun.

SHORT ESSAY B

Traditions

Family traditions is things you do over that your for fathers before you did. For example making a big dinner on a day that someone had done something special that was related to you. Another, would be always saying grace at supper before you eat. One really weird family tradition is drinking the blood of your first deer. That you shot while hunting.

SHORT ESSAY C

Concerts

Concerts are fun for all age groups. Teenagers enjoy concernts because the music is loud and everyone their is about the same age. They can act imature and no one will notice. For the middle age group they enjoy sitting around and to relax at concerts. They don't like to stand and get shoved around. Also they enjoy there music softer and more slow. The older people on the other hand like old music like classical, and jazz, but there are older people that rock and country. That goes the same with younger and middle age people. Younger people feel alive and free. Older people feel complete and self assured and middle age feel freedom and way to escape. Concerts are good for every one because a person can be themself.

SHORT ESSAY D

Jobs

Jobs have there disadvantages, but it also has many advantages. A disadvantage of having a job is that it takes up time. By this I mean that sometimes you may have to give up going to a football game because you have to work. Now some advantages are you get money, it's a great experience, you get to meet new people, and you can save your money and have lots of money for college like me. As you can see here many people would rather have a job than go to a football game or something. The job I had was a great experience for me because I met lots of people from the outside. My job also helped my speech very much because I talked to alot of people each day. My job was very hard to quite because it was such an uprising experience for me. There is also jobs that have bad experiences to. The outcome of the job all depends upon the person and the job.

SHORT ESSAY E

Jobs Teach

Jobs are an important part of growing up. I feel jobs are very necessary through out life, In that people can learn important things such as responsibility, and certain business skills. I have had several jobs, anywhere from grocery stores, fast food resteraunts, and carpentry. The fast food industry isn't all its cracked up to be. I worked in a small hamberger stand for 3 weeks before I coulnd't take it anymore. Although I learned how to cook a hamberger it really wasn't that much of a learning experience. The carpentry job helped me learn how to use tools and about taking orders, even if you don't feel there right. Lastly, my job at the grocery store has taught me alot, I've learned all about produce and how to take care of it. I also learned how to figure the percentage of profit we make from sales. I've learned responsibilty because if I don't take care of the produce they will all spoil. Jobs can teach you alot about life, and most importantly yourself.

SHORT ESSAY F

Spiking the Ball

A volleyball spike is when a player is hitting a set ball over the net. Trying to hit the ball hard so the other team cannot return the ball. The spike must be hit at the right time.

The setter sets the ball. The spiker starts his approach. First the spiker gets back to about the 10 foot line. When the ball reaches its peak. The spiker takes two steps toward the net. Then swings his arms back. Now the spiker is ready to hit the ball. He jumps as high as he can. Then hits the ball with an open hand in a downward direction.

The spiker must hit the ball with great force. So the opponent has difficulty trying to return the ball, if the ball was hit correctly. The ball will usually hit the floor or hit a player that cnanot return the ball. The ball then goes out of bounds.

PERSONAL EXPERIENCE

PERSONAL-EXPERIENCE ESSAY A

Sunday Hero

As a child, I always had fantasies of being star football player on the Green Bay Packers. Every Sunday after church I'd sit down right in front of the television to watch the Packers. I didn't budge until half-time but I always made it back for the start of the second half. Before I watched the game I made sure that I had my Green Bay Packer shirt on and I put my Packer Football on the television for good luck. As I watched these games I pictured myself being out on the field having everyone cheer for me. After the game ended my brother and me would go put our Packer helmust on and go outside to play football. We would pick a packer player that we wanted to be like and pretend we were them. However my brother who is 3 years old than me always picked the guy I wanted. On the other days of the week I collected football cards. My friends and me would trade cards once a week and of course I traded to get all the packers. I didn't stop collecting and trading until I had the starting offense and starting defense. However by the time I had the starting teams the next season was ready to begin and I would have to start over. In some of these cards I would cross out the name and put mine just hoping that someday a little kid like me would do the same on my football card I still fantasize myself being a football start on the Packers but I've settled down since my earlier days. Its funny watching my little cousin do the same things that I did but it doesn't seem like I would do such a thing.

PERSONAL-EXPERIENCE ESSAY B

The Captain

Driving into New York's Kene Valley was an artistic delight. Even though it was a crisp and cool October morning. Chris Carl and I decided the jeep top should be folded down, as not to obstruct out view of the magnificent fall colors. Mothe Nature had surely outdone herself. Colors ranged from subdued browns and rust, to flaming reds and vivid yellows. We were breathtaken as the valley drew us down to the base of the mountain. It should be an excellent day for a hike.

Upond arriving at the trail head we gather our gear and started our journey. After hiking three miles of steadily rising terrain we entered a clearing. Looking toward the moutnain we saw the "wall" facing us. The smooth pyramid like formation, was made of solid granite approximately 300 yards wide at the base, stretching to about 350 yards up, and angling 30-40 degrees. Chris thought it would be fun to leave the train to climb the face to the top. I agreed and we began our ascent.

Without ropes or other safety gear we climbed about 200 yards only the grip of our hiking boots keeps us on the smooth wall. Suddenly I slipped! Laying flat on my stomach with toes gripping I somewhat regained my composure. At that point I realized "where" I was. A flood of terror cascaded over soaking into every fiber of my soul. Shaking and distressed I clung to the side of the mountain like a kitten to a tree. I felt powerless, helpless. Was ther any escape from doom? Things seemed to get ugly quick. The mountain was no longer beautiful, the colors turned to black and white. A rush of ideas resounded through my brain. One wrong move and I could've been dead—but why would I care?

Coming from a dysfunctional family, being divorced, and feeling betrayed by the service had consumed my thoughts for months leaving me disillusioned. Constantly distracting myself I would do anything and everything to avoid confronting my feelings. Each day dying a bit inside I considered euthanasia as an option. I could just let my feet go from under me and tumble to my death relieving my pain.

Then as if by divine intervention my perspective suddenly changed! No matter how outside "demon" forces tried to defeat me, I was in charge. I had the strength. I was master over my own soul. I wanted to live! I wanted to live now more than ever, but still had to reach the top.

Indulging in new found strength, I gathered myself together, and step by step carefully ascended to the top. I had defeated the "demons" and the mountain.

After reaching the top Chris and I promptly started our decent. I noticed a set of captain's bars pinned to his jacket lapel. Both us being enlisted men, I thought it strange he don the mark of a nemesis, and was compelled to inquire. He said that honory rank was bestowed upon him during a mountain climbing expedition. Against seemingly bad odds his team overcame many obstacles to reach the apex. An officer impressed by Chris's skill gave him the bars as a token of respect.

Chris confided he had sensed my fear on the mountain side. Knowing that I over came it he removed the insignia and give them to me. He felt I had earned them. Little did he know how much I learned that day—not only was I a captain of the mountain, but also the captain of my own heart and soul.

PERSONAL-EXPERIENCE ESSAY C

The Soap

Moments after removing my eight year old sister with incinerating profanity, I mounted the appolusa rocking horse with the triumphant poise of a nine year old with soldierly confidence I appraised my newly won ground, Elated sky blue excitement filled my whole world as I rocked. "It's all mine!" I dreamed an enchanted journey that took me away lightening fast. Off to Florida, California, Denver or Greece. My joy and the July sun made it all very possible.

Exploding my twinkling shell with air hammer corce, Momma's voice rang in my ears for weeks.

"Daniel Lee McMan, you get your filthy mouth over here."

Twice as fast as a barn cat's eye my head and total attention snapped toward my boiling mad mother. A wiffet I sat. The horse, which was reluctant to stop, nagged and pulled at me persuading a timely escape.

"I said move, boy!"

With the speed of interspace transporters, on the U.S.S. Enterprise, I was in front of her. All that filled my consciousness was the tunnel of silence through which mother loomed from higher on the stairs. Fear for my body and soul filled every fissure in my shaking head. I pleaded for quick death from the Allmighty before momma got her chance with me. The steps to the bathroom would be my last. With my left ear and ten or twelve neck haird, Momma hoisted me through the door. The tears this caused cannot be counted by even modern computers. Ill with pain, I heard momma's words.

"Pick up that soap."

Crying like a wounded kitten I cried over and over/ "Momma" "Momma" "Momma"

My tears fire hosed.

"Hurry up."

Momma didn't speak twice: ever.

The camay pink bar was mucous like when I picked it up. The executioner's ax was now in my hand.

"Put it in your mouth."

My worst nightmares were never like this. My pleading up turned eyes were met by a lightening fast hand. She shoved the bar all the way to the back. Poison pierced everywhere and stabbed at my throat. Twisting the assulting alien all about, mother said over and over.

"Never again, never again."

"And don't you spit one little bit."

To this day my words are choise not to include the terrible seven.

INFORMATIVE WRITING

INFORMATIVE ESSAY A

On the Road to the NBA

When a boy reaches the age of nine he is usually in the third grade. At this point the kid gets his first chance to play constructive basketball. His coach will teach him the basic fundamentals of the game. His coach will also introduce him to some of the NBA greats by telling the kid to watch the games on television. This is where the fantasy begins. The kid falls head over heals in love wiht a NBA star. He tries to do all the things the star does to become more like him. The kid figures if he can do the same things as the star he too should be able to play in the NBA. After a few more years of playing basketball the kid enters stage two.

Stage two takes place around the age of twelve. This is where the kid thinks that he is the best one on the team. His skills become more advanced than the rest of the kids at his age. He beomces not only the best player on the team but he thinks that he is the best in the league. Because he is the best in the league he thinks he can go on and become an NBA player. He starts to take basketball more serious than before. He goes out and shoots baskets for two hours everyday. This takes play for about three years. The kid then finally reaches stage three of this fantasy.

Stage three takes place around the age of fifteen. This is where reality sets in and the kid realizes that he isn't quite the grade a ballplayer it takes to be in the NBA. The kid still goes on to play basketball in high school but realizes that high school ball is the end of his basketball career.

This childhood fantasy is common in many young boys. The fantasy is short and sweet but at the time it is something very special to the young boy. The fantasy gives the kid a goal to shoot for even though the fantasy was a little bit farfetched it was an important event that took place in the growing up of a child.

INFORMATIVE ESSAY B

Fantasy Games

Fantasy can be an enjoyable way of excaping the rutine of everyday life. Some people play fantasy games like dungens and dragons. They can image their friends that they're in another world where anything can and will happen. Things that are in the game becomes real in a sense that the person must make the right decisions or die. That sense of danger in a game makes it more fun. People want danger in their life to make it exciting. Since they don't get danger in their real life they can resort to fantasy games. Some people play video games to excape reality momentaraly. People can feel the anxiety when they play a video game. It becomes more real because they know if they don't make the right move they will die or blow up. Of course none of that actually happens to them but it feels like it. People usually play new games that come into an arcade because they want a new challange.

Going to a movie in a theater gives a person a way of excaping into a fantasy world also. They can feel what the character is going through if he is injured or surrounded by vicious monsters. Imaginary things have become more real with special effects so a person can believe in what he/she is seeing. Fantasy is needed by everyone without it life would be too boring.

INFORMATIVE ESSAY C

Where Have You Gone, Joe DiMaggio?

My parents generation grew up in much simpler time. Everybody had a nice little house with a white picket fence. The father went to work, the mother stayed home and baked chocolate chip cookies. The kids went to school and played with their friends. American society was very similar to the television show Leave It to Beaver.

Now our society has changed. The divorce rate has sky rocketed, single parent families have become common place. Crime rates have ballooned. However perhaps nothing has changed more than the way we look at our sports heroes especially baseball players.

In the 1940's and 1950's baseball players were nothing less than "Gods" in this country. They were idolized by millions of children. People like Mickey Mantle, Willie Mays, and Sandy Koufax graced the playing field and rarely did anything to tarnish their image and disappoint their fans. They signed autographs willingly and did not demand truly outrageous salaries for playing the game they so dearly loved. They had respect for their fans and respect for their game. Baseball players gave 100% on the field and also fulfilled their duties off of the field to be role models.

This is not the case today. The salaries of baseball players have risen dramatically. Greed has take over the national pastime. The stars of today can earn as much as six million dollars for one season, while mere average players can easily pull down a cool million.

Players don't sign autographs nearly as much as they used to. When they do sign autographs however it is usually at a baseball card show where kids play money to get an autograph of their favorite player.

Drugs are also something that has changed the game of baseball. Too often we hear of players being suspended for the use of drugs. Young baseball fans see their "role models" serving jail time for the possession of drugs. This was never the case a generation ago.

The game of baseball has changed greatly. For today's generation of baseball fans, role models are few and far between. This is a sharp contrast to my father as he grew up. He lived during a time when this county coulf be proud of its baseball heroes, not ashamed.

ARGUMENT

ARGUMENTATIVE ESSAY A

Violent Concerts

Most people don't think of rock concerts as violent but the fact is they are. Rock concerts are very aggressive and violent. It has been a proven fact that the loud sound waves coming out of the very large speakers make people more violent than normal. It has something to do with the beat of your heart and there for causes more anxiety and violence than you normally have. A few years ago there was a large rock concert in which many people were killed because the crowd stampled over them rushing up on stage. Criminal violence is also a problem at concerts many people are stabbed, beaten or even rapped. It cant be said that all concerts are like that classical, rock or opera are anything but violant. It could be the crowd that makes a difference or what people put into themselves such as alcohol or drugs. But the fact remains rock concerts are violent.

ARGUMENTATIVE ESSAY B

Just One Credit

What is meant by the term physical education? I usually think of exercise or an activity that requires some physical activity, and football clearly falls under this classification for most people. Relaxation and Ballroom Dancing have to conjure up some doubts about physical exercise/ Clearly going through a full football season-- which is year around--is as difficult as these other P.E. courses that I mentioned. This leads me to believe that the university should allow a football palyer one credit for every year he is on the team.

Although the P.E. courses that I mentioned earlier are suppose to broaden our horizons; the football team has started a program that lets the players get involved with the public. Football also takes the players to other campuses, teaches them cooperation and teamwork and creates competition just like the classroom.

Once the class room is brought into the case; people will argue that players don't have to pay for football, whereas P.E. classes cost money. Granted the football team is rebuilding, an excellent and exciting team should bring in money to the university.

The university system will have no problem with the grade transcripts because football could be considered a retroactive credit.

Now a problem is that every sport will have to be equal to one credit. So do it. The time required to practice every sport is equal (if not more) to the time spent in P.E. classes.

Although football is totally volunteer there is a choice of P.E. classes. Any class cn be chosen as long as there is no prerequisite. There is no prerequisite for football but I would list it as an advanced course because many people don't have the ability or time (primary education, the reason for no time).

I am all for concentrating on your studies but football will help you become more efficient, and it does look better on your resume than Ballroom dancing.

If the time factor is so important, how dedicated does a player have to be? I speak from experience. The players reported to fall camp on August ninth, studied playbooks and completed tests in running and weightlifting. Once classes started, practices lasted about two hours plus videos once or twice a week. After the season, players lift four times a week (1-2 hours/day), and attend spring practice during april and may.

Regular P.E. classes that are offered as credits don't come close when compared to what football accomplishes. Football is not considered a "blow off" like many P.E. courses, and the time spent on both can't even be compared. As for the physical activity I invite anyone to put forth the effort for just one season of football.

ARGUMENTATIVE ESSAY C

Dogs in the Dorm?

As I walked into my dorm the other day, I caught a glimpse of a four legged animal bounding towards me from down the hall. This four legged creature called Hawkey, lives with my hall director in Towers. Lucky for me, I love animals and was able to catch the dog and play with him for a while. However many people do not feel the same way about dogs or other animals. I have many friends who would shutter at the mere description of a 90 pound black lab, let alone be confronted with one in the lobby. Although residents are not allowed to own pets many hall directors have animals living with them in their apartments.

The resident hall directors live on the first floor of each dorm. They are responsible for enforcing the rules and to keep the dorm problem free. One of the rules they enforce very strictly is the rule that states, no pets allowed in the dorm. I understand this rule is necessary for the good of the residents and the animals but I also believe that the rule should be followed by everyone.

Although the dogs and cats that I have ran into on campus have seemed very well behaved and harmless animals are very unpredictable. Any tame dog could turn on someone especially if evoked. These dogs are family dogs and family dogs will protect their family and their territory if challenged. Hundreds of students walk passed these dogs each day, many of them enjoy yelling at or teasing the dogs as they go by. Although this is not the hall directors fault the dogs could one day react to the teasing by chasing and biting a student.

In most apartment buildings pets are not allowed, the biggest reason is the reason stated above, another reason is that dog make noise. Dogs bark at everything and for the people living directly aboe the dogs area the noise can get very annoying.

Many times the dogs are allowed to run around the lobby. Besides scaring anyone afraid of dogs, there are some obvious health concerns. First when dogs run around they lose hair. This hair settled to the floor but is constantly stirred up by people walking through the lobby. Food including pizza and popcorn is made and served in the same lobby where dog hair is probably floating around. I'm sure you have never heard any complaints about dog hair in the pizza but a few short dog hairs may be easy to miss if you are not paying attention to what you are eating. This hair floating around in the air may also irritate people who are allergic to animal hair and they may feel uncomfortable standing in the lobby.

I understand why hall directors have pets, pets are good companions and add enjoyment to peoples lives. The dogs here have been here all there lives and are somewhat use to the people and the commotion, but like I said previously animals no matter how well trained they are are unpredictable and have minds of there own. So there is always a risk.

Hall directors should not be allowed to have pets in the dorms which serve as a h ome for students for nine months out of the year. This is our home and we spend a

substantial amount of money to live here, students should
be able to comfortable about what is living in the dorm
along with them.

PART FIVE

Keeping Track of Writing Skills and Problems

The following logs will help you see both progress and problems—if you consistently use them. Because writing takes time and sustained practice, novice writers sometimes don't feel as if they are making progress, when in fact they are. The logs will help make progress, as well as persistent problems, more visible. Photocopy these logs as you need them. Be honest and thorough when you fill one out.

REVISION LOG

Name _____

Title _____

Date _____

Strengths of this piece:

Problem Area	What I Have to Do
Controlling Idea	
Development	
Organization	
Transitions	
Sentences	

Questions for Instructor:

EDITING LOG

Name _____

Title _____

Date _____

List the errors in sentence boundaries, punctuation, and usage (agreement between subject and verb, agreement with pronouns, plurals, etc.). Try to figure out why the error occurred (just slipped up, don't know the correct form, etc.). Then make the correction, asking for help as needed. Look for patterns. Chances are you are making the same mistake repeatedly rather than many different types of mistakes. Use this list as an editing guide on your next writing task.

Error	Why It Happened	Corrected

SPELLING LOG

Name _____

Title _____

Date _____

List words misspelled. Indicate why the error occurred. Then examine your list for a pattern. What kind of spelling errors do you tend to make? Use this list as an editing guide on your next writing task.

Correct Spelling	My Spelling	Type/Cause of Error

SOURCES

Page 26: Ad for Tropic Waters Pet Center, Eau Claire, Wisconsin. Reprinted with permission.

Page 27: "Sarah Gives Husband Royal Roasting." From *Eau Claire Leader Telegram,* May 30, 1992, p. 2A.

Pages 42, 43, 68: Sandra Cisneros, From *A House on Mango Street.* New York: Vintage Books, 1991. Reprinted with permission.

Page 49: From Randall Collin and Scott Coltrane, *Sociology of Marriage and the Family: Gender, Love, and Property* (Chicago: Nelson-Hall, 1991), pp. 121–138.

Pages 61–64: "The Kitten" from *Black Boy* by Richard Wright. Copyright © 1937, 1942, 1944, 1945 by Richard Wright. Reprinted by permission of Harper-Collins Publishers.

Pages 66–67: "White Tigers," from *The Woman Warrior* by Maxine Hong Kingston. Copyright © 1975, 1976 by Maxine Hong Kingston. Reprinted by permission of Alfred A. Knopf, Inc.

Pages 71–72: "Mirrors," from *In Another Country* by Susan Kenney. Copyright © 1975, 1980, 1984 by Susan Kenney. Used by permission of Viking Penguin, a division of Penguin Books USA, Inc.

Pages 78–82: From "Blue Winds Dancing" by Thomas Whitecloud, *Scribner's Magazine,* vol. 103, no. 2 (February 1938). Copyright 1938 and renewed © 1966 Charles Scribner's Sons. Reprinted with permission of Charles Scribner's Sons, an imprint of Macmillan Publishing Company.

Pages 123–124: Erma Bombeck, "Big Lies Have Small Beginnings," *Eau Claire Leader–Telegram,* January 30, 1992. Reprinted with permission.

Pages 124–125: Joe Schoenmann, "Cheating May Be on the Upswing at UW–Madison," *Capital Times* (Madison, Wisconsin), February 19, 1992. Reprinted with permission.

Pages 125–126: Anthony Flint, review of Michael Moore's "Cheating 101," *Capital Times* (Madison, Wisconsin), February 19, 1992. Reprinted with permission.

Pages 127–128: Lisa Baumann, "Stressing SAT Brings Criminal Results," *St. Paul Pioneer Press,* November 27, 1992, p. 16A.

Pages 129–131: Robert J. Samuelson, "Teen–agers in Dreamland," *Newsweek,* April 19, 1989. Reprinted with permission.

Pages 133–136, 184: Diane Ravitch, "Back to the Basics: Test Scores Don't Lie," *The New Republic,* May 6, 1989. Reprinted with permission.

Page 151: From Allan Bloom, *The Closing of the American Mind* (New York: Simon & Schuster, 1987), pp. 82–83. Copyright © 1987 by Allan Bloom. Reprinted by permission of Simon & Schuster, Inc.

Pages 154–156: Joan Beck, "Why America's Students Are Falling Behind," *Wisconsin State Journal* (Madison), April 26, 1992, p. 15A. Reprinted by permission: Knight Ridder Tribune.

Pages 156–157: Susan Chira, "Renegade Researchers Offer Rebuttal: U.S. Schools Better Than Many," *The New York Times,* April 8, 1992. Copyright © 1992 by The New York Times Company. Reprinted with permission.

Pages 178–180, 181–182: Lisa Grunwald," If Women Ran America. . . ," LIFE Magazine, June 1992, pp. 39–46. Copyright Time Warner. Reprinted with permission.

Page 183: Carol Gilligan, *In a Different Voice,* Harvard University Press, 1982, pp. 16–17.

Page 187: "America's Family Values," *Eau Claire Leader–Telegram,* October 11, 1992, p. 6H. Reprinted with permission.

Page 205: Charles Schulz, "Peanuts," January 2, 1993. PEANUTS reprinted by permission of UFS, Inc.

Page 210: Terry Mulcher, "No Dummies: Miss America Hopefuls Smash Stereotypes," Associated Press, *Eau Claire Leader–Telegram,* September 19, 1992.

Pages 211–212: Letters from *USA Today,* September 25, 1992.

Pages 223–225: Mike Royko, "Legal Marijuana—A Pot of Gold," *Chicago Tribune.* Reprinted by permission: Tribune Media Services.

Page 295: "Renaissance Man," *Sports Illustrated,* November 30, 1992, p. 68.

Page 296: David Gelman, "The Most Dangerous Man," *Newsweek,* December 4, 1992, p. 66.

Pages 344–346: Excerpt from "To Kill a King" by Sue Gross from *Literary Cavalcade,* Vol. 3, No. 8 (1951). Copyright 1951 by Scholastic, Inc. Reprinted by permission of Scholastic, Inc.

Index